DATE DUE

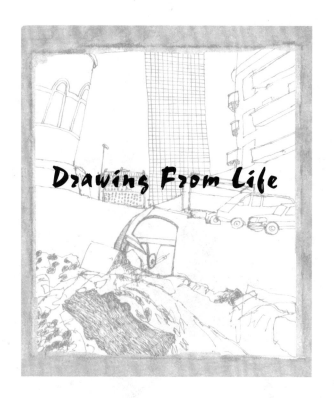

Drawing From Life

Drawing From Life

BY JOEL OPPENHEIMER

EDITED BY ROBERT J. BERTHOLF
AND DAVID W. LANDREY

ASPHODEL PRESS
Wakefield, Rhode Island & London

Published by Asphodel Press

First Edition

LIBRARY OF CONGRESS
CATALOGING-IN-PUBLICATION DATA

Oppenheimer, Joel.
Drawing from life / Joel Oppenheimer.

p.   cm.

I. Title
PS3529.P69D7   1997
814'.54—dc20   96-43470
ISBN 1-55921-197-0   CIP

Printed in the United States of America.
Distributed in North America by Publishers Group West,
P.O. Box 8843, Emeryville, CA 94662, 800-788-3123
(in California 510-658-3453)

Editors' Note

This volume presents a selection of Joel Oppenheimer's columns which appeared in *The Village Voice* from 1969 to 1984.We have chosen pieces which present Joel Oppenheimer's views of his life, and its patterns: from his perspective from Westbeth in the West Village and various other places, new to him, out of the city, as well as his views of society, baseball, and governments. A bibliography including all of Joel Oppenheimer's publications in *The Village Voice* appears after the selection of columns.We have accepted the texts as they were published, but have corrected accidental misprintings.

We acknowledge the generosity of Ross Wetzsteon in granting an interview which we rely on in the Introduction.We also acknowledge the assistance of Susan Michel, Kristin Prevallet, and the staff of The Poetry/Rare Books Collection, State University of New York at Buffalo, in the preparation of the manuscript.

—Robert J. Bertholf
—David W. Landrey

Introduction

At the end of Oppenheimer's life, students at New England College, and other friends, formed "the joel oppenheimer society for arts and letters" and even had a tee-shirt made with the picture of Joel from the cover of his book about the New York Mets, *The Wrong Season*. Beneath the picture is a caption: "be there when it happens," a line which attracts curiosity in parks, gyms, on buses, etc., but which, out of context, suggests a quality almost opposite to his vision. As you will see in this collection, the complete original statement is "let everything come together and be there when it happens." Joel's vision is not one of control; to the contrary, it borders on anarchisim, although that's not quite right either, for he was a man in search of structure, as several of these columns reveal—attempts to reorganize, make lists—and he was always attracted to tradition. What he learned from life is that, if he listened, it would tell him what to do. Did he finally listen? Did he, in fact, let everything come together? Whether he succeeded in daily life is unclear, but in these columns and in his poetry, "it" happened. And he was there.

Joel often quoted Gertrude Stein: "There's no there there." No one else was more deeply aware of what had happened to his "there"; and—whether deliberately or simply by letting every-

thing come together—he became an acute chronicler of the de-
cline of his civilization. One wonders how many readers, during
the sixteen years of these columns, saw the consistency of his
vision, how many shared his pain, how many were redeemed by his
persistent recovery of life's essential simplicity. It was a simplicity
found in several recurring themes: baseball, domestic affairs, the
community of Greenwich Village, lesser-known holidays, and, in
the last years, alternative (to New York City) places, the last one
being Henniker, New Hampshire (as a sign says on the way into
town "the only Henniker in the world")—his final "there," where,
after a struggle, he most profoundly was.

Joel saw his beloved Dodgers move out of and Richard Nixon
move into The City. In the meantime he lived and died with the
Mets, but the world was utterly different. There was Vietnam and
then came Reagan. Still, the Miracle Mets won it all in 1969, and
Joel began writing for the *Voice* that very year. A year later he had
dried out. His vision and wit sharpened; his life and his poetry
changed. What did not change was his sense of permanent loss, or,
as he put it in his column of March 21, 1974, "what a beast i'm
turning into, except that i don't think it's me that's doing the
turning. i can feel myself being turned by them, all of them."
Perhaps the ultimate reason for his column was to identify the
"them," to clarify what they had done to "there," and to provide his
readers and himself an alternative there in the midst of the thereless
there.

Ross Wetzsteon, now engaged in writing a history of Green-
wich Village, was Joel's first editor. In 1969, the *Voice* offices were
on Sheridan Square, on the corner of Christopher Street and 7th
Avenue, directly above Joel's favorite bar, the Lion's Head (often
called, simply, "The Head"). In February '69, Philip Roth's *Port-
noy's Complaint* had been reviewed in the *Voice*. The book and the
review generated considerable discussion in The Head, with Joel at
the center of it. As Wetzsteon puts it in an interview in the fall of
1994, "He was obviously entertaining everybody at the table with

all his jokes and comments and wry asides, and somebody suggested that he write a piece called 'Oppenheimer's Complaint' and take it up to the *Voice*. He was shy, not at all pushy; he was self doubting. They practically pushed him out the door." Wetzsteon goes on to explain that he barely introduced himself when he submitted the piece and that it was "very funny—and very sexist, of course. We weren't as alert or as educated in those things in those days, but it was very funny, so we printed it." Evidently Joel chose Ross Wetzsteon because he had given Joel's play, *The Great American Desert*, a strong review.

"Oppenheimer's Kvetch" appeared on March 6, 1969. In retrospect, it seems an appropriate beginning, for the columns would commonly have the qualities of a "kvetch"; but, as Joel himself, ever fascinated by etymologies, would probably have pointed out, "kvetch" might be heard less as a whining complaint and more as it comes from German and Yiddish words meaning "to squeeze." He would master the art of squeezing the essence from issues in his very legitimate complaints.

Thus it began. There would be only scattered pieces until late 1971, when he began to contribute bi-weekly. Wetzsteon was at first resistant to taking up Joel's suggestion of a regular column of reflections because "the idea of somebody writing reflections on life—this vague kind of thing—made me reluctant. This was a newspaper, after all." But he relented, and the columns quickly found an audience. Wetzsteon says that there was rarely a need to edit within one of the columns but that, early on, "I did only a couple of things to help him." First, because Joel would "meander a little bit," they established what became known as "the Oppenheimer box," a space limited to about 700 words which was inside "little lines around the column. It was the first thing that had that in the paper." Earlier, Charles Olson had called the meandering Joel's "discursive style" and praised him for it. Wetzsteon, as an editor of a newspaper, argued that Joel needed the same kind of form within

which to work as he would require in his poetry. Secondly, Wetzs-
teon explains, "He had the failing of writing a paragraph too long.
It was his 'and thus we see' paragraph, which was basically
summarizing the points he'd made in his piece. I said, 'You came to
the end and that was the end.' At first it made him a little nervous;
it sounded a little truncated to him. I said, 'No, it's not. You're
through; you've said what you have to say. Go.'" In the end, Joel
was to thank him for the box and for the advice.

The columns began, then, on a whim; and, no doubt, Joel
welcomed the small supplement to his income. But he was, after
all, a poet. Every little bit counted. So there appears to have been no
design, no master plan on Joel's part. Yet quickly the columns had
a tone and a consistency of vision which constituted an analysis of
the worsening social circumstances of the 1970s and 1980s. He
needed domestic stability and love, this Village anarchist of the
imagination, and attended to the details of living with the same
views as he attended to the affairs of politics and war. He longed
for a loving human community, freedom of all kinds, and respect
for individuality. He wanted to be a good citizen, and he wanted
governments to act for the good of the people. Then he wrote about
the abuses of his vision of living. He often said that writing the
columns kept the poems free of rant and demands for alleviating
injustices of all kinds. The poems as well as the columns are
informed with an extraordinarily gentle faith, a faith in the simple
ceremonies of communication. He would fight all his life to save
those ceremonies, but he witnessed even their breakdown. In the
column of March 15, 1976 he said:

> we'll find that the beast who talks has lost its ability, its desire, to
> communicate. we'll pull further and further apart while being
> crushed closer and closer together. that's an untenable situation,
> and it needs to be considered and somehow changed. otherwise
> we will stand guilty of having deserted all the generations, and
> of having given each generation the least of all possible worlds.

Could the situation be changed? Might his fight succeed? At Joel's Buffalo State College talk of October 1980, a member of the audience articulated the problem: "There's a kind of superficial magic coming over the verbal clichés created by the media that makes the territory so very difficult that I wonder to what extent the language can be cleaned up at all and for how many people." Joel's response summarized his ambivalent position:

> There are times when I know we can't win, but then I think of Paul Goodman's lovely line that "In many ways the best fight is the long, drawn-out losing fight." . . . Maybe that sounds dumb, but on the other hand, maybe if enough people go into it thinking it may be a long, drawn-out losing fight, maybe we change things a little.

The *Voice* columns became the center of his fight and probably led to the expanded poetry of his last years, especially *names, dates, & places, At Fifty, New Spaces, Why Not, new hampshire journal,* and the remarkable poem about his cancer and chemotherapy, "the uses of adversity." No doubt two fine prose volumes were also made possible by the *Voice* discipline: *The Wrong Season* and *Marilyn Lives,* the latter a brilliantly concise study of the effects of Marilyn Monroe on the lives of individuals and groups he interviewed in the Village.

Each of the recurring themes—baseball, the domestic, Greenwich Village, holidays, and new places—presented alternatives to the clearly identified enemies in his fight, the "them" who were destroying his "there." "They" were (and are) the businessmen and politicians, the manipulators of public opinion for greedy ends, the makers of war—all of whom he liked to characterize as "the old men." (How often he cried out against the persistent killing, yet, ironically, he was intensely fond of war board games such as *Risk* or *The Civil War,* and he studied the history of wars.) In the column of September 14, 1972 he wrote:

i am angry that serious old men make decisions, make decisions, make decisions. nothing the young do can be worse—even murder. it is the old men making decisions who fuel the young mad-men, con the young jocks, fuck up the young heads. we are supposed to be passing on wisdom and understanding and we have none, but everybody breathes a sigh of relief when we do anything that smacks of being a decision.

The old decision-makers included Presidents of the United States, organizers of the Olympic Games, military leaders, baseball owners (there was never any doubt in Joel's mind that the villains in sports world labor disputes were the owners), most teachers and especially their primary spokesperson, Albert Shanker, and landlords. Turning Yeats's line from "Sailing to Byzantium," "That is no country for old men," upside down, Joel wrote: "This is no country for young men, since the old men run it, and decide who dies" (May 17, 1983).

Consider, then, the alternatives. Consider, especially, baseball. In the early eighties, Joel watched many games in Oneonta when he spent more time away from New York City. As the baseball strike of 1981 unfolded, he was pleased to have the minor leagues, and, as his column of July 8–14 reveals, prior to his departure from the city, he had been on a radio call-in show wherein most calls favored the owners. He comments: "We tried talking about market value, but none of these free enterprisers wanted to hear that. Only owners, evidently, are allowed to make a lot of money. To most Americans it seems unseemly, if not Marxist, for workers to make it." The minors provided the game itself, free of economics. He writes:

> So I'll be in the woods, happy with baseball and a couple of books and no news. It will, I hope, be most restorative. And then I can come back and continue complaining—and, if they let me, watch young blood keep swinging. And I can keep on making

metaphors which use baseball and life interchangeably. That, after all, is what human beings do best.

Just what is it that humans do best? Use baseball and life interchangeably? Make metaphors? Perhaps the answer is unimportant, or perhaps the answer is simply: "Yes." As early as the column of April 15, 1971, he had offered a kind of manifesto in response to those who argued that baseball was wasting his time:

> it ain't all bread and circuses. they use it for politics, they use it for profit, they use it for short haircuts, i know that. they use poetry when they like too, baby. but if you can't stop the users, you certainly can't stop the doers. opening day. it's important only because you set up a universe in which it is important, but then you play by those rules. . . . the universe exists if you say it does. it's the only one you can say exists, instead of having it shoved on you.

Creating a universe and playing by the rules: Joel behaved that way within the alternative hope of Greenwich Village. Ross Wetzsteon commented on Joel's curious place in that milieu and therefore at the *Voice*:

> His subjects were very fundamental. Here you have someone in the heart of Bohemia, the quintessential Villager, and here he's writing about family life and seasons and nature and baseball. A hard-drinking Bohemian, a wencher, and he's celebrating spring, baseball, family, picnics. What bothered me at first, and I never quite told him, but I said it to myself, was that, in a way, it was a once-around kind of column: what was he going to do the next time the leaves turned color. But he never ran out.

No doubt he never ran out because elemental values never do. He made clear distinctions between those values and what society had made of them. When his son Nathaniel asked for a bar mitzvah, Joel was thrilled. He says, in his column of December 17, 1979, that he had always doubted what social forms he should lay on his kids, "But Nathaniel, for whatever reason, decided he did want the ceremony—and as a ritualist, if not a good Jew, I understood that." That same column showed his full discovery of the value of the community he had both created and discovered. People came from every period and corner of his life and, whether Jews or not, participated utterly in the ceremony, leading Joel to "feel like a grown-up, and I thank my friends for showing me how."

He also never ran out because he felt just what it was in nature that never ran out. He celebrated "lesser" holidays, those which had lost, in the minds of most, their original impulse. Most important may have been Ground Hog's Day. While nearly everybody who noticed at all were humorously looking for the shadow of Punxsatawney Phil, Joel was contemplating the return of Persephone from Hades, the renewal of life itself. Ross Wetzsteon comments on how angry Joel was at the undermining of elemental values in holiday celebrations: "He was writing when they went to Monday holidays. He hated it."

Wetzsteon succinctly caught what linked these alternative interests and thus what centered Joel's craft:

> Somehow he managed when he was in a home environment to make a small little corner of the world resonate with larger meanings. He had more difficulty when he was only temporarily in a spot. If the world can be found in a grain of sand, it better be on the beach that you know.

So it was that the columns ran and did not run out. He struggled in his new places until he made them beaches that he knew. He did so, and the late New Hampshire pieces resonate as fully as the early Village ones.

Some have thought that newer *Voice* editors were dissatisfied with Joel's techniques, his use of lower case in particular; but, as his column of January 17, 1977 reveals, it was his own decision to change that, realizing that newspaper print created problems in distinguishing ends of sentences without the aid of caps. He never changed in writing his poetry. What did change at the *Voice* was a vision. Ross Wetzsteon summarizes the eventual end of the relationship:

> As the *Voice* altered and changed, he couldn't appear there anymore. It became more of an editor's paper. You can't call on Joel and say, "There's a hot item over there; I want you to look into this." I mean, what's the hot item? The hot item is, "Persephone's returning." So he fell out of favor with the later editors. He seemed anomalous at the *Voice*. He didn't change; the *Voice* changed around him in ways I wasn't entirely happy with. It became much more hip.

But hindsight tells us that the job was done. He had framed a clear vision and changed his life and art. A humorous take on such change is provided by a poem his audiences loved, a characteristic example of "making metaphors which use baseball and life interchangeably":

> eleven years ago
> i stopped making love
> to watch cleon jones
> put the team ahead
> in a crucial game
>
> stopped the act of love
> to watch baseball
> on television
> a ballclub in
> a pennant race
>
> not important except
> to remember committing
> this act life vs art
> art vs art culture vs
> the individual whatever

eleven years later
there is always something
embarrassing to remember
something we did that was
shameful ridiculous and
shameful something
to wish undone
but that marriage is gone
and the team won the pennant

Probably the best summary of the achievement of Joel Oppenheimer's vision (one never felt natural saying "Oppenheimer" the way one might say "Whitman" or "Melville"; such was the way his domesticity absorbed one's own) is a passage from his column of October 28–November 3, 1981, a column in which he seamlessly links the murder of Anwar Sadat, a toothless North Carolinian's murder of his wife and daughter, technology, the changing of the seasons and the clock, and more:

> If one can find a good spot to sit in the winter sunshine one can last out the night; and if one can last out the night the spring will come. But it's lasting out the night that is so hard, that leads to all the frantic partying from now until the spring, that leads to all the frantic inventing—of things, of ideas, of amusements. We have to learn again to sit and muse. The Muses do come if you let them, but they run when you pursue them.

—Robert J. Bertholf
—David Landrey

Charles Olson: 1910–1970

Moby Dick is dead. The big body, six foot seven, 250 to 270 pounds maybe, is gone. Too big for this world, perhaps. Too big for the two generations of poets he created and formed. Too big for the editors and publishers (like the ladies' magazine that published his exquisite Easter poem for Christ as a "bra-stuffer" way in the back of the book in the '40s), and for the readers who kept saying they couldn't understand him. Only the kids knew, the kids he taught at Black Mountain College, at Buffalo, at Storrs, at every reading he gave, in all the poems and essays.

Charles Olson wrote and Charles Olson taught. And he was a man, a mensch. He could dance a courtly dance with a small woman, and he could stay up all night patiently explaining the realities of political life to us little ones, and he had balls enough to correct himself when he was wrong. He held a Pall Mall like you or I hold the stub of a Camel, and once he saved a game for me by falling full-length toward the mound, his foot on the bag, and the bad throw from me just dropping in his outstretched glove. He also cost me a triple because he was discussing Etruscan sculpture with Dan Rice instead of coaching third base.

All this is stupid. A great and good man is lost to us. His work is here, yes, and up until the last week or so he was still adding to "the maximus poems," but the man is gone, and he won't stride up and down the stage at Berkeley any more, handling the mike cord like Sinatra or Belafonte, finally leaving his audience to spend months debating where his head was at. Make no mistake about that, because his head was about 60 miles ahead of all of us. He made mistakes, but when he did it was because he reached too far, even for his size. And the breakthroughs were what counted—not only the whole idea of projective verse, or the best book ever

written on Melville (*Call Me Ishmael*), or the fantastic correspon-
dence that helped germinate 1000 little magazines and a whole lot
more minds, but mainly the re-creation of poet as useful human
being, poet as creator of unified life theory.

The workshops at Black Mountain started at 7:30 and they
ended at 9:00, maybe, or more likely at 12:00 or 2:00 or 3:00. One
day the blackboard held four lines, and Charles just kept saying
what are they? and I still count it a proud moment, and a good one,
when I said at 9:30: it's a map! And he smiled and said, okay, what
map? And a half-hour later we had it nailed down to the Nile, the
Tigris-Euphrates, the Danube, and the Volga, and we spent the
night talking about trade routes and cultural interchanges between
the Northmen and the South, about the way cultures developed and
moved one. Albert Shanker and Ronald Reagan will never under-
stand what he could have meant to American education, just as an
awful lot of people who should have known never did know what
he meant to American letters, but I say we have suffered a terrible
loss.

The last time I saw him, New Year's Day, he was still lucid,
still fighting, preparing a paper for the doctors, planning to tell
them patiently that he was not Zeus, he was Prometheus, and you
had to believe him even while they picked at his liver. He stole fire
from the sky and brought it down to us, and some of us were lucky
enough to take hold, even when we got burned for it.

He was eighteen when the Depression started, and he sailed a
swordfishing boat, and he drove a post office truck, and somehow
he got his education (Wesleyan and Harvard and himself), and he
was in Washington during the war working for the OWI, and
somewhere along the way he became, made himself into, turned
into, a poet. Which is why he never believed that poetry could be
taught, so that he taught us everything else that could let us be
poets. He even had a brief shove at politics, some minor role at the
Democratic National Convention of '44, watching the wires get
cut so that Claude Pepper couldn't put Henry Agard Wallace's

name into nomination. He was running errands essentially, but remember that it wasn't now, and thirty-three, thirty-four was too young to be considered seriously then.

Then he holed up and wrote, and then the teaching began. Maybe it ain't all Spock and Freud and all them guys. Maybe it's a little bit of Charles infused in a hell of a lot of people, and spread across a whole range of life, that taught the "young" what was happening to their world and what they could do about it. Maybe it was Charles writing furiously to Creeley and Duncan and all of us that made it impossible to ignore a whole new school of poetry that insisted that poetry was life and art, and that in the end could not be denied.

The man lived and he died, and Ahab chased him all the way, but Ahab didn't get him. Life got him. Death didn't stand a chance, just like the Pequod. Life got him because he refused not to live it, not to be put upon by it. He sat on a terrace in Germany lighting his cigar with a ten dollar bill a year after he had been woodshedding in Gloucester on God knows how little money, and he knew what he was doing. If it all sounds sentimental, forget it, and if you have to ask what his poetry was about I can only use Jelly Roll's old line: lady, if you got to ask, you'll never know.

If I could say a kaddish for him, I would, but Odin would be more suitable, passing him the cup. Charles just might lower the ocean a bit more than Thor.

no, i can't stay away from opening day

tuesday morning, gray, cold. windy. at 11:30 tex had promised rain, that low moving up. helen all embroiled in family problems, puzzling them out. i had broken in to say please do something for your poor sick old man, work some magic. what, she said. let it be good tomorrow, no rain. mumblings about where the moon was going to be. try, i said.

she had the coffee ready, and an apology. couldn't do much about the weather, she said. sorry. i was too. all morning filled with free-floating anxiety, not even the gameshows helping. philip called. i'll come over if they play. did you hear anything? no. wait it out and see. walt called. tickets. sarah has cold. me go? no, cold too. maybe gordon or david. try them. here're numbers. okay, okay. goodby. bring us a win, damn it. okay. goodby.

two o'clock. let's make a deal ends. channel nine please. thank you. raining at shea. wait it out. game starts around three. raining. twenty-five mile an hour wind blowing straight in. see flag? see how strong wind? mets 4–2 with two outs in bottom of fifth. legal game. mets win if end now. first home opener win ever. starts to hail. delay. keeps raining. five-thirty. game called. mets win. talk to wife and child till six, go out to eat to finish in time to make tom's for knicks play-off on cable. not the same thing. have to watch basketball. have to watch football. have to watch horse-race. baseball only sport can take a nap in, read in, do whatever want. only sport completely artificial time. marvelous idea. nobody understands this. wes furious if i listen to, watch, or go to ballgame. waste of intelligence. right. al thinks waste of moral fiber, game is shill while surrounded by war, race, poor. right.

4

still, artificial time. imagine! essence of game. very impor-
tant. don't have to watch all the time. very important. can play with
statistics all the time. not true anywhere else. very important.

the point in any game is that its limits should be clearly
defined and make sense in the world they define. that's all. then
you can play or watch it, either way. once figured out bocce by
watching italians in houston for two hours without asking ques-
tions. very proud. got slight case of sun poisoning. paying dues. it
ain't all bread and circuses. they use it for politics, they use it for
profit, they use it for short haircuts, i know that. they use poetry
when they like too, baby. but if you can't stop the users, you
certainly can't stop the doers. opening day. it's important only
because you set up a universe in which it is important, but then you
play by those rules. i don't feel insulted that they played in
abominable weather, or cheated, either. i'm sorry for the players,
was anxious in case someone got hurt, but that universe exists if
you say it does. it's the only one you can say exists, instead of
having it shoved on you. that's why games exist. women are used
to changing the universe. men aren't. that's why men invent
games, play them, watch them. cleon, no hits. clendenon, two.
seaver okay except for one inning. swoboda still on bench at end of
game. he'll kill us a couple of times.

no, i can't stay away from opening day. i won't go out and
freeze either, but i'll sit home and watch, and nap for a couple of
innings, and work my own magics. significant that i had helen
work on weather while i worked on game? of course. i know what
i can control, am in touch with, i know what she controls. male
chauvinist.

as a matter of fact mets game far more important than knicks
game because it don't mean anything. knicks game means money
prestige all that. mets game means specified number of idiots
perform specified actions well or badly for no reason in terrible
weather. love idea. much more relevant to life.

lady smiling at television camera at five after three hours in rain knows where head is. me asleep on couch while chub feeney talks old polo grounds talk knows where head is. when game is rained out wjrz plays hillwilliam all day long. right. mets used to have only major league ballplayer named for a poet, robert lowell heise. think about outfield ten twenty years from now.

my son knows cleon is number twenty-one. tanya ripped up his picture. four year old bitch! what's she know? cleon, send us a picture. hit 340 one more time. the outs drone on, the world creates itself because we tell it to. how do you like your blueeyed boy mr death, sd mr cummings. walter thought his uncle was taking him to see the chicago white sox in 1942, he didn't know this was new york in 71. we create our own time. and do our stupidities. baseball i love you.

hanukkah guilt:
the best of one
world twice

she said to me: ha! celebrating hanukkah and christmas! that's cheating! but (this is where she leered) it's the best of two worlds. it would have been fine if she had been in kindergarten or so, or even a gentile of any age, but this was a grown jewish princess. and so, my children, the old rabbi is of a mind to get back onto holidays and what this country does to them for a minute, just to set the record straight.

what has happened while judah the maccabee spins in his grave is that at the same time xmas became $mas, hanukkah turned into whatever you can do we can do better, and here we are again kiddies.

historically hanukkah is the last major holiday added to the jewish calendar, celebrating events of the first century before christ, and as such is not accorded terribly much importance by the orthodox. it is a joyous holiday, celebrating the rededication of the temple, and the restoration of hebrew home rule, after a period of greek, syrian and egyptian rule and culture, and as such the children have always been encouraged to celebrate it with sweets and a mild gambling game (spinning the dreidel) and hanukkah gelt, like a quarter from my uncle harry.

so all of a sudden there are hanukkah bushes and hanukkah cards and hanukkah presents and hanukkah songs in school at the $mas party, and the mayor of new york welcoming the crown to the official lighting of the city's $tree by wishing them a happy hanukkah and a merry $mas in that order which it happens to be, hanukkah falling first.

now look, my old jewish mother who used to tell me that

7

goyim only wanted to hurt me when i went out with charlie welge and kenton osborn in high school, and who spat three times when she was passed by a nun, used to give us $mas presents, for christ's sake!

she theorized that great psychic damage could be done to her precious jewels if the whole world was getting presents on december 25th while hers were not, so she carefully cultivated our knowledge of santa claus (withholding, of course, the non-essential information that he was a saint), and had us hang our stockings on the stove, and filled them with one (l) tangerine, one (l) macintosh apple, some raisins and nuts, useful things like pencils, erasers, and a toy or two, and, also, gave us presents. on the other hand, hanukkah had consisted of a visit to shul on the first night, and the ritual lighting of the candles every night for eight days, plus the aforementioned quarter from uncle harry, and a hebrew school re-enactment of the exploits of judah the hammer.

the system worked fine and i was rather astonished when i worked out the etymology of christmas at the age of ll. my own kids, indeed, seem in no way deprived by being raised under the same rules, and nathaniel, for one, is kind of excited about other people's $mas trees without in the least missing his own. of course, in the new game he makes out like a bandit, since my in-laws opt for hanukkah, so he has two parties a season, or the best of one world twice.

in fact, the more you look at it, the stupider it gets, since it just occurred to me that the wheel as usual has come full circle. what judah was really about was reversing the hellenization of the jews, even to the point of swooping down out of the hills in order to circumcise a whole generation who had chosen to follow the greek style; and now we got a whole generation of jews slathering their holiday with all those goyishe habits until it all becomes one conglomerate mess.

so, i would go so far as to suggest that every citizen of forest hills who held a hanukkah party this past sunday, or who has a hanukkah bush on or around his premises, or who gave his kids more than the obligatory uncle harry's quarter, automatically disqualify himself on moral grounds from opposing the housing project since it obviously isn't threatening to disrupt his religious-ethnic-cultural heritage. and i'd also like to suggest that mayor lindsay be forced to eat one latke on the first day of hanukkah, two on the second, and so on, but that's only because i do a lot of worrying about what wasps eat.

and i'd like to mention that nathaniel wants a fire engine, a bullhorn, a piano, and a ride on a herring boat for $mas, and that he knows that santa claus doesn't come until after you're asleep. next year at this time may we be in miami beach.

mr gruen got sad when famous people acted human

"the '50s? oh yeah, when nobody got laid."
—a young woman in max's kansas city
"they were the good old days. too bad nobody told us so we could've enjoyed them more."
—an old painter in the lion's head

john gruen's book *The Party's Over Now* is subtitled "reminiscences of the fifties—new york's artists, writers, musicians, and their friends." that carefully inserted comma before "and" in that line is misleading, since it would seem to indicate that the writer pays precise attention to detail, whereas, in fact, mr gruen either doesn't even know his birthyear ('26, '27, and '28 are all strong possibilities, according to the text) or he simply can't count. one begins to wonder somewhere in chapter two when mr gruen announces en passant that between 1944 and 1950 he has spent a year at city college, a year in the army, five years in the midwest, and two years hanging around oscar williams's apartment waiting for dylan thomas to show up. thomas finally does, and gets drunk. this saddens mr gruen. but mr gruen is always getting sad when famous people get drunk, or don't talk the way he thinks they ought to, or make scenes, or, indeed, behave like human beings.

but mr gruen says on page four ". . . i can never fathom (people) fully, and . . . i can never fathom myself at all . . ."; and i should have been forewarned. i mean, why does a man who believes this even try to write a book? but i stayed with it. painfully, each day or so, i read a chapter or so. hadn't i myself arrived fresh

and eager at the cedar street tavern in 1953? hadn't i slept in franz
kline's studio, escorted jackson from the artists' club to the cedars,
lusted after ruthie kligman, commiserated with mike goldberg
when con edison finally caught up with his giant space heater, and
kissed frank o'hara at a dreadful party? didn't it behoove me to
follow john and jane down their primrose path?

alas and alas. it's not that their primrose path was different
from mine, i expected that. it's that mr gruen has tried to be as
honest and open and direct in his seeing of their path as he is
capable, and all it does is expose him for what he must be. the book
is bitchy and coy, cruel, romantically mudslinging, and badly
written.

he maintains the fiction of the reporter, but why does he have
to have clem greenberg call kline a bore, when he could've said it
himself if he believed it; franz won't mind. and of what value or
interest is an account of how he saved bill de kooning from the
shakes, when the shakes were no doubt compounded by the im-
pending arrival of gruen to "interview" de kooning. who gives a
shit about poseurs?

there is, after all, only one valid reason for books which deal
in character assassination by personal account, and that is the
strength or technique of the assassin. gruen has neither, and worse
yet, a whole group of human beings who had both are presented as
cardboard figures in a landscape. even mr gruen's wife is no more
than "the tracing of his finger" and damn it he can't draw very well.

one ends up very tired, sad, and old after reading this book, if
one had any contact at all with the scene gruen is attempting (one
feels the same listening to some of the screaming from soho about
poor old jackson). and one shouldn't have to—not that those
people have any special claim on us, but that they were alive and
human and working, and they ought, for christ's sake, to be left in
peace or their own hells, or at least, failing that, be presented by
someone who has a little touch of insight, a smattering of self-
knowledge, and, if a gossip, some wit.

the passover service has a passage dealing with the handing on of tradition to the children, and it describes the four sons: the wise, the wicked, the simple, and "he who hath not capacity to inquire." it doesn't say it there, but god knows the first three might, each in their own way, write interesting books. i read this one with unleavened dread.

heavy hitters,
hard throwers,
& amurricans

the one thing we amurricans can't seem to accept is finesse, and we're always looking for the leader. nixon's popularity in the polls went up right after the mining speech, because it was direct action, a lot of steam on the ball, blow it right past them, and on friday night phil niekro got booed at shea stadium on his way to a three-hit knuckleball win for the braves, and on saturday tom terrific couldn't stop bitching about ralph garr's three-for-three which "didn't make ninety feet between them."

this was new york where, like they say, excellence is appreciated—except when it smacks of conniving instead of strength. the boos came the few times niekro, with a six-nothing lead, threw his floater, a big nothing rising high and dropping around the plate—and the boos were the biggest the one time it dipped over for a perfect strike. shit, i've thrown one, and it bugs everybody, the hitter, sure, but the umpire too, and nobody notices that hardly anyone hits it. i know, i know—rip sewell tried to throw one (he called it the ephus, which is a lovely name for anything) past ted williams in an all-star game, and williams blasted it, but williams was the greatest, and nobody else much that i recall hit it big that season. but it's like betrayal, that a pitcher should throw a pitch that by the very nothingness of it is hard to hit, whereas a rex barney heaving a bullet past you is a hero, even if he hardly ever finds the plate. don't get me wrong, i get suckered by the mystique too, and, indeed, went out to the ball park at asheville north carolina one early spring day in the '50s to see what was to be barney's last appearance in a dodger uniform—throwing smoke, until he threw one ten feet over the catcher's head, and then gave up about six big hits in a row. he put his glove down on the mound and walked to the bench.

the junk pitcher exists by brains alone, fooling you with where the ball is, or might be, and changing speed from slow to slower, and making you supply the muscle, and this is, i'm convinced, what causes all the hostility. if you're going to get beat you want to get beat by a haymaker, not by 10,000 knuckleballers, and indeed, on washington's staff one year which had four knuckleball starters, not three, you would've thought it was a crime against society. the simple fact is that what the game calls for is a pitcher throwing the ball in such a way that it passes through the strike zone and is hard to hit, and it don't say nowhere that the ball has to be a high hard one, or a fast breaking curve.

in garr's case the same holds true, since the hitter's job is to get on base safely, and the fact that garr beat out two bunts and an infield roller, and that he did the same thing all last season ought to be to his credit, as much as kiner hitting homeruns season after season. but we really can't accept that, and we call clemente less than mays or aaron because he hits fewer homeruns, and in san francisco they like willie less than mccovey or cepeda for exactly the same reason. we like goliath, the big lug, is the simple fact; we really hate david deep in our souls. in the same fashion, when the four-minute mile got broken, everybody talked about what a classy runner landy was, but bannister beat him, and good, by brains, and milking more from his maybe lesser talent.

what all this says in terms of populism and the major candidates i haven't the slightest idea, but i'm sure it's something pertinent. maybe it's a question of trust—maybe we just don't believe in the man who throws something that can be hit but isn't or the hitter who dumps one that should be handled but isn't, maybe we can only believe in one kind of perfection: the pitch that can't be seen, the hit that can't be caught. it would be a simpler universe that way, certainly. and yet. and yet. emilio cruz screamed at me all season long, but in 100 at bats he got 98 pops to second, a grounder to short, and a scratch single through the hole, so who won that one, and who was better, if you're counting?

and it's significant that the three met hits were gotten by john milner who's too young to know that niekro's unamerican, and just went up and tried to hit the pitches. mayor lindsay wouldn't give hoyt wilhelm a key to the city if he signed with the mets, but i'd love to see him out there, an old man, with a knuckleball, a lot of wins. a lot of saves, a low era, and a lot of brains, and the hitters bitching. and if he lost, it'd be a goddamned banjo hitter doing it scratching for a hit, screwing around on the bases, and sliding home under the tag. mr kiner, mr seaver, mr fan, mr amurrican, that also happens to be baseball, and fortunately, life.

twenty-five periods, eighty-two commas, and assorted semi-colons, colons, question marks, apostrophes, quotation marks, and dashes.

agnes, antoine, etc.: come again another day

the mexican novelist said that in mexico you knew which four months it was going to rain, and, furthermore, when it did it happened between, and always between, the hours of 2:00 and 5:00. that was nice, i said. the atlantic seaboard i said, from philly to boston, was notorious for changeable weather. i said we have a saying here that if you don't like the weather wait five minutes, it'll change. i did not credit mark twain for this remark. in any event, i said, i really can't explain why it's been raining for two god-damned weeks. we went to lunch, me under my new umbrella, and he striding bare-headed forward. novelists like to walk in the rain—it gives them new material. on the other hand it took this forty-two-year old poet forty-two years to break down and buy an umbrella. poets do not like new material since they are always trying to figure out what the old stuff means.

there is no doubt that tempers have frayed from this siege of weather, and i wish i could report that we are all responding valiantly, as we did during the power blackout. instead we are all drowning. the incidence of marital fights has risen; one of the westbeth pickets actually accused jack kaplan of causing the rain; and even the mice have gone crazy. i caught three in a half-hour at the height of agnes's brush with us, and i'm convinced they just decided to end it all, especially since my neighbor norman who helps me empty the traps (when alone i throw the whole thing away and start over) told me i was being chintzy about the portion of cheese i was serving. he felt they ought to have a chance at a hearty meal—but i was down to canadian cheddar, and what do they want anyway.

even tex antoine is cracking under the strain. i missed the show, but i am informed by a usually reliable source that he flipped the other night and told some anonymous "you" that "you" should stop demonstrating "your" ignorance to your children. i'm sure it was one of us poor bastards asking him about the atomic bomb again. i don't know why this enrages him, but it does, whereas everybody else knows that the bomb is the cause of the weather. maybe he gets mad because he's left out. in any event, it was a rainy day in new hampshire when mrs milsner came running out of camp wah-kee-nah's office to yell that we had dropped the automatic bomb, we had dropped the automatic bomb. that was many years ago, and though i found out twenty seconds later that the word was atomic (she had the times in her hand, so i read it) the initial impression was so strong that i still think of the damned thing as automatic. the point is, however, that tex antoine doesn't like inferences that the weather is controlled by anything but him and since the new york magazine survey showed that he is twenty-two times more valuable to this society than me i suppose i ought to believe him.

so the rain madness goes on and on, with supplemental annoyances like rainouts of baseball games so you can't even securely immure yourself—although it does give cleon and rusty and willie and all a chance to heal their wounds. i, myself, am very upset about the injuries the mets have suffered of late because they all remind me of the "original" mets, rusty and boswell hurting themselves swinging at a pitch, tommie and willie hurting themselves trying to catch balls, and cleon getting it trying to make a put-out at first base. i mean, those are things you're supposed to be able to do without getting hurt, but ever since eli voiced his metsy wail during the big winning streak that "it's no fun to watch anymore, they keep getting five runs in the first," disaster has followed the team—god striking again at hubris, i suppose.

but what's really at bottom of it all is that the magic is all screwed up down the line. mid-summer's night came and went and who could tell? did it even matter that we remembered our dreams for that night when there was no sun before them and none after, when the longest day of the year had less light than the shortest?

and the conventions keep looming ahead. suppose it rains straight through? despite the fact that only the goyim are silly enough to go to miami beach in the summer, it does not bode well.

i like men who fool around within their framework

somewhere in his novel *The Empire City* paul goodman tells the story of the poor jewish new yorker who gets drafted, fucks up all through basic, is useless and hopeless to everyone, himself included, and, finally, on guadalcanal, is stationed, alone, with a machine gun, in a hopeless position, while the army retreats. single-handedly he beats off the jap attack, killing thousands, and saving the day. after, while being congratulated, he is asked what changed him. at last, he says, i'm in business for myself.

all through the build-up for the fischer-spassky match this story became more and more pertinent to me, although, out of cowardice, having taken my lumps for my position in the famous breasted affair, i refrained from mentioning it to the lion's head crowd, which seems to have assumed a moral posture equivalent to our earlier feelings about benedict arnold. in fact, fischer seems to me to be intent on proving the virtues of private enterprise to spassky, and if poor boris isn't sitting there bugged because socialism doesn't let you get that crazy, then i miss my guess.

after all, we live in the very same country where astronauts smuggled envelopes on board the moon mission to privately enrich themselves, and everybody seems to think that that's naughty but understandable, they don't make a lot of money, etc. as a matter of fact, fischer and the baseball strikers are the only thieves america dislikes, which should prove something.

i personally like everything that's happening, although i wish i could be sure that bobby will in fact quit fucking around in time to let the match go to a finish. i ain't at all sure of that, but in the meantime that very indecision does allow me to turn on channel 13

whenever there's a game scheduled, because as long as there's
hope there's shelby lyman, ready to fill the time by discussing. he
is far and away the best discusser i have ever heard, because while
i don't know what he's talking about, he reassures me by checking
in with everybody so much that i think in the end i must be getting
the straight dope. i mean when curt gowdy bullshits or gifford or
meredith expert, or kiner reminisces, you feel like that's all there is
going to be to the subject, even if you disagree. but on channel 13
someone is always popping up with another point of view, whether
it's edmar on the direct line from the marshall chess club, or frank
brady on the line from reykjavik, or the ticker, with its bell ringing
for all the world like the bells on old grocery store doors when they
used to have that, or the panel of assorted chess buffs sitting around
the studio, or the producer running in with ap's latest wire infor-
mation.

now this lends a fluidity to the program which is terribly
refreshing. there's also the fact that there is absolutely nothing else
going on at the time, so you're not missing the game. i mean they
keep running into the plays in football, and in baseball the really
good bullshitting happens when there's a rain delay, which (wait-
ing for rain to stop) is a spectator sport even i find difficult to get
excited about, and during the convention game walter cronkite
kept talking while they were counting votes, which is what my
simplicity led me to believe that game was about, not to mention
sending people down to interview eleanor and muriel as to why one
was smiling and the other sad when the california vote was coming
in. so in this most perfect of television experiences you just sort of
sit there and wait for the grocery store bell to ring which will then
give you thirty seconds of hard-core action. it's terrific. it's also
addictive, about the only thing on television that would beat the
news ticker on cable tv for twenty-four-hour-a-day watching.

in addition, modern technology also does its part, adding to
the suspense immeasurably since the guys feeding the ticker (the
grocery bell, remember?) can't seem to keep their p's and q's

straight, so that poor shelby is in a constant dither as to whether, in fact, the move could be the one we're told it is. sometimes it is and sometimes it aint. as to the moral position started out from, i felt, even when i first read the news item back in the '40s, that ted williams on the field had a perfect right to give the finger to anyone he wanted, and that was when i was in my childhood. i see no reason to change that opinion, and so i must respectfully submit that i like men who fuck around with their own framework, while playing better than anyone. i mean if fischer moved pawns backwards i would be upset—or if he punched the referee without a good reason.

most people think of americans as sports buffs but the treatment of this business shows us to be insufferable liberals with a parochial school ethos beaten into our hides: good guys win, good players win, and when we're lucky, they happen to be good guys, and there aint any morality thank god, read your blake. doesn't anyone at all understand that fischer and mcgovern are the same guy, and nixon and spassky would love each other? ask meade esposito or mayor daley.

the '72 olympics: switching back to real life

Chapter 8   September 14, 1972

on tuesday september 5th, seventeen people died violently at the
olympic games. eight died through some choice: moshe weinberg
and joseph roman who tried to resist, five members of the black
september group of palestinian nationalists who could not have
gone on their mission without assuming the probability of death,
and a west german policeman, the nature of whose calling must
admit the possibility of a violent end; the other nine israeli hostages
died without options. nothing i say can change any of these terrible
facts, nor make life easier.

now it is three days later, and while the west german govern-
ment warns jews not to open packages or letters during the high
holy days lest they contain bombs, the ioc has decided to take away
some medals, to prohibit some athletes from further participation
in the games because they slouched and talked during the playing
of their national anthem, and they have decided that the games will
go on.

decisions, decisions. when the terrorists published a list of
their demands, golda meir decided not to compromise. someone in
the bar decided she was a ballsy woman. the west germans then
made a decision to try to pick off the arabs using five snipers and
long shadows. the snipers missed. abc and cbs had a hell of a time
making decisions over who should get to use the satellite so they
could carry the "news" to us. i am in no position to comment on the
reasons for making these decisions—i am responsible for neither
the existence of israel nor the image of germany—i can know only
that in these circumstances no "decision" could be correct.

decisions like this are made by people in one place about

22

people in another. the members of the norwegian squad who decided to go home because they thought the games had been resumed for purely commercial reasons made their own decision about their own actions. even the egyptians, flying home out of fear, made their own decision about themselves. perhaps even the athletes who continued playing ping-pong while the horror went on made the right decision. what else would you have had them do? should they have lined the fences with the rest of the spectators? even, god damn it, consider the possibility that the terrorists made the right decision, if history will tell our grandchildren so.

i am angry that serious old men make decisions, make decisions, make decisions. nothing the young do can be worse—even murder. it is the old men making decisions who fuel the young mad-men, con the young jocks, fuck up the young heads. we are supposed to be passing on wisdom and understanding and we have none, but everybody breathes a sigh of relief when we do anything that smacks of being a decision. the german sniper who started the firing thought he had a shot at it. he was wrong, but that was what he had been put there to try.

it is silly to ask that death be bigger than the olympics. we so desperately and perhaps properly fear death that we want anything to be bigger than it. a woman called "a.m.new york" tuesday morning and said "i went to sleep last night and i woke up this morning and all this was happening." it was a very simple, very human, and, also, a very stupid, plea. it asked that the world go on without the world's interference. or, like the young canoeist said at kennedy last night, "we were way over at the other end. we didn't know what was going on."

it seems to me that, while these olympics do go on, they have ended. we will never again, i think, be allowed the luxury of so totally watching, simply and with care, a man falling down while trying to lift the heaviest weight in the world, or trying to run faster than anyone in the world, or even trying to beat someone up. we will not see one man toss his enemy over his head backward by main strength, to fall on him and pin him. we will not have this circus any more except in small places where small boys try to stretch themselves. they complain about the jocks. they talk snidely about the runners worried about their training while men were dying—but what, ever, has the juggler been able to present to our lady but his skill?

i ask you to consider this particularly now, because there are so many others for you to judge. judge those who cry for vengeance and those who turn their faces. judge those who condone the terrorists. judge those who call for more guns to protect us from them or them from us. judge the rabbis who this very week will deliver sermons tying this terror to the need to vote for nixon. judge the commentators who already have begun to push and haul the universe until it fits their idea of it—and if i am one of them, judge me, for god's sake.

let us have done with horse shit! chris schenkel switched to volleyball for just a second during the terrible morning, to show us that the games were still in progress. then he said it: i guess we'd better go back to the real world if that's what it is. you bet your sweet ass, chris, not that i'd want to call it that, but what else is it? the real world, where simpletons pick a thing and try to do it well, while geniuses make decisions.

hidden in all this news this week was a tiny item about a court ruling in arizona, where the students of a college had voted the artichoke their team mascot and pink and white its colors. the judge found for the college, allowing them to throw the students' choice out, thus preserving the moral fiber of the cosmos.

the wisdom and understanding i have is this: security is a game, governments are a game, decisions are a game, and unless you understand this you too are a game. pheidippides ran the twenty-six miles because he was hired to do a job he could do better than anyone else. he carried the message and he dropped dead for it. it was a message about men killing each other. of all of them, who died best?

LONG DISTANCE
larry young did
big daddy call? did
the telephone ring in
your lonely head? with
beard and cap and "shades
and baggy shirt," from
the same hometown as
harry s truman "who
also liked to walk," in
that "lonely sport no one
pays any attention to
here," what could he
say to you? could he
tell you you were not a
flower of your place and
time? could he say children
should not emulate you?
or that you ought to
settle down, get a job?
who, after all, could use
the third best thirty
or some mile walker in the
whole wide world, and
what could you do for us?

what kind of toy do they make in hanoi?

david is a friend of mine who wanted out of the corporate rat race so he bought the little toy store on bleecker street when the young couple who'd been running it decided to move to greener fields in the country. he kept the nice yellow front but he changed the name to the breed's hill store and he started learning how to stock it.

i've been helping on a very minor level with suggestions, only because i'm a toy nut. toy stores are even better than supermarkets for impulse buying as far as i'm concerned, and i've never known one personally before.

the problem is, however, that sometimes there are goofs when you're learning, and one just happened in the latest corgi shipment. corgi makes those terrific little cars and they don't cost much so you go bananas collecting them, trading them, racing them. so the salesman told david about those nice "theme" sets of them, six or so cars with accessories. like a racing set with finish markers and officials and drivers, or a highway repair set with heavy construction trucks and workmen, and so on, and he bought a mixed bag of them.

i walked in the store the day after they came in and saw one set and thought someone had accidentally brushed up against it with a lit cigarette. the bus was all sort of smoked up, but then the plastic covering the box wasn't affected at all. so i asked david what the hell was the matter with it. he said, nothing, baby, just look at what it is.

the salesman hadn't mentioned this one. it was the "emergency 999 gift set" and it included one wrecker-tow truck, one police car, one fire-emergency truck, one firechief's car, an ambulance, and a burned-out schoolbus. yup! the picture on the cover of the box showed the bus on its side at the edge of the road, with all the other vehicles parked around helping. the set also included accident signs, road bollards, and "figures." luckily the box was designed so you could only see the cars, so i don't know whether the "figures" were crumpled schoolkids or helpful civil servants.

oh, the kindly toymakers, where are their heads? well, i suspect they're just where they ought to be in the united states of america in this year of our lord 1972.

we got bombing, we got watergate, we got the wheat business, we got all sorts of goodies, and everybody not only seems unconcerned about them, they actually seem to like them. the polls tell us that every time some more people in asia get killed, nixon gets stronger. yesterday there was a news item about one of the pow organizations overwhelmingly endorsing nixon's stand. and how many more pows and mias have there been since the bombing started up again?

i'm not spouting some corny bullshit here about keeping kids away from guns because it's "bad" for them. i don't even think competitive sports are bad for kids. but i am talking about generations of kids growing up who think it's perfectly natural to drop bombs on other people.

when i grew up a soldier was a strange and exotic thing—we even read kipling's poem about the poor neglected tommies and thought how very wrong it was that people didn't like soldiers in peacetime, but deep down inside we knew they must be louts or else they wouldn't be in that crazy business.

now, we got a guy retiring on twenty-five gees a year even though he not only killed people, which is after all a soldier's job, but he killed them when his bosses said not to, which used to be the worst sin a soldier could commit.

it's crazy. nathaniel had a little war going yesterday between his farm animals: the cows on one side, the sheep and pigs and poultry on the other. and all i could do was tell him that only men are fucking idiots enough to make wars, that animals have better sense. tonite they're all sleeping together in the shed we built for them.

and please don't tell me that wrecked schoolbuses are a fact of life and that kids lose if they don't learn from life. golly, gee, i wouldn't for the world deprive nathaniel or lem of a real experience. maybe i can arrange a live bombing run for them.

i forgot to mention that all the vehicles, including the schoolbus, have "track-scorching whizzwheels." terrific.

dancing down the line: jackie robinson 1919–72

jack robinson ran the bases as fast as you can say. as american as can be, he was born in georgia, a football hero in california, he officered in the war to save democracy. heywood hale broun said it the other night: he was a classic hero, and like all classic heroes he carried with him one flaw imposed by fate. he was black. as surely as oedipus or any other of them, his flaw destroyed him, crippling him, blinding him, killing him at fifty-three. as sadly as oedipus or any other of them, why was his flaw a flaw?

by his talents and his forbearance and his flaw, baseball was changed forever. it was a time when we believed the rest of the american game would change too.

in any other universe his life would, perhaps, have not been terribly different, but it would at least have been happier. and the rewards that came to him would have been enjoyed in the peace that should have accompanied them. he was smart, healthy, and handsome. he ought to have lived in that other universe where he would have been less driven, less beset.

and we who cried when we heard of his death, we who write or speak the eulogies, might, then, not have noticed; or merely mentioned it in passing. because good men of ability die every day in this world and there are not enough tears. but men, not symbols, die in such a quiet way.

my generation was young when robby started; in 1947 i was seventeen, and that was very young then. i stood in the stands surrounded by black faces the day he came to brooklyn. that had never happened to me either. from somewhere near me i heard a voice from childhood, a jewish tailor. yankel yankel yankel he yelled, as hard as all his neighbors shouting jack jack jack.

that is very hard to believe in 1972, when that tailor's children live in forest hills.

they tell me robby was not a gentle man; did they expect ernie banks smiling all day long? it takes a long time to enjoy what you are fighting to hold onto, and so i mean no disrespect to banks because i think by now we don't call superstars nigger. in 1947 we did.

what died here with jackie was an era, gasping now these five or 10 years, and now ready to be buried with him. he marks its end as well as any could. it was a time when young people hoped and old men began to realize they could not stop that hope, began to give a little. that time has ended because those once young are old now, because they are scared, because the world is scared.

and so we won't see him rounding third again, or dancing down the line, except in films—startling enough to stop conversations. draw your eye inexorably to the image, even if you don't care. and the lashing out will grow and grow—the same day a schoolbus attacked, teachers robbed, and yes, even two ponies beaten to death. we won't talk about what happened at the higher levels, like what they call government.

we won't talk about adrian constantine "cap" anson who singlehandedly kept baseball pure for whites for near 100 years; we won't even talk about richard m nixon who had the arrogance to put leroy "satchel" paige on his all-time all-star team because he would've been great if he could've played. and we certainly won't talk about the brooklyn fans who booed robby's first error as if it proved them right. we will talk about the stance, the bat held high, the head looming, and the ball bouncing off the wall in deep left center, and the crazy garbage truck run, the pigeon toes.

and in a world where he was clean, and where, yes, dixie walker was clean, too, even with his long-bred hatred, and the point for both was to score the runs and make the flashing play: in that world we will go to the polls, the voice of the people, and we will reelect thieves and liars and murderers to serve us four more years.

i had tried to tell myself i would not tie these two things together. how can i not? did america deserve jackie robinson? i think it didn't, and i know for sure that jackie deserved better than the mass of us.

by the dawn's early light: burrowing in again

the polls closed, and the results rolled in, and the commentators took over. the last thing i remember hearing was something to the effect that mr nixon had caught the tone of the american people, the temper of his time, and that no one could've withstood the land-slide.

i believe this to be true. i believe that the percentages would have changed a little had mr nixon's counterparts muskie and/or humphrey run, and that they would have been about the same had wallace run. after all muskie and humphrey had no choice but to follow nixon's normalcy, and wallace, like mcgovern, would have constituted a threat in '64, and so supplied another common man with a massive victory. the third member of this triumvirate of popular appeal is, of course, warring g harden, the hack apostle.

i believe that the american people keep on indicating that they cannot except in the rarest of circumstances (read: need) accept any kind of aberration. i believe that any man with a touch of lunacy, whether divine or demoniac, can draw only one third of the american vote, no matter how much the rest of the populace may agree with him in general. i believe, in short, that this country has indicated over and over again a distrust, a hatred, of anything that smacks of excellence in any direction. it distrusts the poet, cer-tainly, more than it distrusts the bricklayer, but let me tell you it distrusts an excellent bricklayer just as much as an excellent poet. it is even terrified of the good speller and the grammarian, because these things are more than it is good to know.

and yet, this is not even a question of elitism, since that has always been a phony issue. the problem is not that we great democratic republicans distrust kings, but that we desperately crave common kings. all of us, the vaunted descendants of the dregs of elitist europe, want men on horseback, want leaders, but god forbid that the leaders should have any qualities the least of us does not have. freedom and excellence seem the two greatest threats any american faces.

let me speak, for one moment, to this point in the light of one of mr nixon's campaign stands: the work ethic. let me say that not one invention, those things that constitute what we call progress, and what most americans take to be "good," was made by anything less than a lazy genius. i suspect that in these terms those two words are inextricably tied. i mean simply that the real hard worker is the man who goes by spurts, leaps (forward or sideward or backward, but leaps), who rests in indolence between the great spasms of energy. the plodder invents nothing—and indeed is threatened by every invention, the indoor toilet as much as the printing press. they are all, to him, "work of the devil," and it is not until his sons grow up in a world dominated by these things, and he dies, that they become normal, and inevitable, and absolutely necessary for human life.

but i must go back again and again to the totals of this vote. i must think over and over again of the polks and the fillmores, the arthurs, the hoovers, the buchanans, the pierces, the tafts—and the fifty years of our history out of 180 when we put up with jefferson and jackson, lincoln, cleveland, wilson, roosevelt, kennedy, even with all their faults—and i must think that there's a constant need to burrow in, to draw the covers, to cut off human contact, human growth.

and i must think also of the men we've ground down or driven out, the burrs and houstons and debses and la follettes for just a few, the men with visions that were warped perhaps, but at least were visions. they saw, as the saying goes, beyond the tips of their noses—they showed, as cleopatra said of anthony, their backs above the element they lived in.

don't think for a minute that truman wasn't elected because
we thought he was more of a trustworthy nonentity than dewey—
and when he turned out the slightest bit thorny, we ran to mama
ike. nathaniel told me this morning that some bad kids put stuff on
the street that anybody who walked through it wanted to vote for
nixon. i wish to christ it were that simple, that a theory of evil even
came close to applying. it doesn't. and, lest you missed it, the
wednesday post reported (on page sixty) "heavy strikes on both
sides of the demilitarized zone," the loss of an f-111 over north
vietnam's panhandle with the fate of the crew unknown, and the
wounding of an american in a sapper's attack at long binh. the
savior keeps on killing, keeps on maiming. but that's normal.

a little touch
of harry s. in
the night

while nixon was standing watching harry s be buried the bombers were dropping enormous loads and themselves on hanoi. i am not quite as disturbed by this anomaly between respect paid for the dead in the midst of this death because i would hope that every good man gets mourned well, and that every man gets mourned somehow, but i have been sickened considerably by the official, semi-official, and public mouthing of a comparison between harry & hiroshima and nixon & hanoi.

as i understand it harry s took the oath and was immediately presented with a decision to make, which decision was made on the basis of military, political, and scientific advice, and while i think it was the wrong decision (i. e., as a long-time revisionist it seems to me first that the japanese were beaten and second that there were alternative ways to demonstrate the power of the bomb) there seems at least to be some sane reason for his decision.

richard m can in no way be accused of using reason, nor can he blame his advice. the record shows this. the scars on southeast asia also show this. the problem with harry s was not how he used or abused his power, but that such awesome power had been given to one man. we lucked out with him, in that there were very few "wrong" decisions, and very few shameful ones. but the men who came after him were from a different america, and in this new america it is harder to luck out. i mean that seriously.

i once drew up a list of the three americas: I washington to johnson (andy); II grant to truman; III eisenhower on. there are interesting parallels if you carry this through, and one ends up with a much different view of lincoln and roosevelt, as each turns out to do what yes had to be done but destroys the fabric of the previous nation in so doing. one also gains respect for andy johnson and truman as two men caught in that bind between the dying and the newly born, and desperately trying to make sense and save the fabric. the fact that all three americas start with a bonafide war hero is of course also pertinent. i leave it to you to draw your own ties for king richard, but the letters in the daily news of friday december 29 ran four against nixon, two in favor, which is hardly a significant number but certainly a significant group.

then, for those hoping to drink easier on new year's eve, today's "high official close to the pentagon" intimated that there would be a new year's halt in the bombing, at least for the one day, but not before and not after.

if this all sounds tired, lacking in energy, washed out, it's because it is. my god, there are people asking now, now! what they can do. i will not ask where were you when we needed you, but by jesus if you can figure out a way to stop this mad process at this point you have my blessing. however, it doesn't help that last night a rich man told me with great anger and sorrow that he understood now that we were worse than 1939 germans. i do not know where his mind was in 1965 so i will not judge but i don't think it was getting its ass kicked in demonstrations, and i would prefer to hear this kind of talk from those who have. we had one triumph. we forced a president to give up. that's not a terribly big triumph especially when you spend at least a few minutes every day wishing he was back picking his beagles up by the ears. at least he showed his schwantz to visiting reporters instead of dancing with ll-year old girls.

> hey hey rmn
> how many women, how many men?

> or other similar questions

in any event, i hadn't intended to write an obituary for harry s, since i figured enough people would paw over those remains, but i must say that a long life spent in hiding among the middle americans convinces me that you could at least have bought that used car from harry.

he was a man who rose to greatness in a seat that's filled with power and for that reason he puts to shame as no one else the stink that sits there now jerking off all over the face of the earth.

god bless you harry. may your spirit, even with hiroshima on it, intercede to bring us grace.

and to the
democrat for
whom it stands

Chapter 13   January 11, 1973

the voice $mas party this year, which for reasons beyond my ken
was held after $mas which led to nobody knowing how to say
anything to ed or dan because they were afraid that just saying
happy new year would be interpreted as not wishing a merry $mas
whereas it was kind of silly to wish merry $mas after the fact, was
featured for me by the pinning on my lapel of a small metal new
york city flag by the voice aviation editor. i dug this because i am
after all a new yorker.

   but then people started to tell me that it meant i was for ed
koch—which is not to say that i feel in any way against ed koch.
it's just that they pointed out that the clip to the pin said it was given
to me by ed koch and so it was his symbol. well i got news for ed
koch. he did not give me new york city. i came here from yonkers
a poor boy with two loaves of rye bread under my arm, and now,
twenty years later, i own this city. i have fought for and in it, i have
bred two families here, and i have even fallen asleep drunk in it
thus missing a chance to see the sun rise in brooklyn heights,
wherever that might be.

   i will tell you ed koch who gave me this city. franz kline gave
me this city, who came from mauch chunk pennsylvania via philly,
boston, and london and beat it into himself—just as charles olson
gave it by not being able to handle it. he huddled in his coats and
sweaters the short year or so he lived here, a different kind of cold
than gloucester mass. and my own sons newly arrived from the
west give it to me every day, the one in and out of record stores,
wheeling and dealing, the other still on his mountain in taos.

   this city is my mountain. i have said it over and over again and

38

everybody laughs, but nevertheless it looms beneath me, it fights me, it sustains me—and all this despite its obvious lack of anything human, except the people. are they human? i don't know, i don't look to see. i walk my prescribed beat, the path as well-defined as any indian trail across this island. i will not say i could not write some other place. i think i could. but i write books in my apartment, the kids around, the television going, the phones, the friends, and i think i need that, tho i may be wrong. the suggestions are continually coming in, but they bother me more than the noise in the apartment: i was advised to (a) rent an office, (b) take long bus trips, (c) fly to the islands or out west, or (d) move into a hotel room. my study is a seven-by-eight space under the guest loft—as i write now my oldest son is sleeping up there if he can. a large flag is draped around it to cut it off from traffic. the flag stops neither lem nor nathaniel one whit, but it defines my space. my wife's loom is backed up to my desk, the flag separates us.

what would i do with a book-lined study in the country? that remains to be found out when and if i ever make money—but wouldn't i, just wouldn't i rather have a brownstone? i think i would.

you pick your space to live in, and you live there, if they let you. i need to know where my bar is, where my clean shirts are, and where my lady lives is what i told the cabdriver who was confused because west fourth crossed west tenth, that's all you need to know, how could you find any of them some other place, unless you felt you lived there?

so, dear ed, i have to say i'm wearing the flag of the city of new york for new york and not for you, tho i'm glad you're handing them out. i'm not that upset about flags, myself, and have long considered, for example trying to wrest the american flag back from the american legion and the national football league, since i can't quite understand how it got to be theirs exclusively anyhow. and during our rent troubles i flew my own red white and black flag from the courtyard window as some sort of nation. after all, why not. so i'm pleased to wear this city's flag.

besides, every city needs a couple of poets in residence, because novelists would rather talk than fall down drunk, and what kind of place would that be to live? the new york flag can cover us all.

checkers all over again: we will not be saved

he will get away with it scot-free, which means without paying his dues. the language was as immaculate as the checkers speech, the moral outrage, the attack, always the attack: he will stand for no covering up, no one will be protected.

the president's statement came on tuesday, and by wednesday morning william safire had the guns going in the times. safire had made his first appearance with a regular column earlier in the week, an "essay" indicating among other things that he was not the president's flack, and now in his second column he proved how much the language has changed. what statements like

> "... he wrote out his announcement, read it in a cold stern voice, and left no doubt that he had stepped up to the situation and engaged it frontally"
> and
> "... (unlike Churchill) he is neither magnanimous in victory nor defiant in defeat, but he has often shown himself to be a tower of strength in a crisis"

can be construed as if not flackery i cannot even begin to guess. he also makes reference to this being comeback time which is certainly apt, it being spring and easter and all, but what new gods, what green shoots? thus, there will be nothing from this something, we know that already, so has the world as well as the language changed, and tricky dick will smell of roses once again. perhaps now we will have john mitchell as our martyr, and martha, whose name as well as style elicited cackles not so long ago, will have to be beatified, placed in plaster in a niche, one of those who tried to save us. but we will not be saved.

safire says, "a few will gloat 'I told you so,' and by their misreading of the public mind will help rally public opinion behind the president." he is half right and half wrong. certainly a few will gloat and i will be among them—not only did i tell you so, but the president himself has told you so, and tho some worry about seeing the presidency splattered with mud, i worry about the emperor's new clothes and a curious blindness to mud on the presidency when even the president is trying to brush it off. but safire is wrong if he thinks my writing down such thoughts will help rally public opinion behind the president.

it will not, because public opinion needs no such rallying. the last year has demonstrated amply that half the public doesn't care as long as dick's our man, and the other half is desperately frightened that the walls will come crumbling down and so will tolerate any abuse. blend this with the basic underlying feeling that they're all dirty anyhow so what difference does it make, and you begin to see a genuine marxian analysis of why the capitalist system will disappear. that's pat, but not nearly as pat as nixon's statement.

i am trying to be reasonable about this, in the hope of being heard by someone who doesn't ordinarily agree with me, but all the time a voice is screaming inside me, because it is very hard to rationally announce to the passengers that the ship is taking water at an alarming rate. excuse me, sir, but that iceberg is now in the engine room.

the problem is not the watergate itself, it is that which comes now, otherwise known as the snow job. and it will succeed, you'd better believe it. nixon spoke out, finally, because the party needed it, the erosion of credibility was too much for them to bear; now the saner minds will speak out to save the presidency; they will say, and will be believed, that it must not be tarnished, it must be preserved. but who will save that ideal called democracy?

if the form is more important than the substance, the thing

dies. we know this, we know this, we know this. yet we will continue to cherish the form and cover our eyes to the rot, and so the thing will have to die. and if we kill ourselves or they kill us, in the end, indeed, they will bury us.

into the heart-lands: no one will march

the road to cortland new york is paved with new jersey and the borscht circuit, when country fades out after liberty but the knicks can be picked up on wnbc almost 'til binghamton, and even come in, weakly and fading, late at night in cortland itself.

driving through jersey one has to think of the weird houses people must live in in the garden state. one looks at the roadside emporia and draws conclusions. every house must have at least four breakfast nooks and six fireplaces, else why would there be so many dinette and fireplace shops? there's a place called schatzi's delicatessen, and i quiver to think of the spellings on the menu but i'll never know, since we kept plowing ahead on our journey.

we didn't stop until into the borscht circuit itself, when a food-gas-lodging cut-off beckoned just as my bladder reached the danger point. with my luck the place we picked turned out to be american, with four middle-aged gents scowling at me as i asked for the john. shots and beers were in front of them, the ball game was on the set, why could there not be commerce between us? instead the looks followed me to the john, and the conversation started up the minute i re-emerged, heads together, furiously discussing anything. fearing to intrude i murmured a polite thank-you and headed for the door. once i got there, behind me, the owner's voice burst into a furious "you're welcome." to which i thought not to respond, but then, equally furious, i snapped "i said thank you." and left. this is known as a mind like a steel trap. a minor incident, and some touches of paranoia, yes? oh but i am what nixon protects them from, and like the germans with hitler they are so afraid of the enemy that the enemy becomes their friend, no matter what he does

to their lives. so the car rolled and the knicks rolled and i arrived in
cortland, and did my stint, a week of working with young kids in
writing. what we taught each other must remain a secret until i get
a book written. but i did get to watch nixon from the perspective of
a college bar and am happy to report that the wit is as sharp as ever.
but the mood is defeat. their paranoia has lapsed, or fallen again,
more precisely, into catatonia, and the quips cannot save the
dreadful feeling that nothing can be done. not that we in this city
will do anything, either, don't misunderstand me, but the bitching
here seems more positive, more an american right. out there it's as
bitter as gall and no one will march.

on thursday and friday i participated in a conference on open
education, its motto: making the schools safe for diversity. i didn't
find out until thursday that the keynote speaker was al shanker and
since i had a workshop to run i was spared him. but i'd still like to
know why he was even invited, since, as far as i can tell, his idea of
open education would be to get rid of the kids so the teachers
wouldn't have to worry about the little bastards. someone said that
the ultimate symptom of the social disease was the appearance of a
shanker. my workshops concerned the various methods and tech-
niques of teaching children creative writing. since it is my belief
that there are no ways, and indeed no need, to teach this to children,
the workshops went very well.

the one concrete result of our meetings was to formulate
precisely objectives for teachers which can be drummed into every
administrator's head, and posted on the bulletin boards in every
teachers' college.

        each june
        each child shall be
        one year older
        and one year smarter
        and alive

the teachers loved it, i love it, you can love it too. but it won't happen. we will go on turning our children into surly believers; and, equally, it will never be possible to leave "this little world, this precious tone set in the silver sea, which serves it in the office of a wall or as a moat defensive to a house, against the envy of less happier lands, this blessed plot . . .," without feeling palpably the heartland turned against us, the good gone down, the world turned topsy-turvy.

on the way back in, when we hit the west side drive, i turned to george and said "why don't we pick up some chinese on the way home," and he said "i could always eat chinese food." we were home, and the bowels relaxed.

let's put the
holy day back
in holiday

this piece was written on the longest day of the year. at 9.01 a.m. today, thursday, june 21st, summer began officially. i am telling you this because i assume no one else will, aside from noting it on the news as a lead-in to the weather report.

but on that same news, this morning, was the report that the city schools are going to teevee lunches for the kids, presumably for "better nutrition" like they say, and on "a.m. new york" a psychologist with a proper gray beard and all was talking about his "new" diet which depends on your body's appetites, and of course we've just finished celebrating, in less than a week, two of the great archetypal holidays, father's day and flag day. so nature is taking a beating as usual. i'll leave the food questions for a cooler day, but i'd like to talk about the time problem.

there won't be any bonfires tonight welcoming the sun, unless they're accidental or arsonistical, and who of us knows or cares what we dreamed last night, so who knows what the year holds for us?

the point is that even computers are quite often programmed to "meaningful time sequences," so why can't we do it for ourselves? why can't we ride out tonight in joy and mystery, fuck dance and sing, we've got the sun back. why didn't school end yesterday? flag day indeed!

what i am asking for is atavism in the purest sense, a return to the commonest of senses, that of the world and its infinite glory and terror. does it make you feel any better to know that the sun will continue coming back for x billion years? do you sleep better not marking such dates? a sense of holiday, holy day, is what is needed.

herewith, as suggestions for summer contemplation, a list of holidays to be observed, strengthened, enjoyed:

midsummer eve: dream the dream that will take you through the year.

midsummer night: celebrate the shortest night of the year by staying up. occupy yourself appropriately.

july fourth and labor day: the thirteen weeks of summer ought no doubt to be punctuated by long weekends, so why not these two, since neither has much relationship any more to either independence or labor—the point being simply to have one on the seventh weekend and one on the thirteenth, to signal an end.

harvest holidays: halloween, certainly, with its homage to the mother, and to the mysteries of death while the crops are being harvested; thanksgiving, when the crops are in. eat, grow strong, it will be a long winter.

winter: the old idea, yule, saturnalia, the twelve days of christmas—in other words a statement that yes, winter is here, the sun has gone away, the feasting, the dancing, the fucking, is all desperate now, the gift-buying, making, giving, is all a hedge against eternity. and let it culminate in what we call new year's day, the day of adding up, starting out, sobering to the long haul of winter.

pre-spring holidays: as said before, groundhog day as good as any, and better than most. a recognition that the spring will come, no matter what we do, or what the winter does to us. and valentine's day, or, simply put, love day, so that after the blackness of the winter and the clutching for warmth only we can recognize some pleasure also in our mutual company.

spring: the seeding, the beginning. the idea of easter and of passover as endlessly man-handled by religionists. the seeding of the soil, the soul, the mating in the furrows. a week of brightness. why not new clothes?

and so back to summer, in that magic circle of the year.

for additional consideration: the fool's day, where it all hangs out, hostility, love, whatever's left from winter; and self, or human, day may l, because isn't that what the revolution is about, and the maypole?

understand, you still could bitch about these, that's part of it, no one has to celebrate them, but you damn well ought to know what it is you're turning your back on. that's a celebration too.

who do we bribe to get these laws passed? do you have any connections? or, maybe, we just start celebrating them. there's a precedent for that, you know. out of the cave mama, the sun is back.

fair play: getting in the spirit

*Swooping down on the brood of vultures comprising the alien
IWWs, the Anarchists and the Socialists, everywhere hatching
discontent and misery, the great American Eagle is driving 'em
out!*

*Every loyal American in every walk of life should help the
sturdy beak and talons in the unrelenting fight.*

Start to-day!

To-morrow may be too late!

which are the beginning and end of a poster reproduced in
this year's anarchist-revolutionary calendar. it's a splendid thing to
see before descending to the times and the hearings. it rings in the
head as i read the admonitions of all my fellow americans to all
their fellow americans to keep the hearings pure, to make sure that
the hearing room not be turned into a "circus" or "carnival."

and every time sam or howard asks that the customers refrain
from applauding, i think again about the good old american spirit
of fair play. i think of how often i've hungered for this spirit only to
find it a bit evanescent in the way of spirits everywhere. and i've
noticed that it seems to apply best while the establishment is
winning. for instance, altho i don't know anything about the merits
of the positions in the fuentes fight, i do notice that his supporters
are accused of using unfair means, while all those nice people in
the south and canarsie and around detroit play fair.

i remember an editorial in the news in the early '60s announc-
ing a pacifist demonstration against the first nuclear sub up in
connecticut and i remember the news calling on all good americans
to go up and break some heads.

i remember the fair play at the robeson rally in peekskill, and i remember the fair hearings of the mccarthy era.

and i remember too the fair play macarthur gave the veterans in the bonus army, and how rational the cavalry and tanks and machine guns were. i remember, just to be corny, sacco and vanzetti, and my heart throbbles in my throat.

what i see is that we are dealing with beasts who countenance and practice burglary and theft, character assassination, blackmail, and assorted other malfeasances, all in the name of national security, who indeed are proud of what they do, because they are saving the country. and i wonder why we worry about fair play for them, when we don't give it to people who want bread or education or change in the power structure or to get high.

what i'm trying to say is that much as i would like to live in a world where there was such a thing as fair play, i understand that i don't, and so, when the people roar with laughter at ehrlichman's obfuscations, or when they cheer sam ervin as he takes his seat, i'm not surprised. it's the sort of thing people in this country have always done. we're a nation of fans, and also great believers in bandwagons, and when we hear what we want to hear we yell about it. but it ain't only us who make the problem. it's them that laid the groundwork: i, like ehrlichman, believe in national security, and if i ever saw a threat to it it's nixon and his gang and i believe any means necessary, and i can't draw any lines, ought to be used to get them out of the way. i mean this sort of talk might be misconstrued if you listened to it on a tape, but that's not what i meant at all when i wrote it, and it's out of context anyhow.

and what i'm saying is that they've always had this double standard about fair play, and now it's permeated the whole atmosphere. what else was cowens saying that night when he tackled walt frazier in a losing game, except that when you're mvp and white and a boston celtic you're supposed to win the championship and if you're losing it then fuck fair play. or like we used to say fair play, and its cousin the good loser, only applies to those who ought to lose. winners got no rules, because they're the good guys.

which thought leads me back to the calendar, where i find

> *Lacking the power to reason, they have become wolfish and vicious.*
>
> *Refusing to reform and become decent, law abiding Americans, they have no rights under the American Constitution.*
>
> *The old Eagle has his eye on 'em and he's going to sweep 'em out.*

and people are worrying because the crown is hostile to ehrlichman? have they chained and gagged him yet? or even let him see the inside of a cell? let's be fair, fellows, and let the hearings go on, let the crowds at the stadiums boo nixon's name, let the audiences chuckle with uncle sam, it's all part of the good old american tradition. and i'm fully aware of the implications that ehrlichman et al may never be prosecuted if the "hostile" atmosphere persists. since when has such a thing interfered with a fair trial the american people wanted?

people you could ask include henry aaron and hank greenberg, chief joseph and sitting bull, susan b anthony, eugene v debs, joe hill, and john ehrlichman's grandfather, to mention only noncriminal defendants.

the little american: the era of john j. wilson

just as graham greene supplied the world with a usable definition of us guys for the '50s with his "ugly american," john j wilson may very well have served the '70s. the little jap, after all, is an old story from wilson's ilk, but the little american is too good to die, what with tricky dick being turned down on his steak order by his own butcher for the visiting jap's dinner, and the gnomish swiss and the greasy arabs and the porcine krauts all making money on the u.s. dollar, and the fat chink and the ugly russki jest asittin back and smiling.

so we can relax now, having been named, and even inouye (who could laugh, according to the times, when sam rayburn, on being introduced to him for the first time, said: i know who you are, how many one-armed japs do you think we have in the house?) must now realize that it don't make no difference, they've all named themselves as well.

like nature imitating art, the day my last voice piece appeared containing solemn maunderings about the meaning of "fair play," the little american went and proved the whole thesis out, and now i can only laugh. i am not, by the way, concerned with the "racial epithet" as such. we're all used to that—but i am concerned with the very real venom with which he used it, this little american, and the singling out of this particular senator, because indeed it would be difficult to use a racial epithet with a lowell weicker, and most of all its use by this particular man, who had spent the last several days making use of every letter of the law, and none of the spirit of it.

the point is that only the most hopeless liberals will at this point maintain that racial epithets are not a part of our (or any) language; but one must then begin to carefully elucidate the hows and why of their use. and the little american demonstrated clearly to any and all that his primary recognition of any other human being depends on race and size. it was not only the cry of the racist, it was the cry of the "fair play" bully—he's a shrimp, so why should i take shit from him? that's the real horror, might making right again, with only the rule of law to save us, and this son of a bitch quoting that law to his own warped ends.

and, of course, the argument that this little american is an unfortunate single example just won't wash either. he is the appointed legal representative of not one but two of the triumvirate which has ruled america for four years. you don't get picked for such jobs because you happen to be walking down the street at the right time. in fact, lawyers get picked as much for the possibility of client-attorney communication as for specific ability, at least in the workaday world i live in.

all of which is why foolish people like me refuse to put down the radical left when it engages in or talks about violence and terrorism, or why other foolish people do feel "better" when mugged by a poor "minority" member than by a middle-class white teenager, since there are very real distinctions. because people like the little american do have power, are in control, do have it all knocked up, and don't hesitate to step on anybody who gets out of their idea of the lines. they are the judges and the juries, and to work within their law, and their idea of fair play, is only to get your ass kicked.

the little american is indeed the silent majority, but he's very far from what lincoln thought he was talking about when he mentioned the common man. the little american has very little idea of what being human is, and doesn't care that he doesn't know. john j wilson may even really believe that to call inouye a little jap is not an insult—and as i've indicated, i'm not sure it is myself—but the venom in john j wilson is the insult, and it is an insult to all of us.

these men, the wilsons, the ehrlichmans with their moral indignation, the haldemans with their cool calculations, must be destroyed, taken out of power, simply because they have the deathdrive to destroy everyone else. it's implicit in their view of the universe, they say things like who is not with me is against me—and if it comes to that, i would rather see the apocalypse run by the have-nots than by the haves.

the morality of the have-nots is really much more acceptable: get off my back or i'll kill you. the morality of the little americans is much too orotund: get out from underfoot so i can make a better world for the good people. and, like willie howard used to say, comes the revolution you'll eat peaches and cream and like it!

dog-day madness: our synapses one scrambled

only the poets don't lie.

"i have a bureau-drawer full of unanswered letters & have a nervous breakdown whenever i open it . . . i don't have any title yet, being only a monk—which word is extremely mis-leading/chinese term is 'cloud/water' viz. a wandering zen student training in a monastery. the training scrambles all my synapses temporarily. . . ."

which is a much better answer than "to the best of my recollection in the march period of the year," in itself an indication of unadmitted scrambled synapses.

only the poets don't steal.

"we're all having much flu & working hard . . . me on part III of 'letter' and 'introductions to other people's books'!! hell of a way to spend time, but as you know, we get caught. . . ."

and they not only usually don't get caught, but when they do they either get away with it, or we decline to push it, because it would damage the nation.

only the poets don't cheat.

"the painting is going fine or crude which is more of what i'm doing. and i have a lot of painting that i need to do before i leave here. i really feel like a tourist out here so i am painting where the tourists go. the beach with all the french painting they did on that domestic subject. people on the beach has something to sink myself into and come up with some fresh air, not that i'm holding my breath and staying under water. i'm on the beach and mingling. and there is such a fine line between the sky and the water that the clouds are coming right down onto the beach and sitting right next to the people. . . ."

only the poets don't kill.

"i'm forty-five years old and all i want is there should be a book out with the poems in it for people to look at after i die. . . ."

so i sit and read the mail, stuck here in the dogdays in the big city, the undefined high anchored somewhere off the coast, the weather change pressing in too slowly, too weakly, and followed up by heat in canada, the plains, the great southwest. i read my mail and it cheers me, as i read the times and it angers me.

what shall i say to william p clements jr who thinks the bombing of cambodian targets and the subsequent bald-faced lying was a "first-class military operation . . . i don't think anybody has anything to apologize about for this. . . ."

what shall i say to the likes of agnew and nixon, what shall i say to ms brownmiller, defending the court's position on censorship, what shall i say to judge di lorenzo accused of perjury, to elmer wayne henley, 17, admitted slayer for sex, for sex!, what shall i say to richard bell, deputy assistant secretary of agriculture, when he tells us there will be less wheat this crop, so food prices will remain "strong," which means higher, and finally, what shall i say to the eighth infantry division command which has announced it is dropping its plan of "counterdissidence" because it is "inappropriate?"

inappropriate, shit, it's snooping, prying, fascism, dictatorship, paternalism, any fucking thing you want to call it except inappropriate. it's also illegal, but the principle seems to have been somewhat eroded.

only the poets do their work outside the profit and the public instant, so it's not that they are cleaner than the rest, it's just that they can't get nothing by being dirty.

like the great whales they swim solitary, singing to not be alone, beaching occasionally, running from the world more often. when they mate it is over in a minute, yet they keep coming back each season for more and more. in between perhaps that is what they sing about.

like the whales everybody believes them marvelous mythic
creatures and no one will believe they have either a function or a
right to exist. they exist so that the lord will see a few solitary souls
who do not lie, cheat steal or murder—except, of course, for art or
passion, but never for profit, never for standing, never for peace or
health or morality. like whales poets cannot sleep since something
must be always feeding in, their metabolism demands it. if they
steal, then, they steal for bread.

since money is the only language of the rest of the world, this
is a crime.

> "pregnant you wander
> barefoot you wander
> battered by drunk men you wander
> you kill on steel tables
> you birth in black beds
> fetus you tore out stiffens in snow
> you moan in your sleep
>
> digging for yams you wander
> looking for dope you wander
> playing for birds you wander
> chipping at stone you wander"
> diane di prima, "loba" part l

which says some of what i mean, altho it was written about
woman and not poet. so there is not time enough for the front page
of the times, for the filth the court allows, the clouds are coming
down onto the beach next to the people, we are busy writing
introductions to other people's poems, our synapses are scrambled.
we want to leave a book, we want to meet in that mating of one
minute that sustains us all year, we do not want to leave dead bodies
behind us.

losses

hateful though it is to admit it, nevertheless i must confess that life in general has not been that bad to me, not nearly as cruel and malicious as i would like to think most days. the losses have either been predictable or otherwise acceptable, and somehow i've learned to live with them, one after the other. sometimes they all pile up, and that becomes a problem, but you rank them by their priorities and live with them one by one.

innocence was lost at some early age, perhaps four, since i was not yet going to school. presented with the choice between going to shul with my mother—still an exciting and desirable object in those days, to be together and apart up in the ladies' balcony, among the smells and sounds of women in go-to-meeting clothes, and still to be able to sneak downstairs, crawl into the space between my father and my uncle harry, or better yet between uncle harry and uncle manny—between the magic option, and the two new passenger coaches for the lionels that for some reason (i can't think of any holiday near my birthday, nor did we go to shul for chanukkah—perhaps, then, a pre-wedding ceremony, with the pelting of the groom with nuts and raisins, the wild scramble by the kids, each to get as many bags as possible, while the men grumbled and the women smiled), i sat, four years old, unable to decide, until my mother left in anger, leaving me with the trains, totally unsatisfying. decisions, decisions, ever since, i can't make up my mind, and gifts have ended up a disappointment.

virginity, losing which is usually considered glorious by males at least, also a problem. waiting 'til twenty, tormented by doubts as to my own sexual stance, when it came it was filled with love and very little sex, and took a while to get used to, fifteen years perhaps.

then, in order to save my liver, i had to lose (give up, but still a loss) the only crutch i ever found that worked, that slowed me down, but helped me walk or limp my way through difficult passages, had to learn to walk without it.

i lost my first wife—though there we both lost our first loves, more like, but maybe that is straightening itself out now, with one son back in town, the other off into his world, and so, perhaps, i have a good deal more than many who have stayed together that twenty years or so.

my ideals went in my 20s, as they must, though some cling on tenaciously. the energy went then too, eight hours a day at the job, two kids a year and a half apart, the poems at night; and then it came back a little in the 30s, and i started in again, with poems and kids and chasing hours.

i lost the country several times, each time a chunk of it chipping off, mccarthy, the assassinations, vietnam, nixon, but i stay here, still claiming citizenship, still trying to dredge up some hope for what we live in, what we dreamed of.

the hair stays, but even that thins down, the beard is getting scruffy where it once was full, the muscle tone was never ever there, the fast ball wasn't either, nor the legs, so they are all just the same, no losses.

the eye and ear remain, at least, whatever they have been, and they let me hang in there, wherever that turns out to be. i can still laugh at jokes sometimes, and the heart rouses, as is evident, for women and good men. the poems remain, or rather, keep coming, and i suspect that words will be the last thing to desert my one-sided brain.

but now my teeth have gone, at least the top half of them, and i feel profoundly that loss, and i thought to write something for them, so they'd know my dentist is saving them in a little envelope, memorabilia he says with a wry smile hidden behind his surgical mask, and i wonder if they can be used to make the plates that are coming. how else will anyone know me without that fucked-up smile, the gaps i hid for years without success. what will celery taste like and apples?

they are gone, the ganglionated cyst on my wrist that marked me for twenty years is gone, only the wart on my nose still stays, the oppenheimer wart. it appeared a year after my grandmother died, to replace hers in this world, and it marks me. but to have no teeth at forty-three is to know loss as well as anomie, that is, the conscious feeling as opposed to just lacking something. they are gone, the world goes on, i will adjust the dentist says. other people have he says. what has that got to do with loss, with knowing that somehow the world will never be the same, that there is no returning, in fine knowing that you will survive, but wondering why it had to be this way, and how it would have been the other.

they went easily, at the end, and they have a good home.

piece with honor:
on the language
of sex

the op-ed page of the times, as a part of its constant and useful effort to keep my bile flowing at a healthy active rate, has come up now with a person named barbara lawrence, whose credit notes her as "a former editor . . . (and now) associate professor of humanities at the state university, old westbury." ms lawrence is certainly not what you would call your run of the mill fuzzy-minded liberal feminist humanitarian. or any of the above.

her piece (you should pardon the expression, since ms lawrence probably wouldn't) is devoted to telling us that all the words we've been using to speak of sexual activity are bad, like my mother used to say. and all those we thought we'd stopped using, like copulate and intercourse and making love, are good.

she claims a "sadistic" root for fuck, which may even be true, altho my sources seem much less definite about it than hers, but which ignores the main point. the people she is talking to, us, were all raised on a different root meaning—even if it was incorrect. everyone i know who thought about roots at all was told somewhere along the line that fuck came from an old celtic word meaning to plant seeds in the ground. and we thought how romantic and beautiful that was, and how unlike all those sterile words the official world used. understand me, she may be right. it may indeed come instead from words meaning to strike. to hit, etc., but we all thought we were saying something else.

in addition, ms lawrence misunderstands the war. no writer i know who uses "dirty" words is using them to "deny women their biological identity, their individuality, their humanness." maybe some use them to deny it to people, but not to women per se, and most use them for exactly the opposite purpose. in fact, we use such words for two reasons. first because they are there in the air and language around us, far more than those words she suggests are "better" whatever that might mean in the context of language (and it might help here if she seemed to have an ear as well as an intellect). and secondly because, indeed, we are attempting something political.

we are trying once and for all and again and again to answer those who stifle our own humanness, those who for some 100 years (the victorian age through world war II) have attempted to mask every human activity in obfuscation and sterility. the very reason young people can talk today of making love is because there was a twenty-five year moratorium on that particular usage which allowed the phrase to be rescued from the mire of bad language, bad thinking, and, indeed, bad art.

of course making love is better than fucking. but who could have known that in recent years? and what of copulation? "to bind or join together"! that's terrific if you're s-m. ms lawrence prefers "testes" to "the obscene equivalent of this word which suggests little more than a mechanical shape," by which i assume she means balls, although conceivably it's nuts she's bugged about. i would suggest that in any real universe balls and nuts both have more real relationship to that conglomeration of tissues than testes ever dreamed of having.

she says the words in question are "arrogantly self-involved" and perhaps they are. perhaps in order to make love one must be so arrogantly self-involved that one can go outside oneself to another. perhaps the physical interacting of the erectile penile tissue and that of the lubricated vaginal complex will lead to such humble disengagement of self that indeed intercourse will transpire, or maybe not.

that is all so much cowshit. that a teacher should be laying out a totally abstracted and unreal language to students at this date is unforgivable, no matter what the political or philosophical reasoning behind it. that we need new words for a real relationship between people is without question, but to re-institute the words that have held men and women slaves these many years is ridiculous. language changes the world, but the world also changes language. there can be no absolute dicta.

one might just as well write about truth and beauty, and shill, with nixon, for the dignity of labor, which is where it is. you and i know that truth and beauty and the dignity of labor are worthy objects of our attention. but they have stolen the words from us, so we will have to do with what we can. perhaps in a better world talking straight about sex will allow for some options, but right now we're trying to figure out how to touch each other. and talk while doing it.

silver linings for our times

ralph nader says that there isn't any energy crisis at all. that it's all a hype, to maintain outrageous profits for the oil companies. barry commoner says that it's probably a hype, but that there's an energy crisis nevertheless, and unless it's solved the environment is done for. the department of the interior says that there's a crisis, too, but they want us to tighten our belts, put on sweaters, and start getting tough now that the going is. and the oil industry says that the crisis is so bad they need alaska, wyoming, and colorado.

so the situation is, to say the least, unclear. meanwhile middle america is showing its mettle, and its devotion to the america for which it stands. the truckers are stopping their trucks, southern california is asking for a variance because "our culture depends on gasoline," and a guy in fort wayne said, well, there ain't no law yet. all this is going on while the radical subversive, and un-american states of the northeast are indeed tightening their belts and at least trying to make sense, and the best, of the situation.

so some of us here have been turning our attention to the good things that can flow when the oil doesn't. tom wicker ran a piece the other day about the probable loss of jobs for a sizeable part of the population. and in the course of it he predicted the demise of the motel-mart-mcdonald strips outside the smaller cities and towns. channel 2 had a featurette on how buildings will change, what with architects paying some attention to energy needs. instead of just "designing."

i've come up with my own list of possible benefits and present them here.

1. *the re-flowering of towns and cities and the concomitant demise of the suburbs.*

wicker doesn't go far enough when he foresees the asphalt

strips dying. what will actually happen is that all those middle-class intellectuals who destroyed the cities by moving to the outlying towns and villages, which they then destroyed by trying to make them into small greenwich villages or brooklyn heights or upper west sides, will come back to the cities when they discover that they can't go anywhere, and it's a drag to huddle in front of a fire when you have to instead of by choice.

this will allow the towns and villages to re-flower in the original image. with only those people who genuinely like that kind of living living there. in addition all the weekend visitors will stop flooding in and the leaves will be able to fall in their own time and without supplying kicks for voyeurs.

when these middle-class intellectuals do indeed flow back to the cities, the cities will find themselves re-invigorated, or at least so every sociological tome and civic report i've read in the last ten years seems to believe.

the suburbs will wither of their own weight due to a number of obvious factors, among which are the impossibility of setting up an efficient bus service to and from shopping centers, the unfeasibility of entertaining one's self and family inside the house, and the inability of an entire generation of young people to move, socialize, or mate without a car.

2. *the re-emergence of the chair as an object on which to sit. and other aspects of non-travel.*

never mind the buildings. designers will have to re-align their thinking in regard to much simpler forms. the chair, which will again be used for sitting, will have to have its form follow its function once more, just as god intended. no one who has to spend his time at home instead of in a car is going to put up with aesthetics when it's his ass that's involved.

the sitting, of course, may lead to a renewal of reading and thinking. which may be just as well. after all, we've had twenty-five years of extensive travel opportunities, and most polls seem to show that instead of broadening it narrows. i know of only two people who have had their horizons widened in all that time—and one case involved the discovery of the basket number in tangiers two years after i had read about it in an olympia press book.

whether or not the current plague of impotence will be affected i have no way of telling. but my guess would be that people who sit still and think tend to have more hard-ons than people who are always running around drinking strange water. on the other hand, the sexual revolution is probably done for, what with having to spend most of your time with the same people.

3. *the upgrading of colleges far and near, partly helped by the healing of the ears.*

without the possibility of jumping on a plane at any hour and at a student discount, people will have to decide whether they really want to study in walla walla, or whether they'd rather take advantage of the brilliant minds at city. if they go to walla walla they're going to have to stay there except for $mas and the summer, which, after all, may be a great idea, but you'd better make the decision, and be right.

since there'll be a severe cutback in electric instruments, high-powered stereos, and the dreaded amplifier, ears will hopefully regain some of their normal capacity to hear, and the art of conversation, and, indeed, the dialogue itself, may revive. this can only help the educational process, whether in a formal or self-taught manner.

4. *the re-identification of the enemy, and as a corollary the re-growth of the revolution.*

this point may well be the most crucial. if the gas crunch continues, and the car sales follow the pattern already established, in which large luxury cars keep selling at their normal rate to the wealthy, while middle-priced big cars are being abandoned in favor of small ones by the middle and lower classes, we will once again be able to point to and hate rich men.

something went out of this society when everybody looked affluent, and it was possible to deny the existence of need. we can look for a resurgence of, at first, petty harassment of cadillacs, imperials, and continentals, which ought to escalate rapidly into a full-scale attack on such blatant symbols of conspicuous consumption by the haves, and then on the haves themselves.

this is obviously a fruitful field for further speculation, and i'll try to keep you apprised of new developments. in the meantime, while, obviously, i can't guarantee you the kingdom of heaven just because of the energy crisis, i do have high hopes. i keep thinking of the rabbi's instructions to his congregation when the world learned that the polar icecap was melting and the entire world would be flooded to a depth of twelve feet within fourteen days. he said, we got two weeks to learn to live under water.

any wednesday

under the assault of the seasons i look at the calendar and find spring and henrik ibsen both born on the same day, and even though that don't equal march 30 which has moses maimonides, paul verlaine, and sean o'casey for god's sake, it's not bad. the onslaught of spring takes us all in different ways any year, but it's got to be odd for everyone this time, regardless of license plates.

the time is out of joint like willy said, and the seasons turn around and around, but what will you do with a mild winter and a short one, and the clock fucked up, and the world gone to hell in an oilbucket, and the eternal truths down the drain? there's no burrowing out from under this spring because we've gotten so far into it we live there. and while the recession may be only a downturn in the economy the depression is real and fierce.

maybe dickiebird is getting us clear of the gurry and now we're in the natural order of things, the second law of thermodynamics proving oh so true, entropy: everything going to shit. is there a horror we haven't learned to put up with?

spring this year isn't coming in green but blue. even spring training means nothing. the sports pages worry about a football strike and the times ran a special series on college recruiting, and so, instead of headlines, there are squibs in the corners of the backpages about that wonderful mythical florida where the sun is warm and winter leaves the bones. kriegel whirls on me asking my picks and i have to stop and think of the names of the teams.

then there is a phone call about a painful and unnecessary death close to us and all i can think of god save me, is how it intrudes on our lives. or at least that's the first thought. what a beast i'm turning into, except that i don't think it's me that's doing the turning. i can feel myself being turned by them, all of them. all of the day-by-day assaults on all of us. no faith, no hope, no charity. no boy scout virtues, no what we used to call morality. and it

wasn't spock that did it, or freud, or marx. no sir. it was all them
decent people. all them god-fearing ones, except they never did tell
us what god it was they feared, did they?

it's easy to know what god ibsen feared. and maimonides and
verlaine and o'casey. they kept putting it down in words for all of
us to see. not one of their phrases was inoperative. wrong or foolish
maybe, but that's allowed anyone if he's able to allow it himself. so
i think i'll think about them and about li po who seduced the
emperor's favorite concubine, showed up late and drunk, fell
asleep on her bosom without performing, was exiled for it anyhow,
lived his life out in the hills writing poems and drinking, dove into
the yellow river one night to fuck the moon because he loved her,
and drowned. or peire vidal of whom they said "he sang better than
any man in the world, and made good songs, and he was the biggest
fool who ever lived because he believed that whatever was made in
verse was what was" and he loved three women at the same time
with all his heart, or so he tells us in one simple stanza, so i think he
was the biggest fool who ever lived.

it's people like this you ought to think of in spring, and to see
the stars in their courses changing, and human beings and trees
alike opening, beginning to bud and spread. and yes, for god's sake,
even think of spring training, what it means, a loosening up, warm up
your arm, begin to throw a little after a long winter's holding back,
begin to run. the scientists begin to think that testosterone produc-
tion's at its lowest in the spring. why not? why would you need that
artificial impetus when the whole world's calling you?

but as ibsen knew and the calendar doesn't this year, the
world is saying go away. helen's off to help a friend survive a
funeral, people like dying, the violence continues unabated, the
lying continues in high places and in low. we are murdering the
spring, and we will pay for it. o western wind, when will you blow
that the small rains down can rain? christ, that my love were in my
arms and i in my bed again. which is what we seem to have
forgotten.

the all stars

it is hard to admit it, but the members of the house judiciary committee may be restoring some small part of my faith in the american experiment. it is hard to sit and watch and listen to these men in my normal state of paranoid cynicism without being moved by their responses to the question before them.

it may indeed be as we keep being told that they are acting politically, that is, that they have at last heard the voice of the people, or seen which way the wind blows, or are intent on cutting losses, or are jealously protecting their own prerogatives, but, nevertheless, they are doing something i believe to be absolutely necessary, and something that is very difficult. they are trying to cauterize their and the nation's wounds. it is too late perhaps to save anything, perhaps indeed the nation can survive neither verdict: nixon innocent and the country, led, slides further into the fascism of our time. nixon guilty and the country, leaderless, slides deeper into the economic morass we already are foundered in. but, certainly, for anyone nurtured on what this country should and could be, at least the ideas can be saved: of all men equal before the law, of public offices being public trusts, of checks and balances. all these ideas have been subverted truly and deeply since the '30s, and increasingly we have lived in a dream of democracy, within a superstate.

now, perhaps, at least that dream can be preserved, to be re-built like they say at some future date. because it is impossible to watch men like mcclory and railsback of illinois turn back to the lessons of their childhood and not have hope. they are saying, simply, that somehow this country did not turn out to be what they were promised it would always be, and they are moved to make one last effort to bring it back.

one can see those moral precepts of their childhood looming large before them, and they are responding. sure, i am proud of my

guys, the jordans and the kastenmeiers and all, who are saying
what i want them to say, but men like these other two must be
listened to by the others, the ones who don't have my dream of
america.

men like these two—and, indeed, most of the members of the
committee—are the closest to what we charmingly call average
joes that we're likely to see in this brouhaha. the senators, ole uncle
sam and his boys, and the cabinet, and the administrators like
hoover and gray, they're the power, they're the superstars. these
guys could be you and me except that they're lawyers, but they're
still little guys. don't i shop with ed koch, watch bella float through
the bar? the house of representatives is the last touch with reality
within the structure of these united states. and sure, that reality isn't
always mine, i recognize that fact, but what i'm trying to say is that
even when the guys with my reality get up to the senate and that
rarefied air, we ain't in touch either.

so, these two come from that other america where they
believe in profits and exploitation and charity and all the trappings
of free enterprise, but they also used to believe in freedom, and law,
in a free market of ideas and emotions as well as of goods, and it is
here that mcclory and railsback are responding. they are saying that
an america cannot stand for any of us if these simple principles are
subverted. they are, in other words, willing to let things go only so
far, even too far, yes, but they will finally stand up and be counted.

it is an admirable thing, one my father told me and told me
was to be found in this country, in this structure. i have not found it
until now. we will not any longer change the world, we lost our
chance for that, but we may, just may, change ourselves. no matter
that ford looms on the horizon—or even that we kept being told
that thornton's speech would tell us what wilbur mills thought. or
that any revolution is miles away. we may yet learn to handle the
fords and the millses from this beginning. in other words we may
yet learn to stand up. that was the whole point, the one that kept

getting lost while we talked about our standard of living, and our place among the great nations of the world.

i consider myself a good and decent and evil american, because i want my vision of america to be the one that wins, within that framework that lets men stand up. i believe this is what mcclory and railsback said in their opening speeches. i believe they stood up and said: enough!

getting the bastard out will not be enough. i know that, as i know that this is a romantic piece. but getting the bastard out will be at least a start, a beginning of things. it may give us strength enough to go further, to re-build this country while this country bumbles or more properly lumbers on. all is not perfect in columbia god knows, but the dream of free men in free communion for the general welfare may just have received its first boost in years.

we may even survive long enough to say: look! we have come through! and at least we'll have tried. the all-stars are the ones who do more than you or they thought they were capable of.

language &
sexism in today's
world: a code
of honor

                                          September 26, 1974

there was this big spread in the times this week announcing mcgraw-hill's decision to try to eliminate male-female stereotypes from its non-fiction publications, including textbooks, reference works, trade journals, children's books, and educational materials. the lead paragraph of the article by grace glueck proclaimed "a new, non-sexist era . . . dawning" at mcgraw-hill, and we were further informed that the house had issued an eleven page set of guidelines which included a list of forbidden phrases and practices to be avoided.

the immediate reaction in this corner, and, i suspect, in most corners occupied by writers, was to writhe a little in embarrassment, and a little in anguish. i mean it's certainly censorship, whether it's good or bad, since it is telling people what they can and cannot write and read. it's also classically dumb, since like the southrons keep telling us you can't change things just by making laws. but then on more mature consideration, i started coming to different conclusions, reacting in the reverse way.

look, it's essentially been these kinds of writings—and by extension, the equivalent kinds of institutions—which have preserved the old shibboleths, the status quo, the sexism, and the racism, and all the isms. these are the code writings, the writings which have nothing to do with language or literature or human activity. and these are precisely the writings in which the stereotypes are preserved because the powers in this society want them preserved.

74

paul goodman, among others, talked a good deal about the difference between reading as we'd like to understand the word, and reading the code, which is what the american system teaches most of us. reading the code means you can go into a supermarket and tell whether you're buying lima beans or carrots by reading the words on the label of the can. reading the code can be taught very easily by force and threats, as when goodman suggested that if the army was really upset about soldiers not being able to understand simple instruction booklets, all they had to do was threaten the guys with vietnam duty if they didn't learn to read them in six weeks. but reading as reading is a different matter. it's taught by care and attention and example, and once you get the habit you don't lose it.

mcgraw-hill's editors, and their cohorts across the breadth of the publishing industry, have been screaming for code-writers and code-readers for fifty years, and that's why we have so many, and that's why their books are filled with offensive material. the code keeps changing. slowly, and not too perceptively, but it does keep changing. what is acceptable in code now won't be ten years from now probably, and certainly won't be twenty-five years from now. and since, in fact, they're the ones who are perpetuating the code (in this case the sexism) they're the ones who have to make big announcements that they're "changing" it. look, everyone knows that mailer is a sexist pig, and so what happens every time he drops one of his loaded statements is that there's a lot of screaming and yelling and some sensible shaking down and everyone comes out of it a little wiser maybe, and generally pretty exhilarated. but when the sexism is slipped in the code books then you grow up believing it.

and, of course, the writers struggling to communicate in the code fields get screamed at when they try to write non-code (whatever it is that year) while non-code (read: creative) writers have constantly to struggle against the code society's implanted in them.

of all the reading i've assigned at city college the one writer who runs the women up the wall on first acquaintance is d h lawrence—and it's his literary criticism i've assigned, not his novels. and yet, of course, in the first quarter of this century there wasn't one writer, male or female, anywhere in this world, who did more to break down the victorian concept of the "good and bad women," who did more to set in motion the sexual revolution, women's lib, radical feminism, and the like. of course by today's standards he's sexist, but then we don't know what he'd be writing like if he were a young writer now, do we? but we do know what mcgraw-hill's non-fiction writers will be writing like—they'll be writing like the editors tell them to: either sexist or non-sexist, left or right, collectivist or individualist, whatever the power and the money says is the code.

so it seems to me we needn't worry yet about this being censorship, and we might even applaud a little. it's probably just bullshit on their part, and most likely also not too workable, and, after all, even if they are riding with the tide for their own purposes, for once it's a useful tide, and it might even help us all a little. i mean it might be nice for nathaniel and lem to find women doctors and bricklayers like they know in real life also appearing in their textbooks for once. and when they read a poem, whether it's mine or muriel's or whoever's they'll know how to read that too.

meanwhile, down in the gap: sports, children and philosophy

it's that season of the year, with days and baseball getting crisper, and i find inside me a softening. it's not that i've modified my stand about the yankees—i still say it'll take another ten years of suffering before yankee fans become bearable (1984!)—but that i've begun reacting differently when it comes to the kids i see everyday here in westbeth who are yankee fans.

we've been here close to five years now, and i've seen myself and them growing older. i date changes in lem, now that he's three, by what i remember of nathaniel when we first moved in, for instance, and in the past summer i began seeing more of all those kids that live around us here. part of it is that lem is three now and socializing with his own gang, while nathaniel at three first had to learn how to make friends; and nathaniel, approaching eight, has now begun to be accepted by the big kids as a friend in that magical alliance of eight to twelve-year-olds; and so i've begun also to know the kids in the building better, as well as be more aware of them.

and when kirk and michel and marco gleefully pass me in the hall with the results of a yankee win or bug me about the mets's chances, i just don't have the heart to snap back at them. i mean, these kids have died with the yankees for more than half their life, just like i've died with the mets and dodgers for more than half of mine, and their glee with the winning is the pure glee of innocence, not the tainted arrogance of old. it's never occurred to them that they're entitled to win, and so when their team is hot it's pure pleasure.

i can even accept, now, nathaniel seriously saying that he
loves both clubs, and when he finds it natural to equate murcer and
jones as love objects, my stomach doesn't twist like it used to. the
kids, as so many times before, may yet restore my humanity. i felt
like a genuine shit, for example, when michel showed nathaniel his
picture with blomberg, taken on photography day at shea, knowing
that if i was any real sort of a dad, i'd've had nathaniel there too.
and it didn't make any difference that the grownups told me that the
yankees had been like of old, with the kids being seated for a
second and a half and then snatched away, without a chance to talk
to the heroes. that's politics, and the game of life, and we know all
about that. the picture itself is what kids and baseball is about.

meanwhile, they are all growing. the kids who were six and
seven when we moved in are now eleven and twelve, and the shy
locked-in behavior, the tendency to run back to the known, has
been replaced by a curiosity, a willingness to take a stand, and, of
course, an occasional need to break balls. they ask me now about
"the wrong season"; they're pleased, i think, to know someone
who wrote a book about baseball, even if it's not their club, and
they're open to the little ones, too. there's a care demonstrated
toward lem and little john when the two three-year-olds wander
into the view of the twelve-year-olds—not that they'd go out of
their way for them, but the kids are no threat now, and indeed
sometimes cute.

and nathaniel stands in the middle of this, accepted, now, as i
said, because after all he can play baseball, catch, throw, hit with at
least the beginnings of authority, and he knows the rules to board
games, or at least can learn them, and so he's ready for the long
rites of initiation. he's running with them, a little behind, a little
scared, but he's learning. the other day he was over at a school
chum's for the afternoon, and when i picked him up there i saw the
kid had a younger brother, around nathaniel's size, and on the way
home i asked about this brother. ahh, nathaniel said , he's ok. how
old is he, i asked. ahh, he's eight. and that was the end of it, though

i said in vain, nathaniel, that's how old you are. it was the ten-year-old was his buddy. he's moving up in class, because he wants to, now, while lem, more often than not says: i not big boy, i little baby, i got tiny ears. because at three he's not yet sure he wants to leave it all behind. he wants desperately to know that helen and i and even the dread nathaniel are here for him, the house is here for him, and the cat and goldfish too. the world out there, that gingerbread world, is lovely and beckoning, but here is safer.

they grow up, and all the kids around them, too, and we sit in the middle of it, not too often noticing. the gains for us are things like no more pampers, no more bottles, help around the house, the startling appearance of new abilities, new knowledges, but the real growing, the changing into other goes unnoticed most of the time. we lose by it. but if we watched too closely, would they change? and would we?

master of
deceit & other
sports news

as if we needed further proof that god is dead and that the older order changeth giving way to the new and that the system doesn't work, we're in the middle of the first all-california world series ever, and to make matters worse it's being held under the auspices of wily walter o'malley and callous charley o finley.

o'malley, who destroyed a city and broke ten million hearts in the process, celebrated his birthday while the dodgers beat the pirates, and across the continent finley was cavorting in his box as usual, making sure that the manager knew how to run the ball club. it's a hard choice to make between those two, but the series is, after all, and after a long long season, the only game in town.

i have to go with the dodgers, and if i get my druthers, the results will be in by the time this hits the stands, with la's golden boys winning in four straight, but if i don't write it down i won't be on record. i've got a lot of semi-hard reasons for picking them, and like most semi-hard things they don't help, especially since they're all emotionally based. but i have to root national league first of all; and there is the lingering memory of the real dodgers (this is, for us purists, the first meeting ever between the brooklyns and the philadelphia athletics, and one could wish indeed to see connie mack locking horns with wilbert robinson instead of o'm and charley, but that's for us dreamers); but most of all i want to see charley throw a genuine fit of pique complete with tantrums when the a's get wiped out.

i realize that that's not terribly sporting of me, but then those two gentlemen have never been terribly sporting themselves, and, indeed, one could if one wanted to make a case for the moral basis of the watergate et al lying in the corruption of our national game; after all wasn't waterloo determined on the playing fields of eton?

but in any event, we'll see whether the stands are full in oakland (which classic california construction has to be the only ball field where it's impossible to play decently during the day, because of the sun angles), and we'll see what the neilsens are for the series as a whole. i was angered and "i-told-you-so" pleased when i discovered that channel 4 ran only one of the two play-off games on its sunday line-up, so it could show a football game too, and i was reminded that it was charles o finley who pushed for the weekend day, midweek night, series format so that "the great american working public" wouldn't be deprived of the games. leonard koppett, most notably, and a few other sportswriters did mention that the very unavailability of the series heretofore with its casual placing on the schedule lent a mysterious magic, and a genuine interest, that i don't think will ever be matched by the current set-up. there was something to arranging your lunch hour or your appointment schedule or a radio to hang an ear on so you could catch some of the game even while adding to the gross national product that's missing from sitting at home. you certainly aint going to go running out in the street when mazeroski homers now.

but the series is the series and i will live with it. i like the dodgers for more than the emotional reasons—i was particularly disturbed by a colleague who characterized the oakland-baltimore match-up as "the two best baseball teams in america" since the dodgers have looked frighteningly solid since last year. they've decent fielding, good pitching, great relief pitching, fantastic hitting, good power, great speed. how much more does anybody want from a club? of course they don't have the class of a brooks robinson whatever that is, or the charisma of a reggie jackson (the only superstar in history with a lifetime average below 270), and like most national league pennant winners all they can do is play baseball good.

for them to win in four games straight is just a dream of mine, of course, but i look for them in six, because i'm worried about holtzman and blue, oriented as i am to minority groups. and speaking of minority groups, dave markson reminds me that last week in the wrap-up column, i forgot to mention rod carew who took his fourth batting title, a considerable feat, since only a few guys like cobb and hornsby and williams and heilmann have won that many or more; and, of course i didn't really think it was necessary to mention mike marshall's rather astonishing season, or to note that he's clearly deserving of the cy young award even if he is a "reliever." i've also been chided for not mentioning nolan ryan's third no-hitter and third over 300 strike out year. all i can say is which nolan ryan is that? or: is he still in the league?

new old
lifestyles

my fall mini-tour was a success, readings in four colleges with a total student body of 1780, in four new england towns with a population of maybe 4000 altogether. the readings were both good and fun, the audiences attentive, the towns possible, and the weather fantastic—maybe the last beautiful fall week in maine and new hampshire, the week before the six month winter sets in.

it was a good chance to check up on the drop-outs, the old friends who picked up and went, and have long since stopped writing me, calling me, telling me about how i ought to be there. i don't know what i expected to find, but i warned them all by card or phone that i'd be up their way, and hoped to see them. tony sent a card by return mail. it said among other things that time would be tight because his gilts were having their first estrous. i astounded helen by knowing what that meant, and got further points in heaven by not answering tony with a card telling him that estrous with the o in it was the adjectival form, and that he meant to say estrus. first of all tony's a fellow writer, or was, and a damned good one, too, so i didn't want to sound snotty, but more importantly, he's out there raising the damned pigs, and using the language, and i'm sitting here as usual reading about it. and even i can get excited about the possibility of young sows going into their first heat so, in the end, tony and i talked for a long time on the phone, with no chance for a meet. there are a lot of things to do on a farm on the vermont new hampshire border when hawk's coming—it ain't like westbeth where all i got to do is get the coats back from the cleaners and put the mortite up on the windows.

my friend charlie just put up the "gone for a while" sign on the old print shop and came over to the reading at franconia. the typesetting shop that he owned and i managed here in the apple is long gone, but he's sitting in north conway now, with a small shop, and gigging weekends as a piano player in the ski joints. new hampshire may not think he's new hampshire yet, since he's only been there eight years, but he sure as hell looks like new hampshire to me.

and dear old sam, who split for the new mexico communes in the '60s, and then gave up on that bad idea and came back to start another one in new hampshire a couple of years ago is thriving too. the farm is doing well, with more melons than anyone's ever seen, and if his car hadn't broken down, he'd have been to the reading in henniker. but sam was a classics professor once and now he was fixing his own car. this is all frightening to me at the same time that it's awe-inspiring, and one can't help wondering about the possibilities for oneself. not the romanticism of it, at all, at all, but the possibility that one might indeed learn to take care of one's own life, at least in some small ways, that one might not be dependent on all the things we spend our lives bitching about.

so with my mind turning that way i got to bar harbor maine, and spent two days looking around the island, and thinking things like gee, is it possible? and then, into the reading that third night walked cliff and frances and the baby, now a boy, grown up just like mine. these two lost east side poets who wandered around st marks's years ago, and then disappeared to run some kind of social service program out on the island, and then moved to maine. and here they were, with a farm, with frances turning herself into a puppeteer instead of a poet, making the circuit of county fairs up there every summer, with cliff learning how to make his own ax handles, because he won't pay the inflated price for new unusable ones, with the two of them growing things unheard of in maine like eggplants and broccoli (their sixty-eight-year old neighbor, old maine scotsman, showing up at the house in the middle of october, his own fields cleared three weeks earlier, asking for some more of that green stuff he and his wife had tasted for the first time ever a month earlier, and he, the scotsman laughing then when cliff said they'd grow 'til november, back now, asking, offering to pay!, for some more of that green stuff, broccoli, in maine, in november!), in other words, the three of them making it, rooted in that hard cold soil.

frances saying you get used to the cold, it's been two winters now, and she survives, and cliff still heating with their own selected wood, no oil bills, living out of their fields and their greenhouse, only a few staples each month to buy, bartering a lot, learning to build, to make, to be.

i said, listen, cliff, i'm forty-four years old, i ain't got the energy or the strength to build a farm from scratch, but damn it, some day if there are enough of you, maybe you can use a teacher, a writer, maybe some day i can trade that off so we can live, if it is a reasonable universe, and had a picture of myself on a skinny old mare, like ichabod himself, pulling into cliff's yard while everybody laughed.

and i came back here thinking jesus, some of them didn't go off half-cocked, some of them went to live there, and are.

rich man,
poor man

it's the end of november, the year is almost over, and the senators assure us that rocky will be confirmed before christmas. i know that others have spoken out earlier and often, but i've held my tongue. it's been a fear, really, that the man would take the state back, and then where would we all be? now it begins to look like carey will take office, and while that may not make us safe, it at least will preclude any possibilities of a rockefeller coup, i should think. there's still a possibility, i suppose, that the stuffed and mounted figure of wilson could be moved out of the governor's mansion and decently planted, and rocky moved back in, but it seems unlikely at this point.

so i can say what's been gnawing at me for the last several months, ever since he left happy up in maine to go flying to his appointment with destiny and the reporters when that feller ford nominated him. it's simply the generation gap again, i suppose, and i'm on the wrong side of it, too. the people who grew me, people like my father for instance, must be spinning in their graves right now. i can't imagine one of them who would've allowed even the idea of a rich man in office. now we're surrounded by people who ask is he to be disallowed simply because he has money?

yes, yes, yes, a long line of americans answers, except that they're all dead. what was taken for granted in this democracy as founded was not only a divine mistrust of unilateral rulers, but of rich men in visible control. no one ever doubted the power of the rich, that's why they weren't given office. they were known to work behind the scenes, they were thought to be pulling all the strings, maybe they were even expected to do all this. but the jump from expecting such a thing to making it an actuality is both enormous and qualitative. the dream before was to be able to say yes, you own my ass, but i can at least pretend to be free and independent. now, since the second world war, increasingly we've said: take it all, run it, have the money and the pomp also. and it doesn't much matter whether we're electing good guys like harriman or bad guys like rocky. it's money.

the country's always wanted a king i suppose, the peerless leader on the white horse, but it was embarrassed to say so. now there's no more embarrassment.

i figured up in my head what it would cost to buy a yes vote from the senate and the house. a million dollars a senator, and a hundred thousand a congressman leaves about 80,000,000 bucks in rocky's kick, and doesn't touch the family fortune at all. which is not to suggest what's going down—it's only to say exactly what that kind of wealth is, what it can do. as phil tracy and lots of other reporters have pointed out, it's not what rocky "buys" with his money, it's what people like ronan and logue et all think that they've sold.

the kennedys at least wanted in quick, in one generation— the money was still comparatively new and the style was compounded equally of rich and still struggling, the desperate attempt to be "somebody"—and, too, politics was as much a family inheritance as joe's money. but rockefeller? unless you want to consider the robber barons to be both politicos and paragons, the process of anointing rocky smells more like the divine right of money than any part of the natural order.

and what the disquieting public quiescence with rocky's appointment indicates most strongly is the non-existence in this country any more of a true middle class of small merchants, farmers, professionals. only a country that believes in such things as agri-business, industrial military complexes, and the like, and which insists on breeding managers, managers, managers in place of that middle class, would even want a rich man for its leader, and would find excuses to make it morally right.

can't we just offer him a big white house up on the hill somewhere else, and pretend to call him massa when he appears among us?

in the dark
month

win a couple lose a couple is generally the story of everybody's life so i don't know why i'm so depressed and downcast at the latest politicizing in the world of poetry. after all, it's a bare two weeks or so since imamu baraka came out via the times, after some lesser publicized statements over the past month or two, in favor of an integrated black and white marxist-leninist approach to the problems of our declaring black nationalism a movement which no longer has any meaning and, in my sense of it, he's come back.

i have no delusions that baraka is going to change back into the leroi jones i knew and called my friend ten or so years ago. i don't believe that we'll be sitting down drinking like we did in the good old days or that we'll ever run together again the way we did then. but i think we could probably talk now, and i'm glad for that. he did what he had to do for himself, and for his beliefs—and he got a hell of a lot done, too. no, he didn't ever really build a viable political base, i guess. at least if i believe the times, but he started things moving in newark, he did his job. and i took it for granted when he started that chips would fall, eggs would break. a lot of other friends reached breaking points with him. there was this particular statement, or that one, or this action, or another, and they would say well! now he's gone too far. i never said that, because i believe that when you have a cause, the definition of too far is a tricky thing. it's also one reason it's hard for me to have causes, i suppose. but it does help me to respect those that do if i believe they're serious. then i can just lament the excesses.

i believe adrienne rich has a cause too, and a good one, and her letter in answer to m. l. rosenthal's review of the current state of poetry (the review a couple of weeks ago in times magazine section and the letter in the december 29 magazine) was much needed, much to the point, and well-directed. but then the cause takes over. rosenthal had quoted something from charles olson: "lazily/the weight of breasts": ms rich says "who is charles olson to say how women are to move?" damn it, you can lay onto rosenthal all you want, and hang charles for what he's guilty of, but you really can't mean that one.

first of all there's the question of what a poet looks at and how, of course, but beyond that is it really a question of olson or any of us telling anyone how to move? we try to see, we try to make sense of what we see, and then we try to write it down. but the cause is building up steam, and it will run over everything until finally the coming together happens, slowly, and quietly, but as it must.

this is not to say that women haven't been dominated, oppressed, even denied, in masculine poetry. of course it's happened, and it's happened a lot, and it shouldn't happen any more. but to accuse an olson of malevolence on the basis of those two innocent (yes, i said that) lines is waste, is awful, is exactly what we have always done amongst ourselves, attacking, attacking, instead of going after the real enemies.

no, olson's maleness or masculinity or his manhood is not the cause of the woman poet's problems, any more than his whiteness or his norseness was the cause of the black poet's problems. but i know that it will be seen that way, i know that all male poets must be targets until such a time as things have indeed changed. i'm sorry for it, that's all.

good poems are good poems and good causes are good causes, and i'm glad that ms rich, and ms rukeyser, and ms levertov, and all the other woman poets are writing, and that the feminist presses and magazines that ms rich mentions exist. they make life fuller and better. but i'm not going to stop looking at the way a woman moves any more than i would stop listening to the way she talks or reading what she writes and i don't think that any of the magazines or the poets really want anyone to perceive less.

and i do wish the critics would stay out of it, and just let the poems get directly to the audiences. as i mentioned, the letter to rosenthal was not only well-taken, but desperately needed. go out and read the poems and we may not need the walls.

the free market

these days every time a table suggestion as to the economy is made by the president or the congress or the great mass of us known as the consumer the screams of rage go up from the business world and the bankers. we've been accused of tampering with or worse yet suppressing the free market and we've been lectured on how all good things flow from it. which would be terrific if the free market really existed and things did indeed flow from it, except that all the evidence seems to suggest that if it does exist all things in fact flow toward it.

for example, their answer to the oil problem is generally phrased so: if we offer enough free market inducements to the oil companies, like tax abatements and subsidies and the like, they will go out exploring and find whole lots of new oil deposits and we won't need the nasty arabs any more. the fact that there is a finite supply of oil in the nature of things, and the additional fact that the rate we're using it at guarantees an end to that finite supply doesn't seem to bother the free marketers in the least. they really seem to believe that the right inducements will make more oil flow from the bowels of the earth.

but as it is we're told we need the oil from the alaska fields because there isn't any oil left down here, but on the other hand if there's enough money to gain there'll be oil here, and then there are all those ads about the new ways of getting oil out of old wells, and by chewing up colorado, and by blowing tunnels in the rockies and so on and so forth. what's needed is an economy that runs on something besides or in addition to oil, but this seems not to bother the businessmen at all.

other examples of the free market in operation include the food business, specifically sugar, which is not only making cuba a viable economic entity now, but is also allowing amstar to make astronomical profits by supplying less and less, and beef, which has added its own fillip to the market by selling for two prices, dear and dearer. this is accomplished by developing expensive methods of feeding, thus ensuring a high price to begin with, and then, if production gets too high, by slaughtering and burying carcasses. the process is accompanied by public advertising to show us how much we need beef in our diets, and how in fact beef is the cheapest way to eat. somehow it seems cheaper in the end to let the cows eat grass, and us eat them only once in a while.

things have moved quite briskly since those halcyon days in the age of enlightenment when the economy was indeed expanding and there might very well have been a free market: i.e., a real genuine place where people brought their wares and displayed them at whatever they thought was a reasonable price for their products, and other people came and bought what they thought looked good. there was a corollary law in effect then, called supply and demand, and if a lot of people wanted something in short supply, its price went up, and people started trying to make more of it which caused the price to come down, and things went on quite merrily.

today, if you're big enough, it doesn't matter how much of what you make, or how much people want it. if you're not making enough money then you get governmental support, so that the free market won't collapse. this seems to miss the point.

the process is all tied in with the wage and price spiral, which dictates that people ought to get paid enough to buy the products they are making, except that these days every time they do, the prices go up again. there is a good deal of common sense in the municipal unions' position, which is against firing anyone, since whether or not any of those people are doing anything, in fact if they get fired there won't be anyone left with enough money to buy anything in the city. while those opposing early retirement are right about the waste of human lives by discarding them too soon, at least the retirees would be getting their pension money while the younger workers would be getting their wages, and the money might flow. but then, on the other hand, if people don't put their money in banks, there ain't going to be any construction funds, and the market will slump too, and we're in the big again.

this would exactly duplicate the situation with ford's new proposals, which seem to consist of giving people back some money to spend and then tacking on enough built-in increases to guarantee that the money they have won't help.

it's interesting to note that recent investigation indicates that the middle ages saw the benighted peasants working about twenty hours a week to earn their keep, and that studies among deprived pygmies of africa, living in marginal areas, show that they have to work about four or five hours a week to feed, clothe, and shelter themselves. such is the price of progress, which seems to be the only product on sale at the free market these days.

answers, god knows, aren't easy, not when we have russia and china to show us their economic madnesses as well, and in fact one wonders if under the present rules the only economic entity guaranteed to work is switzerland, which has given up on producing and supplying real things and deals only in the money madness of the rest of the world. but then if we all tried that it wouldn't work either, as you will see if you refer back to supply and demand, so we're back where we started. what this country needs is a good five cent anything.

waltz us around again, jerry

with the images of the kids starving to death in phnom penh still fresh on the screens the man gets up in front of the press conference and talks about the bloodshed and the horror and the tragedy going on in cambodia, and lectures us about how a communist takeover will make it worse. i doubt it. i think probably a lot of "political enemies" are going to get lined up and shot but i don't think the kids aren't going to get some food. i don't think the carpenter i saw the other morning is going to have to keep cranking out coffins from american ammunition cases, three cases per coffin.

the lie never dies. the lie keeps building and building. now the dominoes are back in action. if we desert cambodia (whatever deserting lon nol might mean) then all our allies will lose faith in us, in our ability to keep our word. jesus, if the starving kids aren't enough to make them lose faith in us when we do keep our word . . . and especially since the kids are starving because lon nol's boys are making money off the rice we're sending in, and there's plenty of everything in phnom penh if you just got the bread baby!

then the news report comes through that thailand has ordered planes out of the country, and the pentagon issues a statement that says it's probably because they want to cut ties to protect themselves since they see we're not honoring our commitment to cambodia, and it sounds just like a simpleminded ploy devised by the cia to convince congress that they got to spend the money . . .

we're past cynicism now, we're into some gut-level nausea or conditioned reflexes or some such. the buildup begins, the publicity, the strings get pulled and we all react. reps fenwick and abzug come back from their fact-finding trip and they are fighting between themselves over whether it should be just "humanitarian" aid or military aid too. ms fenwick even says the men know more about military matters! so much for the revolution, so much for the '60s. and on the news day after day everybody mentions how this time there is no light at the end of the tunnel, it's just a matter of letting lon nol hold on until some sort of reasonable, what a word, settlement can be made. and how lon nol got in in the first place is still covered with colby murk, and sihanouk sits in peking issuing statements, and who can care at this point which "leader" is anywhere.

people are indeed dying in cambodia and kennedyjohnson-nixonford's solution is to kill more people, and for christ's sake it doesn't even have to do anymore with benefiting our economy. at least in the old days they used to make wars to sell papers or fill the shops or capture the rice crop—which incidentally is pretty much what both the viet cong and the khmer rouge have been doing for twenty years. we keep fighting to hold one man's power for him, or to demonstrate our unanimity behind our leader. how senseless, how much more senseless can we get?

meanwhile kissinger issues his standard statement about the latest arab terrorism, this time in tel aviv, calling it as usual "senseless" which does in the language once more. obviously those attacks make more sense than our support of cambodia, since every time they pull one off the plo gains ground. and since their objective is indeed to gain ground in the truest sense of that phrase, the attacks can't be "senseless." but kissinger keeps flying, people keep dying in israel, will die in lebanese villages, die in the streets of phnom penh. and each month that goes by finds us in less and less of a position to even be generous to the victims of our principles. it used to be we could rebuild germany and japan for them. now we can't even rebuild our own cities, or even stranger, our own railroads, and there it's business getting hurt. you never thought you'd see the day where business would get hurt here too, did you? hosannah, the millenium.

but he keeps using the same words, saying the lies over and over again. so that the press conference sounded like, and the printed text of it read like, all the press conferences about southeast asia for the last ten years, and the comments on the economy sound like all those from the last two years. and for god's sake they're even advertising a diet dog food on television. that's where we're at now, in the glorious world of make-believe, or is it being packaged for all the people who can't afford peoplefood anymore and have found that eating straight dogfood puts too much filler in their diet?

spring is coming and this time april may indeed turn out the cruelest month, filled with images of dying while the trees and flowers start to bloom. we are drying up our roots. we are running sapless. someone has to stop this charade in which the children keep dying, and there is no peace, no food, no life.

the question of
victory

once, for a very brief time, i had possession of a rare and curious book, a history of the catawba county soldier in the civil war. It was rare because only a dozen or so copies had been left of the original edition, the remainder burning up in a barn fire, said barn being where they had been stored prior to distribution. the book was written and printed by a gentle soul in the county, in the middle of north carolina, who had wanted, somehow, to memorialize those men who had gone off to fight in the war between the states. he spent years interviewing, questioning, checking, through the '20s and '30s, dealing with memories, old journals, and scraps of old news. it was a beautiful labor of love, and i was awed by it, by the labor and the love, and by what was left of those old men.

one of them, i can't remember his name, recounted his own journey "to see the elephant." he'd fought, been wounded, fought again, seen friends and neighbors die, killed his enemies he thought but couldn't be sure, and ended his memoir with: i came home, went to farming, and have been there ever since.

that simple. and he was one of the losers. he had been defeated. he had seen his generals hand their swords over, his president lose his power. he came home, went to farming, and had been there ever since. and now he's in my mind. i've tried to maintain a balance, a sanity, in my thinking and my writing about this horrible war, about our part in it, and about their part in it. i've no delusions about the red menace, just as i've no delusions about the american dream. i know the commies kill their enemies, i know the good guys kill theirs. i know governments in our time exist to use people up. but i know that men who go to fight in hopes of a better world want to live in that better world. they want to go to farming, and be there ever since.

there are people in vietnam who are close to forty and have never known that simple act, who have fought the french, the japanese, the french again, their brothers, the americans, and now will find some peace. there are children who will see their first spring without the sound of guns next year. there is a country that can start to heal, regardless of its government.

this is what i believe most of the population of vietnam was about, this was what i was about. so there is a quiet jubilation growing in me. not because we lost (for the first time! he said. oh yeah?), and not because they won, but because maybe it is over now. maybe people can go to farming now, and stay there. maybe now the farm market will deal in green things and not m-16's and dope and penicillin. isn't he romantic? of course he is, how else do you live?

i wasn't there, ever, i can't talk from that experience; i don't know who killed who in hue; and i certainly don't know how many will die now in the aftermath, in the "bloodbaths." i don't know how many vietnamese who worked with us will be carried out with us, some say a million, some say "only" a hundred and fifty thousand. i don't know how many of the orphans will make it here to have their names, their religions, and their diets changed, to grow into whatever this country will be calling them twenty years from now. i know that the living will have some peace, some chance to live another way.

so it is a victory, it is a victory of the obduracy and persever-ance and simple staying power of people burrowed in under bombs dropped from the sky, people moving under orders from the government, people watching their friends and families dropping around them. there's a story from the second world war about a russian colonel who took the surrender of konigsberg from a german field marshal. all through the talking he answered with sneers and scorn, and finally the german asked the translator why the russian was acting that way. the russian, about to accept the key to german strength in the east, after a siege of three days, said: i was at stalingrad. i stayed. we won.

obduracy. adamantive unwillingness, finally, to give up. a need to say i will not stop, i will not go, i stay. governments don't legislate or order that. people do that when they have enough at stake, when they don't they run, and they blame everybody else.

i welcome my brothers to peace. i hope i may achieve it here. i wish them well. if there are parades i hope they enjoy them, but i suspect most will go to farming and enjoy that more.

we have our own farming to attend to now. we have our own dead to bury, our own ravaged children, our own destroyed cities. we have work to do.

i asked a friend last night, has saigon fallen yet? you're not going to start gloating now are you? he asked. no, no gloating, but i want it over. i want the peace to begin. i want old men and women to be able to go back to farming. i want somehow to erase our own disgraceful participation, to wipe out fifteen years of leaders who led us down the wrong road. i want the vietnamese to have peace, and us to find the right road.

simple pleasures

there come times when you've had enough of civilized pleasures, and so you don't want to talk about politics, sex, or sports any more, you just want to rest a little. sometimes it's reading you fall back on, sometimes it's just sitting. this last two weeks for me it's been a mixture of both, taken slowly and steadily, rebuilding the self. and then a little outer directed action, like they say.

a drive up to cortland, my almost annual reading trip, tuesday, the day all the civilized people have their taxes due. for the first time in my life mine was in two weeks early. i don't know why, maybe a sign of advancing age and the concomitant fears, maybe just a change of style. in any event, a gray day after four or five lovely ones here in the city. as we climb past the catskills and up into the far reaches of route 17 i start noticing snow on the hillsides, or ice hanging from cuts in the side of the roadway. spring has not yet come here. the temperature's not that bad, but it sure ain't that good either.

but wednesday morning the sun is shining and the thermometer's climbing. i have a day to kill with another reading coming that night and i spend the morning over breakfast and coffee with old friends, investigating the whirl of things they do, keep doing, start doing to keep themselves sane in the upcountry winter. books, paintings, a small business even; i get tired thinking of the energy being expended while i stare at the walls in the city and creep to the typewriter for an hour or two. when i leave their house it's almost noon, the temperature is fifty-two, the breeze is gentle, and the sky is clear.

by two i'm sitting outside the student union enjoying spring with two students, the male who runs the creative writing series, and, praise the lord, a female. one ought, despite the fact that it's 1975, to greet the spring with some company of the opposite sex. we sit on a stone bench, jackets off, turned toward the sun. the snow is still on the hillsides surrounding us, but it is the day the season breaks, changes, starts moving on. we talk for two hours about poems and people, about how nice it would be to be biking now, or how nice it is we aren't. we even discuss the snow. while here in the city we had a week of cold and wind, they had cold and wind and a foot of snow. now we can look back on it. it's history. meanwhile, all around us students appear, coming out of winter, shedding clothes, stretching.

that night there's a workshop and reading at a community college. i don't know at all what to expect, and an afternoon in the sun has knocked me out. dinner is with some transplanted new yorkers, up there five years, their little girl exactly lem's age. a lovely dinner, doubly so after the college dining room the night before, and then an early start on the work. there are thirty or so students waiting, a classic community college mix, ages from teens to fifties, maybe sixties. and all great stone faces, waiting for me to earn my keep i suppose. the first few efforts at jolly camaraderie fall flat on their face, and then, suddenly, the poems themselves start doing it. soon we are talking, all of us, and the pot is bubbling. an hour of reading, an hour of talking about poetry itself, who i read, who i started with, what's important, what's not. half of them have never heard of william carlos williams, but they'll read him now. they're writing down the names of my books, my publisher. if my publisher ever gets books up there they may even buy some. but we're all excited by something else, the muse may even have come in the room to sit for a while.

there's a break for wine and cheese, and then an hour spent with their work. and it's good work. thirty people in a small town near the finger lakes and they're writing real. the revolution may be winning after all. one of the older women hands in a poem about remembered fragrances and the first four stanzas are terrific. the last two fall away into horrendous made-up "poetry" straight out of a bad textbook. i take a deep breath, this is the first one i'm going to attack strongly all night, but i have to; if i don't half the group will suspect me, will start reading hypocrisy into every line. i say what i think, that she got scared and decided she had to end the poem with an official ending. i wait. she smiles and says she felt that way too, but she didn't really know how to end the poem. we talk about ways to do that, and then we keep moving on. a half hour after we're supposed to finish, the leader calls time. we start breaking up and one young guy tells me he doesn't like my poetry but he likes what i have to say and he's glad i came. i tell him that if i told him my poetry and what i have to say are the same thing i'd be stealing the pleasure of a future discovery from him and he shrugs and says what i mean is i think you'd be a terrific prose writer and he walks off. okay.

all that's left now is a four-hour drive back to the city. actually it takes four and a half, because at 12:30 we pull off 17 into monticello and find a diner open. we sit for a while. drinking coffee, watching the short-order man handle his grill. listening to the old diner code words roll about, coming back to me. forty-two over, adam and eve on a raft draw four, and even a strawberry burn. there's always some young lush who still uses milkshakes after a night of drinking.

the car radio says the next day will be sunny and clear and pleasant. we pull into the city at 2:30 and i'm in bed by 3:00. i even feel a little like talking about sex, politics, sports. i wonder what's fallen while i've been away. i'm civilized again, i suppose.

guile 1, rape 0: england no yes?

somewhere in brendan behan's collected works there's a line to the effect that he had never seen a bad situation that the arrival of the police had not immediately made worse. this sensitive perception must now be broadened to include the blue's good gray partners, the judges. in two separate decisions, announced fittingly enough on may 1 (hooray, hooray, the first of may, outdoor fucking starts today) a manhattan supreme court justice and britain's law lords (their supreme court) have added their own glue to an already over-sticky situation.

justice edward greenfield was ruling in the case of martin jules evans, a cable tv interviewer, who was accused of rape by a twenty-one-year-old college student. she said that she and evans had met at la guardia airport, that he had told her he was a famous psychologist named martin sage who was working on a book about women. he offered her a ride into the city, took her to maxwell's plum for a drink, whereupon she seems to have discovered that she'd missed the last train to white plains, her destination. he then suggested she accompany him to an apartment in lincoln plaza towers where he said he could pick up a car key to give her a lift home. once there he started doing research, using her. there were three acts of intercourse and oral sodomy, him on her, finishing up at or about 7:00 a.m. she testified that he held her down "by the weight of his body." no force or violence was attributed by her or him, but he did say such things as "how do you know i am who i say i am? how do you know i am a psychologist? you are in the apartment of a strange man. i could kill you. i could rape you. i could harm you physically." the student claimed that statements such as these constituted rape, since she believed he would've killed her. my own feeling is that having believed he was a famous psychologist, having believed that they would stop for just one drink, having believed he would get her to the train on time, and having believed they were going to the apartment for a car key, she was perfectly capable of believing the moon to be blue cheese. and on the surface, his behavior seems only to be that of the classic singles schmuck. in fact, it turns out that the apartment itself wasn't even his or a friend's, but one he had gotten keys to from a friend who baby-sat there. and then it developed further, as it always does, that the real dr. martin sage had, on several occasions over the last year or two, received calls from women who claimed they had met him on airplanes, and who wanted to continue the dalliances that started there, and, in addition, reports started to come in from women who had with varying degrees of pleasure or displeasure also run into the guy. so that put another dimension on the case. i mean, a one-shot line is one thing, but making a career of it is sick.

so, justice greenfield donned his solomon's robes and ruled that evans was guilty of conquest by conjob, which is not a crime. he went on to say that, "it is a fact that since before the dawn of history men with clubs have grabbed women willingly or unwillingly by their hair to have their way with them." and that, "as we have become more civilized, we have come to condemn the more overt, aggressive, and outrageous behavior of some men toward women and labeled it rape," and then went on to a discussion of "seduction," "guile," etc. leaving aside the fact that the good justice's reading of the descent of man is more victorian myth than demonstrable history, to be talking these days about dragging anyone, least of all women, off by the hair for any purpose, is crazy. up until this decision i really thought that it was okay to come on to a female, that that was how one made acquaintanceships and, possibly, relationships. now i'm resigned to sitting back and letting chemistry, in the form of pheromones or sex rays or whatever, work unabetted by me. the justice has reduced the whole sexual war to a simplism that makes it no longer possible to participate.

on the same day, in england, the supreme court ruled that if a woman says no in a way that the man thinks means yes, rape is not possible. we see here the nutcracker effect so often observed in course of law, lately known as catch 22, since the net result of adding up the two rulings is that there ain't any such animal as rape, there's only seduction, and no matter what the woman says or does, she ought to lay back and enjoy it.

the english case involved three airmen whose defense in a rape case was that they had been told the girl would fight and scream because that was the way she was turned on. curiously, having delivered the above opinion, the lords upheld the men's convictions because they didn't believe the facts supported the defense, but in england they always do one thing while they say another. what will go down as precedent however, is not the particular case, but the general opinion, and so what's a woman to do?

i know i'm going to hear both that i'm taking the new york case too seriously, by men, and the english case too lightly, by women, but what i'm trying to say is that as a relatively healthy male, i am outraged, offended, and angry at 1) a guy who has to become someone else in order to get laid, 2) a justice who thinks that seduction of the female by the male is the only way to consummate a sexual union, 3) young men who believe that fighting and screaming are a general and normal female response to sex, and 4) courts that rule that men are innocent of rape if they believe the woman was consenting to the intercourse.

and i would hope that other sane men and women are as bugged by these underlying theses as they are amused by the apparent hopelessness of the individual people involved in the cases.

this series was top-10 stuff

so i said boston would win in seven games. so they lost. it was still a hell of a series and it did go seven games. i was half right, but the old rule says that if there's one thing better than watching a good, tight, well-played world series, it's watching a badly played one that your team wins. since i insist on thinking like a fan instead of a sportswriter, wednesday night's baseball game, going to the reds in the ninth inning and giving them the series, was a disappointment to me.

carl yastrzemski came to bat in the bottom of the ninth with two outs and boston down by one run, and we all knew how glorious and how fitting it would be for him to clobber one into the right center field stands to tie it up and send the game on. alas, no one had any magic left, all the psychic energy having been expended the night before, getting carbo's homer off, up and away, to put boston back in the running. i sat before my set, unable to move one minim of energy across the miles to fenway, and carl made out and the world series was over.

they keep saying it was a series nobody should have lost, and of course they're right. cincinnati played good smart baseball and did what it had to: i think of the two keys, bench beating boston and bill lee with a wrong field double, and morgan's seventh-game-winning bloop into center field; both of them not freak hits but the acts of professionals hitting very good pitches the best they could to make them count. that's better than perez's home run, or even fisk's. it's what the game is really about, performance under pressure, even when it ain't graceful.

so, the last game was indeed an anti-climax. tuesday night saw both teams reach physical and psychic heights, saw both teams make spectacular plays, saw both teams play maximum ball.

george foster, the reds's leftfielder, and not a terribly great fielder at that, made a perfect throw on a difficult catch to take the game out of boston's hands in the ninth, and then, three innings later, dwight evans one-upped him to save the game for the sox. evans's catch must certainly rank with the great ones, gionfriddo, mays on wertz, swoboda and agee against baltimore, and it's one that will stay in our heads like those. of course, there were faults with this series, large ones, but they had nothing to do with the players—despite a few regrettable lapses on boston's part in the field, the missed double play in the seventh game, most notably, which allowed tony perez to crank up on bill lee's ephus pitch and send it out of the park. peter rose, as so many times before, set that error up, sliding hard into second base and sending doyle straight up in the air from whence he let go a throw that ended in the dugout. it was a heart-breaker, but we've seen it happen before, it's what you expect when you play cincy, and you do your things to counteract it. no the fault was with the management of baseball, and with the team managers, and with the network. curt gowdy is a shame. even non-baseball fans were asking me why he talked so much, and about such irrelevancies (for just one sample, when, in the ninth inning of the last game, boston sent its second string catcher up to pinch-hit, a man almost no one had ever seen play, gowdy told us that he liked model railroads, and then added, but he's thinking of other things right now!). he was abetted by such gems as the boston announcer telling us that bill lee, boston's resident freak, liked honey, ginseng, transcendental meditation, and "read kurt vonnegut."

the umpiring was competent at best, and awful on several occasions such as the celebrated non-interference call on armbrister, which cost boston a game. the umpires' union had dictated a rotation of men for the world series, and this series ended up with six guys who had never called a series game before, and with not a hell of a lot of experience among them in regular games. commissioner bowie kuhn lived up to his splendid non-reputation by pandering to television again, so that the last two games were played at night in the cold (relative cold, of course, but one shivers to think of how bad it could have been) instead of during two glorious boston afternoons.

and, despite the crowing of the television crew, darrell johnson and sparky anderson showed me much less than inspired managing. in fact, i'd not say anything about them at all were it not for gowdy's insistent pimping for their brilliance. anderson dithered about gullett, preferring to keep his young ace away from tiant, and almost blew the series because of that, since, if the rains hadn't come, delaying the sixth and seventh games, he'd have had gullett pitching with two days' rest because of it; and, in gullett's games, anderson twice waited far too long to pull him out, and paid once with a loss, and lucked out the second time. johnson did nothing remarkably bad, but nothing remarkably good either. sending montgomery up to bat for doyle, the only player on either side to hit in every game was not so much stupid as puzzling, and his patience with cecil cooper despite his repeated failure at bat cannot be faulted either, given cooper's year-long record, but basically the players were the ones who did it all in this match.

both clubs need pitching but both clubs are superb. i must add, despite my hostile feelings toward him, that bench made fisk (who's surely the second or third best catcher around) look like a fool behind the plate. after watching bench, one had the feeling that fisk was sort of another choo choo coleman, even while one's head told one that that was ridiculous. nevertheless i look to see boston the power in the american league for a while to come, and cincinnati obviously has several years left also. it was a splendid series and i thank them all for letting me see them play this game i love so well.

let's say farewell to the endless summer

the weather changed over night this october between wednesday the 29th and thursday the 30th. oh, yeah, the mornings had been crisp, occasionally the wind had blown a little, and once in a while you needed a coat instead of just a jacket on a couple of the nights, but most of the days had been either pleasant or downright warm, and the extra blankets i'd taken out back in september when there was a false alarm of three days of cold had ended up kicked to the foot of the beds or down on the floor all these weeks.

mornings and nights were bad for me only because it's impossible to tell the real weather by looking out the window here at westbeth. the wind comes off the hudson and stirs things around and you dress to meet it only to discover that hudson street and more easterly environs are twenty degrees warmer. so lem kept going off to playschool overdressed, and the nights that the kids were with their mother and i was free i'd go swinging out in my brand new trenchcoat and end up sweltering.

wednesday evening was like that. i'd been up at city teaching and i had my sheepskin-lined suede jacket on—the "fall" jacket, since i live by rituals and it was fall—and number one son, nick, came to pick me up in the balmy air, in just his shirtsleeves, and i felt a fool. after all, one's son comes in from the mountains of new mexico and one wants to look a mensch for him, even if he doesn't remember what "mensch" translates out to.

he and his friend were in the pick-up with the house on back that they'd built and driven here; the three dogs were inside waiting to meet me. the warmth was in the hearts and the air, and the chill was only in the gut, what with everyone at city buzzing about jerry's speech, and whether there would still be a city college at all after christmas, and in that air, all the while we worried, the construction kept going on on the new performing arts center, all those good union men pulling in their wages while one could feel the place grinding to a halt.

anyhow, we drove downtown, and spent the night talking, talking, talking, while nathaniel and lem showed off and screamed the joy that their big brother had finally arrived. nick is sporting a full dark beard now, and the boy in him is gone i guess. i showed susan baby pictures of him just like daddy, and disputed his far-off mother who had told susan he had been a quiet child. damn it he knew six words at just one year, i said: cold which meant good by an etymology too complex to go into, wow, jesuschrist (which he said everytime he opened a present at his first birthday while my mother palpitated), mommy, daddy, no. you could live a life with that vocabulary, and he has.

so thursday came and the morning was cold but this time the day didn't get warmer. by nightfall the radio was calling for the first freeze of the season, and friday morning indeed the temperature was 31 degrees at seven thirty.

it was halloween, this friday, the day the witches say ends this year. we've got so many year-ends you can take your choice: this, and the harvest festival of thanksgiving, december 21st, when the sun's the farthest from us and starts to turn to bring spring back, and even new year's eve. but the weather change makes this the right one this year. they're all gone now, the good times of summer. the weather killed them, jerry ford killed them, the witches danced with the children helping. it's a new year. i've got three of my sons here, the fourth is on his way in from the coast, we'll all burrow in.

thursday night the blankets stayed tucked in. the jack-o-lantern that we'd carved glowed its candlelight orange. nathaniel experimented with the make-up crayons to get the ghastliest set of hands for the next night's frightening, and then, being almost nine, he washed it all right off, to keep it in its place. lem on the other hand spent the whole week between his batman cape and his captain marvel costume—yes i know it's called shazam, but not to me—and said thursday morning "i never remember to put my lem costume on."

the weather has turned, the city is dying, the feds are telling us not to eat anything colored red—hell, it's the first time since 1953 for me that i'm facing the winter with an empty bed and i don't think i care, either. there's nothing to do but duck the head in the shoulders and keep on moving. i wrote a thirteen-page poem about my cactuses on monday, that'll have to hold us all 'til groundhog day comes 'round.

this year they've even let the clock go back where it's supposed to be for the first time in two years: it's like they knew we needed something to help us all along. the weather's changed, the days are dark early, i've got some family, some friends, some poems cooking. the hell with the rest of it, we'll burrow in.

how to lose a
school system

 November 24, 1975

the bicentennial is beginning with a strong possibility that educa-
tion as we have known it here will be washed down the drain, the
baby thrown out with the bath water, and the tub, too. the great
american dream of an educated and literated citizenry capable of
making wise decisions and thus enabling the democratic process to
function will be over—not that it's worked out so well anyhow,
what with the government admitting to a twenty per cent illiteracy
rate and indices such as the college boards showing less and less
proficiency among the graduates. but at least the dream was there,
we believed it was possible.

   now, under a combination of enormous pressures, and speeded
by the worldwide economic situation, the dream is in danger of
being washed away in spirit as well as in practice.

   consider new york now, and, by extension, the rest of the
country ten years from now: the city university, at this time next
year, will in all likelihood be either a part of the state university
system, specializing in technical training, or, if still nominally a
city institution, much smaller, still trade-oriented, and available
only to the rich and the poor but not the middle classes.

   the public school system will be in actuality what it's headed
for all these years, a detention system to keep kids off the streets
and out of the labor or crime market.

   and the day-care system will be reduced to a tiny entity
serving again the rich and the welfare clients, with the working
poor and the shrinking middle class again ineligible.

   what's happened? simply that the children and the idea of
education itself are being ground down between a rock and a very
hard place. the rock is the vested interests of the concerned direc-
tors of the system: government, business, labor, the educational

establishment. government wants, in these increasingly central-
ized, authoritarian, "efficient" times a center that will guarantee a
passive or at least controlled population. business wants, as it
always has, a trained and docile labor pool, large enough to allow
it to pick and choose in a buyer's market. labor, of course, wants
that pool to be small, to set up a seller's market, which has meant
traditionally a lengthening of the years spent in the learning pro-
cess, years which are extended further by a phony apprenticeship
program within the skills themselves. and the enormous educa-
tional establishment which has sprung up over the years of massive
public education wants to perpetuate itself, and doesn't much care
any longer about the process which spawned it.

and the hard place that's become the grinding edge is money,
the whole economics of the situation. business complains that the
kids aren't trained to read, write, add, can't in fact serve their
purposes as a labor pool. labor sees its bastions of the previous
century weakening day by day, done in by the shifts in world trade,
by technological advances in automation, by the cartelization of
everything, and by the swing of money away from its traditional
centers. government finds that even with their weak education the
younger people of the postwar years have been able to destroy
presidents, and even chip away at the economic structure of the
country via mass assaults like the ecology movement, and fringe
nibbling like the communes, the dropouts, and the countercultures.
the schools, even while working badly, have provided a steady
stream of "revolutionaries" who insist, however romantically, on
being "freethinkers."

but now there's no money, and nothing seems likely to
replace those enormous resources, that tremendous yankee inge-
nuity that combined to give us something to dominate the world's
economy with; and without that money, or the possibility of it, why
should any of those three forces care about education? and the one
organized body that might serve as counterpoise, the teaching
establishment, has indicated over and over, as i've said, only that

obdurate belief that they deserve to hold onto their jobs. it doesn't matter that they do them badly, or that a lot of them are not only unnecessary, or even counterproductive, or just bad for the kids, they're jobs that have existed heretofore and therefore must continue.

meanwhile, the graduate schools continue to churn out diplomas in enormous numbers; most of them end up working in bookstores, while the teachers' unions fight to the death for seniority, and fight to the death against any increase in quality, because it interferes with what they've done before. every time a step forward is attempted, even as blatantly a political one as open admissions, the teachers' establishment manages to sabotage it, and, as the recent strike in the public schools demonstrated, to protect seniority and prerogatives they're willing to do anything except teach. to settle a school strike by taking time away from the kids has to be one of the strangest anomalies of our time.

day-care presents a new and different problem: it raises the highly emotional issue of the destruction of the american family, as if that hadn't disappeared in the flight to the suburbs and the ruination of the farms thirty years ago. to many americans day-care means simply communism, the systematic brainwashing of the new generation before it can even think. no use to talk of what happens to kids who otherwise would be isolated in a world they cannot understand when they are put in a warm and loving situation with their peers and given a world they can understand. no use to talk of the enormous gains intellectually as well as emotionally these kids undergo—it still smacks of taking them away from momma and turning them into creatures of the state. the fact that only the chain day-care centers, in the business to make money, are willing to live by the insane rules promulgated by the government and the aforementioned establishment, and so approach that cold rigidity, and that the small individual places fight constantly to maintain some fluidity of development, fight constantly to develop better methods for the kids despite the rules, gets ignored in the irrational gut-level opposition that can be and is raised every time the issue comes to a vote.

the upshot is that we will have schools which are more and more inadequate to do any job, whether the job is really teaching, by which i mean opening the minds of people, or, on the other hand, narrowly defined technical training. what will be left will be places abuzz with busywork, entangled in outmoded regulations, and geared only to keep some sort of system limping along. teachers, administrators, psychologists, psychiatrists, sociologists, social workers, custodians, dieticians, and the like will have their kids, papers, theories, rugs, brooms, and slop to push around; the kids will be produced year by year and pronounced ready for the big world, and that big world, business, labor, government, will keep muddling ahead more and more slowly to its own death.

answers? there are no easy ones. but there must be some. what we need to do now is to start searching for them—we, the parents, the kids, those few teachers who still care. there's no hope left for help from anyone in the big world, because their own dance toward destruction is too intricate, too interesting to them, and too predetermined.

as charles olson said, in his essay on "the human universe," "value is perishing from the earth because no one cares to fight down to it. . . ."

franco is dead,
viva la muerte

francisco franco is dead, finally. sometime in the last month, depending on your definition of death, he died. and, depending on your view of history, he died ten years ago, or twenty, or thirty, when world war II ended. but the only problem with that theory is that he didn't, at least not for spain. the rest of the world moved on, somehow, but not his spain. franco's spain was still safe from godless communism, and it was still some fragile iron shell that held down within it people and beliefs that might have died in some more open, co-optive society. so i suppose we have to thank him for something, but i won't.

maybe you have to have been born between the two wars, the one to end all wars and the one to make the world safe for democracy, to be unforgiving about a political leader. i mean, we live in this best of all possible times in this best of all possible worlds, and we've learned that nobody's perfect and that nobody's perfectly awful either. but franco, the generalissimo (how we laughed at the balls of that, as if general wasn't enough of a title for that ego), the caudillo, outlived his time, and kept his power, even to the last breach, and the old hate still boils in me, and i'm a kid of my time again, knowing gods and devils.

when hirohito visited here a couple of weeks ago, there were, then, a few letters to various editors from sad old voices wanting to know how we could entertain him after pearl harbor, but i couldn't raise any anger over that silly old man who started out a god, and ends a japanese tourist watching the jets lose. franco, though, is a different story, as any spaniard would be glad to tell you. there were attempts to spread a rumor that he'd been kept alive this last month by a cabal of leftist doctors, intent on punishing him here and now for all the evil he'd committed by sentencing him to unremitting pain, but the jokes didn't work, because he had, even hooked up to the machines, an awesome control, and even a powerless unwanted king had to be named with great great care.

the roots of my emotion are in that halcyon time between the wars, when hitler, mussolini, stalin, hirohito, franco, were the enemies, especially for the unsophisticated. even the moderates knew that dictators were bad. and i remember the headlines and the pictures of that preparatory war, in which every nation tried out its hardware on spanish peasants. i remember the picture in life of an american freighter, its decks lashed with tanks and planes, dashing for the three-mile limit covered by the coast guard, desperately trying to make it before the embargo slammed shut on our supplies for the republicans.

i don't remember guernica from then, not until the late '40s when i discovered art, but now guernica is just art, not politics, and maniacs attack it. and it wasn't 'til the '50s that i found out about the other war, the fascists joined with the communists against the anarchists; and then in the '60s i discovered the basques and catalans, stolidly plowing ahead with their wars that had gone on for centuries against the spaniards themselves. franco crystallized all this, men forced to war for politics, for church, for language, because he had his god-given vision of the good.

so while i have had to learn, intellectually, to add up pluses and minuses with the leaders of our day, at base there is always that hard emotional core that fears, distrusts, and hates the strong man, the man who knows what's right. that core makes it hard for me to buy any leader at all, and it's supported even more as the revisionists keep coming in about the likes of roosevelt and churchill. they were all bastards, and they all promised us the light.

and what matters now, for me, is that those old ones who knew enough to distrust such men back then have kept up the fight, and have handed on the tradition. the basques still go on, the catalans go on, and we shall, i think, be hearing from the spanish anarcho-syndicalists also. perhaps, without franco, without the falange, they would have withered and died, subsumed by the general glop; but he and his rule guaranteed that they survive to face his successor.

and that very existence in this world of ours, now, is a beacon. it is a living proof that we can win if we have strength and patience. but it takes an enemy to call it forth i guess. radio free basque was still broadcasting in the hills in '51, somehow; in '55 the republic of catalonia (dead what? 500 years?) was still appointing envoys to carry their official messages. and do you think that black side of spanish anarchy that burned and buried haciendas complete because they would not use anything that came from evil, do you think that dark line is gone?

franco is dead. i am glad. nil nisi bonum is a luxury the postwar years taught me to forget, but there doesn't seem anyone worth hating like that any more. hate nixon or ford or lyndon b or khrushchev or mao or tito or all those funny little fascists, socialists, anythings we have around today? you don't hate a worm you want to squash, do you? franco was the last genuine all-fired ogre still alive, and now he's dead. even spain survived him, somehow. and now, as my beloved spanish anarchists were wont to say in those days: *viva la muerte!*

stuff it

i dreamt i served this big $mas meal for my family, my friends, and a few assorted people from the real world. i had invited william ferracone, president of the corporate chemical division of crompton & knowles, for one, and to my astonishment he showed up. his company makes all those lovely things they put in our food to make it taste like food, and he was featured in an article in the times on december 10th, so i never thought he'd spend his holiday meal with a freaky voice writer, but there he was.

in the times piece he'd bragged about his breakfast: "Eggbeaters, breakfast strips (ersatz bacon), Tang and a nondairy creamer in my coffee. And it was just great. Everything tasted just right." since i'm quoting him i'll use his or the times's capitalization. but that's just to prove that i'm not a hard-nosed guy, and certainly not a kook tilting at windmills.

also at the meal were the inventor of pringles newfangled potato chips, which state agriculture commissioner john s. dyson describes as "not chips at all but dehydrated potato flakes reconstituted into liquid and flash fried into a 'perfect' shape no chip ever had"; and the unnamed spokesman for miles laboratories who claimed that their brand name "morningstar farms," used for their bacon and sausage substitutes, was (just) a brand name and that the products certainly used farm products, despite the state's contention that the use of the word "farm" was intended to con us.

then there was that guy from the feds who says that the statistical jump in the number of cancer deaths can't possibly come from food additives because they wouldn't all show up at once like this. I was also going to ask the guy that sat on the report about lead emissions from gasoline killing kids but figured he'd probably use a big official limousine to come so that it was hardly worth the risk.

i served turkey shot full of stuff to make the turkey plump and keepable, cranberry sauce laced with red dye #2 for a nice bright color, sweet potatoes made with raisins which had been dried and preserved with sulfur dioxide, and coated them with reddi-whip straight out of the can. we had home-style cider so loaded with chemicals that it wouldn't harden if you let it sit for a year, and we finished up with decaffeinated instant coffee, which had been made so with something that might release a carcinogen, but the evidence isn't in yet, so why worry. there was sugar in everything.

everybody asked for more, and the only interruptions of the lip-smackings and contented belches were the phone calls. like the one from the student who needed some hand-holding. he couldn't understand why his father had died of cancer at forty-eight while his great-grandparents were still alive in greece in their nineties. and my mother wanting to know how come one relative had died of cancer at fifty-one a year or so ago, and now another at thirty-eight. i put the guy from agriculture on with them, so the others could keep scoffing up the goodies.

we talked a little over the artificial mints about the women dying from the estrogen treatments, but the consensus was that all the women who didn't die from them had had much easier menopauses, so what the hell. ferracone pointed out the humane nature of his work when he mentioned that without crompton & knowles's dedication there wouldn't be enough natural vanilla flavoring in the whole world to satisfy america's want for vanilla ice cream.

these guys really seemed to love the meal, and we, the kids and my friends and i, sort of enjoyed watching them, while we ate our freshly-ground peanut butter and homebaked bread, washed down with organic apple juice (all except nathaniel, who had just the bread because he won't eat any kind of peanut butter and never has and never will) and i thought how i used to think people like that were kooks, but then i believed that the cia was trying to overturn foreign governments, and that the fbi was spying on people illegally, and so i thought maybe i was just born to be a kook no matter what.

like i say, it was a dream, and i'm probably going to eat all that other stuff myself for $mas, because i haven't got the energy or the moral fiber or the plain old unadulterated gumption to do anything else. but i sure am turning into a puritan these days. i'm not so sure that we're supposed to be progressing all so much, and that maybe life isn't supposed to be easy. i mean, maybe we ain't supposed to have all the vanilla ice cream that we want.

maybe, even god forbid, some things are supposed to hurt, maybe not everything is supposed to be able to stay fresh on the supermarket shelf all the time. maybe we're just supposed to eat what grows around us, at the season it grows in, and the way it tastes to begin with, and looking the color it is. that's a vain hope with all the problems of feeding the world, but then, after enough people die off in the new plague, maybe there'll be few enough of us around to try it.

does it change?
can it hurt?

it's an old and honored tradition to start things over by making them new—whether it's a list of new year's resolutions or a spring housecleaning. so here i am doing things like finally entering all those phone numbers written down on scraps of paper, backs of matchbooks and store receipts that have been falling out of my phone book for the year. this involved considerable effort, since i also decided to edit the whole damned list, so that the twelve addresses for mike stephens would be down to the current one, and the couples split up would each be entered under their own name, and all the people who wanted to pay me countless thousands of dollars for screenplays and reading tours would be reconsigned to the limbo of my fantasies. the editing demanded that i tour the local stationery stores looking for the right kind of six-holed paper. this took up the antepenultimate and penultimate days of the old year, and the transcription of the miscellaneous numbers to fresh sheets took the ultimate morning. i finished at noon and wandered out to meet a young poet who wanted to know where to get published so as to meet people who would offer her countless thousands of dollars for screenplays and reading tours. by 12:30 i had three more scraps of paper and a matchbook cover in my pocket to add to the phone book. and i think mike stephens is getting ready to move again.

the process of organizing the phone book was accompanied by records played on my new stereo—the first stereo, nay phonograph, i've ever owned, ever gotten all for myself. i am not terribly musical, as any one who has ever heard me attempt to hum, sing or whistle can attest, and i'm from that last generation to whom phonographs were not a necessity but a luxury.

that combination of factors had led me in the past to set my dial at our favorite all-news station, or our favorite all-country station, and to let a steady drone of one or the other fill my ears and my days. but shortly after i broke up with my wife i realized i had been left with my slim but select record collection, and that i did want to hear them, to play them, maybe (and probably) to assert my own space. it took nine months, as any proper new thing should, but i finally got the stereo a couple of weeks ago. now, sometimes, i remember to play a record for me. this morning it's blind willie mctell, but shortly dan will be up and god only knows what he will play. we've had only one generational fight so far, which was when i realized that someone named keith jarrett had played the same phrase over and over for twenty minutes or so, but then he's had to put up with an awful lot of jimmy rodgers and several ecstatic renditions of "four saints in three acts" so i guess we're even.

my son dan's presence in the house hasn't changed things as much as one might expect, aside from the music. putting a forty-five-year-old set in his ways together with a sturdy and vital twenty-year-old who haven't lived together in sixteen years might have been expected to lead to some clashes, differences in style, and all that, but we seem wary of jerking each other around too much and things flow nicely. the emotional needs engendered between father and son are different too, and of course, from those of a couple in love or out of it. i remember a woman i lived with who spent the first six months of our relationship systematically, albeit unconsciously, breaking every object in the house that had been given to me by another woman, ashtrays, whiskey glasses, pens, whatever, if they had come into that place via a female friend they disappeared one by one. the same objects when purchased by me, or given me by a male friend, or scrounged on the street, somehow never got scratched. it was the most fantastic exhibition of making it new i've ever witnessed, and since she generally replaced what she had broken with equivalent objects, and since she did have very good taste, it was not nearly as upsetting as it might have been. sure was curious though.

the whole need to renew ourselves or the things around us is even more curious though—to take a particular day as the turn of the year and focus on it by shifting things around, throwing things out . . . and the most curious thing is that it works, even a little. the mail is all racked up to be answered, and will be answered, promptly, at least for a couple of weeks; the phone book is clean and usable, the poems are going to come spilling out like never before. that's the feeling that comes, even if nothing does change, even if march will find me bogged down in the same old morass.

meanwhile this new year opens up, and the wisdom influencing the week for the beginning of january in my i ching day book says "one should approach the future with joy and devotion." that sounds like an awfully easy way out.

angry at the
hall of fame

the hot stove league, by its very name, evokes all sorts of cheery winter images: the boys sitting around the store on sacks of flour, drinking coffee, whiling the time away until spring training, chewing over the past season, and staring into a cheery warm stove. but it's 1976 now, and the cheery stove that heats westbeth is twenty feet underground and can't be seen, and besides it's 2°, having risen from -1° in the first two hours of my day, and that cheery stove don't do no good at all when the temperature drops below twenty anyhow—and in good old days there wasn't a new virus every winter to lay the kids out, and, oh hell, i'm just a sour old man today, and angry at the hall of fame, for my hot stove heat.

lemon and roberts are in; that's fine. two good good pitchers, the best of their time, and that's part of the criteria. that they were even better than that i can only guess, but i think so—i think they would have been starters any day of any year for any club. so that doesn't get me angry, although if they had gone in earlier it might have made me happier, since roberts had to wait four years and lemon an incredible twelve, despite his thirteen-year career, 200 plus wins, and seven twenty-game seasons.

no, it's not them, it's the vote count that follows them down the list of those still in the running that's getting to me. the point with the hall of fame, i'd thought, is that it's a place for rewarding some special kind of excellence. it ain't supposed to be a political reward, or even a religious ceremony. but third on the list this year, and stronger than the year before, is gil hodges. he's there for two reasons, really. he's there because he had a lot of exposure with the dodgers and the mets, and because a bunch of writers and fans, led now by our mr. young of the daily news, have decided it will be morally good for america to have a "man of his caliber" installed.

he was clean-living and serious, and in these dissolute days we need images like that.

which is not to say i didn't live and die with him all through the dodgers's glory days, and which isn't to take his ability and his stats away from him either. a brilliant fielder, maybe the classiest first baseman ever, a joy to watch, one of the few men who played that traditional butcher's position with grace and agility; and a batter that could destroy you: seven years of more than 100 rbis, 370 home runs, with six years over thirty, two over forty, well what do you want, oppenheimer? i want a batting average higher than .273, a slugging average higher than .487, i want maybe numbers like .312 and .562, which belong to johnny mize, who hasn't made it yet, and won't now unless the old-timers vote him in. i suppose it's all because he doesn't have sterling moral qualities, because he's bitter about the game now.

or, on the hype front, still in there fighting, and still getting shilled for every year are phil rizzuto and peewee reese, while arky vaughan lies with mize moldering on the old-timers' lists. sure, reese could be my shortstop any day of the week, but not if arky vaughan is sitting on the bench. fellers, let's be fair. i know the brooklyns and the yankees from our childhoods were better than chocolate halvah, but there were some other guys playing baseball too. and even on these clubs there are serious inequities bobbing up. how come the duke only gets 159 votes to hodges's 233? the duke was a legitimate slugger with a batting average twenty-five points higher than hodges, a slugging average of .540, and a great fielder to boot. the measure, it seems to me, is: faced with picking one or the other to start a team, who do you go for? and snider wins that one hands down.

the one hopeful sign is that enos slaughter placed fourth. maybe he'll make it, if time doesn't run out on him. mize and slaughter not only meant baseball to a whole lot of people, they meant a particular kind of devastating play, the other kind of baseball from the perfection of the yankees and the flash of the dodgers; they were classic ogres to haunt your nights as they kept coming, kept coming, kept coming.

i suppose what i'm asking is impossible in 1976, that some things should stay pure, not be hypes, not be public relations, not be "good for us," but just be good, and that excellence ought to merit some sort of reward, just by itself.

and that excellence itself is seen less and less in our time. the same day the hall of fame vote is announced the obituary appears for charles reznikoff, poet. eighty-one years old, a new yorker, he spent his life making poems about that life and this city. the poems were good, the line was clean, the ear and eye were magical, and nobody paid much attention, except the other poets. he wrote: "i will write songs against you,/ enemies of my people; i will pelt you/ with the winged seeds of the dandelion;/i will marshall against you/the fireflies of the dusk."

the occasions of excellence in our times ought to be celebrated and not covered in the muck of the popular con; if you think that a clean swing is more or less than a good poem, you lose by it; if you think that either is less than what passes for the best, these days, you are lost even more.

the tin ear
listens

a man with an inability to carry any tune anywhere, aside from a verse and a half of "i ride an old paint," and my own idiosyncratic version of "i was born in east virginia," and with a long string of abandoned instruments behind me, and only the slide whistle ahead as a possible vehicle for the music that must be in my soul or else how would it keep coming out in the poems, i spent most of a week involved willy-nilly with music and musicians.

the first two nights of the stretch were spent listening to tapes by and talking with bobbie bridger, the thirty-two-year-old folk-singer who left nashville for austin after a fling with the big-time scene, and settled in in time to become loosely attached to and identified with but not part of the "new" country scene there deep in the heart of texas. he was up here trying to peddle a big new concept album he's got on tape, about the history of the west. the first part is called "jim bridger and the seekers of the fleece" and that's what we listened to. it's a dynamite piece of work, following the story of the mountain men through the life of jim bridger, who may or may not have been one of bobbie's ancestors, and it uses a "poetic" narrative interspersed with songs about bridger, hugh glass, jedediah smith, and it talks to the particular place these strange and wonderful anarchists filled in the opening of the west. the second section will deal with the indians's side, basically through an interpretation of *Black Elk Speaks*, and the third will cover the present, starting with buffalo bill and sitting bull in their traveling circus.

bobbie's commitment is like we say intense—he's going to get this damned record out somehow, even if nobody does want to listen to a continuous narrative in these days of disc jockeys who talk all through the three-minute song. he'll get it done commercially or he'll tie it in with the bicentennial, he just doesn't care, as long as it gets out. i used to know poets and painters like that, in the good old days.

then, on saturday night, after much urging by dan, we went to hear sonny rollins in concert at carnegie hall. dan asked me how long it had been since i'd been to a concert and i had to answer "oh, about 19 ought and four," and it may well have been close to that. but sonny's a tie that jumps the generation gap for us—i remember sneaking out on dan when he was two or three to pick up sonny at one of the village clubs, and if "wagonwheels" isn't imprinted in dan's memory cells from all the times he heard it as a toddler then all the psychologists are crazy. dan's come to him now on his own, of course, since he's been listening in a way that he could only have inherited from his mother's side. so we sat there together knocked out by this guy my age who's just kept growing, coming on stronger and stronger. we had fantastic seats, up close, and toward the middle, and we were listening to the instruments, not the speakers. and we could see sonny up close as he worked away. and work he did, changing his shirt three times in the two sets as the sweat soaked through. the face is still the same one that got him called newk in the old days, and the mad and beautiful doodling solos that lead into the numbers still send chills down your spine.

man, he's forty-five or so and he ain't stopped looking, trying. the group behind him was good, tony williams, hubert laws, masuo, and the others, but they were young, when everything's a gas. what i mean is that sonny knows it's hard work, but that it has to be done. and he's doing it.

then two nights later i went over to the cookery to hear "the other" joe turner, the old stride pianist who's been in europe for twenty or so years. sitting at the table in the big bare chromy place, with just that old man and his piano, i kept thinking of anthony quinn near the end of "la strada," the act the only thing he's got to go on. turner plays genuine and genuinely beautiful old stride numbers, the bass walking while the treble fucks around, mixed in with sort of '40s standards that tickle old memories and serve admirably to trickle in behind the ears, and then, always, throws in some horrid showbiz thing like louie's version of "hello dolly" or a lush "gone with the wind," and one sees constantly the old man, hanging on, the teeth flashing, the desperate attempt to please.

that part of it is very sad, and makes the rest less by it. you want to say "just play the piano old man, screw the audience," but you don't, because you're well aware that he's too old to scuffle, too old to change the act. there was enough good playing to bring me back again, i don't want to sound like you shouldn't go, but be warned that you may cringe a little too.

i don't think sonny'll ever be at this particular place, going through the motions; i think he's going to be fighting with his art, his ax, himself, all the way. and while it's too soon to say it about bobbie, i don't think he will either; i think he'll always have a dream ahead he has to get out, for him, for us, and he won't be able to settle for an act.

what i know is, you end up doing what you can and must, you can't fake it beyond that. and we, in the audience, we sit and listen. and what they have to give us is there if we open our ears. if we don't, like we used to say, shame on us. and if we do listen the music may even make us shake something beside our ass, once in a while.

ageism comes home

the young hate the old, the old fear the young, and the ones in the middle wish everyone else would go away. our noble experiment has led us this far these days.

these thoughts were triggered by an article in the good gray times a couple of weeks ago, about a "retirement" community in arizona called youngtown, which has embarked upon a campaign to keep itself pure. it was set up some twenty years ago as a place for older people to spend their golden years; it featured houses geared to retirees and available at a reasonable purchase price, and it was predicated on a low tax rate that pensioners could both afford to pay and trust not to rise too precipitously. well, the twenty years have passed; some of the original owners have died and passed their houses on to heirs, there are young couples with children creeping in, and now the oldsters are counterattacking.

according to the times, there's been telephone harassment featuring threats to the children, and a case of breaking and entering, too, to vandalize a christmas tree and steal the children's presents. the article was loaded; everyone i know, including myself, reacted in horror and disbelief. of course, hidden deep in the piece was the economic justification: the tax rate didn't allow for schools, playgrounds, the kind of community services that families with children need. so one finished reading filled with emotional outrage, and yet hedged with intellectual doubts.

we're a people who've taken the old, standard, only-to-be-expected generation gap and twisted it in on itself; we've spent so much energy driving enormous wedges between the generations, in the name, i suppose, of "freedom" and "independence." all generations have had to fight the ones before them, and then, of course, have turned around and found a need to lay their own loads,

the things they've "learned" on the generation coming after. but
we—my generation, the one born between the two great wars—
seem to have had to do this more emphatically: the world had
changed, qualitatively, and our parents, for the most part, didn't
know it. so we threw out all the old ways, all the old ties, or tried to
anyhow, and we swore we'd never hand our kids up the same way,
we'd teach them their own worth at least. we didn't want our kids
to go through the same hell we'd gone through, not realizing that
that particular hell was gone anyhow, and so we didn't lay a social
code on them, but laid, instead, each in our own way, some
theoretical, abstract code that might or might not have bearing on
the new world.

we did it in our homes, we asked for it in our public institu-
tions, whether school, church, or government, and we made it
stick. concomitantly, because it fit in, we bought an advertising
hype about the young, about youth, about being "alive," about how
being "old" was bad. and so we effectively separated out what had
been, willy-nilly, for better or for worse, at least some sort of
integrated culture. the idea of respect for old people, love for young
ones, and responsibility for those in the middle, may be both
simplistic and limiting, but at least it's an idea, and it gives a frame
to work on. it also allowed ties between the age groups that are no
longer possible, like genuine friendship between kids and old
people. and so, now, we get places like youngtown, and middle-
aged dropouts (and mid-career crises), and "amoral youth." simply
put, no one knows their function any more, and no one has a way to
find it out.

a healthy culture trains its young to do what living in that
culture demands: the orangutan raises its child with no sense of
social grace, no code of "manners," because the orang will spend
its life alone, with no need for such things. the eskimos raise their
old to greet their deaths with welcome because they know they
cannot waste their families' necessities if they can no longer
function in that family. it's not that we're to try either of these

solutions for ourselves, it's that we're supposed to see in such possibilities of adjustment some possibilities of adjustment for ourselves.

must grandparents be alienated from the children and the grandchildren? must grandchildren be as distant from the grandparents as their parents are? must the parents be so desperately involved in what ought to be a natural relationship? dare we allow ourselves such luxuries? i think not. i think we'll find more and more youngtowns, and more and more separation, and we'll find that the beast who talks has lost its ability, its desire, to communicate. we'll pull further and further apart while being crushed closer and closer together. that's an untenable situation, and it needs to be considered and somehow changed. otherwise we will stand guilty of having deserted all the generations, and of having given each generation the least of all possible worlds.

poet digs out

the annual oppenheimer poetry mini-circuit took place in march this year, with readings in north carolina and upstate new york. north carolina, not visited since the glory days of good old black mountain, back in '54, is still the old north state like they say: enough city and mountain to keep it from being the deep south, enough sun and grits to keep it from being yankee.

feeling like sulzberger in ulan bator, i keep my eyes and ears open trying to determine what goes on in the new south, and, indeed, america. on that level, fortunately, i have nothing to report—only once did i hear someone moaning about the northern liberals hating jimmy carter, and that was from an aging history professor. everybody else seemed quite human.

i spent my time there among the students and faculty of three quite different schools: a small "experimental" college, a small "traditional" college, and a small college hung up between a traditional administration and an experimental faculty. in all cases people were working, and working hard, and reaching out, too. my own audiences were good both in size and interest, and everybody had done their homework, which is to say they'd read some of the work, so that the question periods were alive and intense. there were several solid sessions on my use of four-letter words in "the woman poems," and i got pushed into making some new evalua-tions for myself. the young women were perhaps just becoming aware of the real issues of liberation, but many of the young men seemed already to have accepted, and even welcomed, the fact that things are changed already. nobody down there was really aston-ished that i'm single-parenting it three or four days a week, and that i'm doing it all myself, while many of my hip friends up here are vaguely upset by it.

the dirty word question was all the more interesting in the light of an article in the raleigh newspaper that appeared the day i

left, about how they and other papers in the state censor x-rated
movie ads. practically every drive-in i passed on the road was
showing one or another x title, and the papers have taken to
dropping "suggestive" words—teenage lust becomes t. lust to
calm aroused passions—and to draping via airbrush any illustra-
tions that seem too raw. there's also been, i'm told, a continuing
series of efforts by state and local authorities to kill the traffic
altogether, but it goes on; it's the same with grass. i was told that the
police on all levels are very rough on possession, but on the other
hand everybody seems to have more than enough to smoke when-
ever they want it, so i guess it's the usual truce.

but the main thing that was different for me, both in terms of
new york city, and in terms of time elapsed, is that the idea of us as
an energy center now seems out of date. there are real people in
these small colleges in these small towns. they want, i think, visits
from the outside world such as people like me represent, but only
for additional input and not because they're starving without us.
the same was true for me in the four stops upstate: there now seems
to be that energy net across the country in strange, small places that
people diverse as sikorsky with his helicopter, fuller with his
spaceship, and olson with his poems predicted.

the simple fact is that the city as such is now just another part
of that net, and not the focus of it. out there some of them still think
we're tapped in to some fantastic socket, but what i see is people
alert and aware in a way most of us here can't imagine. people
wanted to talk there, and about interesting things, too; not like here
where, as my friend the specialist in the seventeenth-century french
novel says, "you go visit a dear friend you haven't seen in a while,
and you discuss jobs, rape, and arson."

upstate new york has, of course a fair percentage of dropouts
from the city, and they are interested in the above statistics, but
everybody else seems vaguely sorry for the city, not angry or
hostile, just sorry; and they've sort of written it off as a possibility
except for a few incorrigible romantics.

the best and the worst of the visits was, for once, the weather. north carolina was the recipient of the same mild weather we had in february, but its more southerly lie meant that spring was already busting out all over, and i fell in love with a particular redbud tree that stood all magenta in the middle of one of the campuses. at the other extreme, the second day in upstate new york i nearly got nailed by a six-inch snowstorm, complete with zero degrees and high winds, and escaped down route 17 as fast as i could. but, again, the weather was real, not like here: the juices came alive in the north carolina glow, and the head went into the shoulders in the cayuga cold. it all made the city seem a one-temperature climate somehow, because the urban sprawl and the greenhouse effect seem to have smoothed out the differences: there's no abruptness, really, here, as we slide from day to day, so there's no weathering, either.

the last night in carolina i was at a party when midnight struck and i turned to the woman whose house i was sleeping at and suggested that maybe it was time to go since i had to get up early for my plane. from across the room one of the students asked, "how can you go back to new york?"

the knee-jerk responses started to pour out, but for the first time in my life a switch clicked, and the "right" answers slowed down and ground to a halt and i heard myself saying, "well, nobody's offered me a job down here yet . . ." sure, i love my city, and i won't take any shit about it from "them," and i don't really want to move. but, maybe, now, if the right offer came, at least i'd listen, this time. maybe it is possible to do your work somewhere else. it never seemed likely before.

the plot thickens

for the past four or five terms i've had this class up at city called "introduction to creative writing." it consists of about thirty undergraduates who are in it either because they need it for a prerequisite for more advanced writing courses, or because they think it sounds like an interesting elective, or because they've heard i'm easy.

but whatever their reasons, almost all of them have one thing in common: they plot like crazy. ask them to write a simple vignette describing an incident on a subway ride to school and it turns into science fiction or gothic romance. they just can't let reality be; they have to screw around with it and make it keep happening. i yell at them. i tell them that a world where we can send men to the moon, and then have one of those men up there hit a golf ball, doesn't need invention; i tell them reality is so far ahead of their inventions that theirs just seem ridiculous. it doesn't help. they keep on plotting more furiously than harold robbins and jacqueline susann put together.

it's hard to know whether this comes from television or the movies or kurt vonnegut or what—maybe it's a natural human endeavor, since it obviously worked in the nineteenth century—but in any event, i can't stop them—no matter what reality does to prove itself.

so along comes "mary hartman." if i were writing scripts for that damned show, and i walked mary into a store and had her get in a fight with the clerk because the clerk wanted cash and she wanted to pay by credit card, and then i had her sit down, and then the police came, and then they checked and found old traffic tickets, and then they took her to the stationhouse and frisked her, and then they found some cocaine on her, i wouldn't be writing scripts for them any more. they'd laugh me off the set. they'd say, hey, come on, opps (that's what they'd call me in video world if i were working there), this show is supposed to have some bearing on reality, cool it, stop going bananas.

now that it's really happened they can work it in, and i guess it'll show up somehow in the third series, since the second is already being shot. but they couldn't've even thought about it before. for me, the glory of the show is in its willingness to avoid plot in favor of reality. the other day roberta the ex-social worker was trying to get some advice from gramps the flasher, while he rummaged around the kitchen, obviously desperately searching for something. finally she asked him to stop and listen, what she was asking was important. he looked at her and he said: listen, when you're my age and nothing's moved for three days and you can't find the prunes, that's important.

lots of people think that that sort of thing is 1) implausible, 2) unimportant, and 3) not funny. i think it's just the opposite in all three cases, and that's why i fell off my seat.

what's unrealistic is the shock, horror, and mealy-mouthed apologism in the newspaper headlines, the police statements, and the television columns, not to mention the unnamed stars who talk about how everybody else in hollywood is using cocaine, as in: they all wear little spoons around their necks. i'm not crazy about the idea of louise lasser or anyone else using c, but as one who spent twenty-five years on lush (making my own plots as it were), i'm not about to start moralizing.

some of the columns have in fact been terrifying, implying that louise/mary is in danger of life and/or soul because she discusses orgasms on television. what else is there to talk about, sometimes? unless you want to discuss prunes or yellow wax buildup.

the problem is, i guess, that reality used to be, to some extent, predictable, and so we had to go on and on inventing, talking about the improbable, the abstract. but that's all changed now, there are new rules, and no invention of ours hasn't been prefigured, or isn't quickly duplicated, by real people who don't even know about our inventions, and don't care.

my favorite definition of how to write a poem goes: let everything come together, and be there when it happens. what you need these days is a good set of eyes and ears; the imagination will be taken care of by the world.

get ready and fall

so it begins again; this round of the calendar. labor day, as sure as any other arbitrary point, serves to start a year. i've picked up my handy-dandy pocket-sized academic year calendar for 1976–1977, which will allow me to keep this busy time, with three separate school schedules, somehow ordered. at least i say it will, and for now at least am dutifully noting down readings, invitations, birthdays, and the like. this will last, with luck, until october 15th or so, when i will revert to scraps of paper and vague memories of commitments.

the weather has helped this year—that cold snap in the last week of august sort of convinced everybody that it was fall already, and bodies, heads, and clothing adjusted. but my first visit to the westchester campus where i'll be teaching one course a week brought me back into summer; it was the day after labor day and the weather had milded again. gardeners were out trimming hedges, the air was soft and warm, and everybody was in summer dress. nevertheless, emotionally i'm ready for fall.

the kids and i got back from maine in the middle of august; we'd already had seven weeks up there, so that felt like a full summer. they went off to their mom's for two weeks and i went into a veritable frenzy of household organizing. i've never done spring cleaning in the fall. perhaps it was the stabilizing, finally, of my situation with the kids that triggered it; perhaps it was the final burial of the ghost of the old relationship, a year and a half after the actual breakup. but i've spent the last four weeks throwing things out—in an ecological fashion, because here at westbeth anything that gets put in one of the garbage bays gets scavenged within minutes, so there's very little waste—and i've moved things around with a new freedom.

i have the kids six days a week now, after a year and a half of half a week, half a week, half a week onward, and the fact that most of my time will be spent here with them in this house has fostered a genuine nesting instinct for the first time in my life. for the last eighteen months i've been acutely conscious, for obvious reasons, of the attention being paid to this particular situation: articles in the times about split custody and its problems; greenwich house's questionnaire, asking, among other things, whether i'd be interested in rap groups about being a single expectant father, or about the children's relationship with a live-in friend; young mothers smile knowingly at me, ask how much time i'm going to put into p.s. 3 now that lem's starting kindergarten. but the reality is something quite different from the articles and the theories, as always.

this new season is serving to focus that reality. i've even bought a jewish calendar and day book, deluding myself that we will spend a little time regaining that heritage, the jewish year is, after all, the only year i know of that officially starts in autumn. and, curiously, although i don't believe it, i suppose starting this new way of living at forty-six is the same thing—it's labor day in my life and i'm ready to push on through the busy fall.

i haven't read gail sheehy's book on age rhythms in adults yet, just sections of it that were excerpted in new york, and it's on my list for reading in its entirety, but what i've read made sense, and now i see this part of my life falling in with what she talks about there. ma, i'm finally settling down, i think.

of course, with my impeccable sense of timing, the new career of teaching is disappearing from the world around me, just when i'm getting in the swing of it—as i remember, this is the age when one feels most deeply the need to pass things on to the younger generation. and that's certainly been true in my case, whether the younger generation cares about it or not. so i'll be at city college for the fall at least, and at new rochelle also. and there are my own kids, although how much one can teach his own kids is always problematic.

that four weeks of throwing things out has actually seen me

getting rid of toys and clothes and books, those things that were always sacred possessions before. and as if in reward for that act, last week, miraculously, i got two glass-fronted bookcases—something i've lusted after all these years. my good brother, moving and restating his own life, sent them down with nephew george, nathaniel cleaned them yesterday with lemon oil and windex, and tomorrow i will fill one with my own collected works, and the other with my dirty library. i think that i may finally have caught up with the books now, and have room for all of them on shelves. that organization will take months and months, but now i'm ready for it.

a is for anker,
b is for banker

sinking slowly in a sea of shankers, ankers, and bankers, it's of interest to note that a congressional committee is now concerned that the monies of the various city pension funds which were used to buy big mac bonds have been badly invested. there is no committee in congress or anywhere else concerned about the investment of our children.

just as the nursing homes and day-care centers exist to enrich landlords and speculators, just as ballparks are built to pay off politicians, and just as roads and public buildings are designed to keep the construction unions happy, so, it seems, the schools are run to benefit the power policies of a few men and the retirement plans of a few teachers.

nathaniel and lem are both in the public schools now, at p.s. 3 here in the village, an "experimental" school in a "high-class" district. and if i, and they, and their principal, and their teachers are all unhappy, what's it like in the jail-like schools in the districts no one cares about? nathaniel lost his teacher four days after the term began—we think he now has the teacher he will stay with this year, maybe. there's a gigantic form of teacher roulette going on, with bumpers and bumpees, and, i'm told, masses of teachers being shoved hither and yon like cattle. the children, i suppose, are the forage, too—and with class sizes what they are, they're stacked like forage, too.

and while the shifting and bumping are going on, the teachers being forced out or held from ever entering the profession are the young and eager ones—the ones who might actually teach for a year or two or three before being ground down.

it's hard to write coolly about this subject when one is in the middle of it; one wants the best for one's own, of course—but some of us realize (all those centuries of humanization) that ours can't have anything if the others don't. children have a right to know who their teacher is; they have a right to a full week of school, not eighty per cent of one; they have a right to be in classes small enough—and well enough staffed—that they can conceivably get some attention.

none of these things is happening now.

a school system that admits that it can't properly teach most of its students to read now has stripped away even the corollary activities—music, art, sports, etc.—that might make the passing of time in a custodial situation not only bearable but possibly profitable for some. meanwhile, we have a city full of teachers out of work; older, skilled people in forced retirement; young, trained people held off the market. has it ever occurred to any of ford's economic advisors that a fully working educational machine might also produce some gross national product, or does that theory only work for the defense complex?

but economics can't be blamed for it all: anker and shanker must share the blame with the bankers for their parts in maintaining and developing bureaucracies that exist only to perpetuate themselves. they are the status quo, they have the power, and they will not budge. it's time, i think, for parents, children, and those few teachers and administrators who care, to begin the process of destroying those two bureaucracies.

how? i'm not sure. certainly that tearing down involves a lot of disruption, and yes, a lot of mistakes. but the system we are all caught up in means that that disruption and those mistakes may be necessary in order to finally end up with a school system that is interested in teaching the children rather than in feathering its own nest, protecting its own interests, wielding political power, and ripping off its consumers.

of course, all this restructuring might lead to some dangerous rethinking about this great country of ours—about an economic system that wants an elite working class surrounded by a huge mass of unemployed. and i'm not talking about welfare cases, either, because they're just the tip of the iceberg. the rest of that iceberg consists of forced early retirement, featherbedding, sexual and racial prejudices, and the sham that college and graduate study has become, to keep the younger people off the market.

but, whether that rethinking comes now or later, what has to come right now is some voice—some control—over our children's fates in their schools. they are, after all, the children's schools, not the teachers', not the administrators', not the union's, and certainly not the bankers'.

but all those people—teachers, administrators, the union, and the bankers—are fully aware that they are dealing with consumers who haven't yet made up their minds. they know that an awful lot of us will settle for custodial schools because we're busy earning our livings or just trying to stay alive and that, my friends, is the crux of it; because until we reorder our own priorities, and indeed, rethink how we want to live, that great they out there will keep running our lives for us, and our children's schools.

to tip a cap

remembering always that charles olson said "the only thing that does not change is the will to change," i face the new year considering possibilities. first of all, the kids and i are off to a new adventure: a month's residency in north carolina while I teach and the kids get out of the wintry blasts. i've thought, and written too, about this kind of move for three or four years now; to be getting out of the city, seeing how the world is out there. i had originally assumed it would be for a year, but i'll settle for a month, especially when the month is january.

while i'm down there i want to think about another major change in or for myself. my first poem was published twenty-five years ago, in 1952, and as far as i've been able to control it, every word i've published since has been lowercase. i've given the reasons so many times i'm sick of explaining, but i suppose i might as well one more time.

one of the things i did at black mountain college was to learn the art of printing. it had always excited me, the notion of extending the act of thinking to talking to writing one step further into printing. but in that act, i became physically conscious of what lowercase was, what uppercase was: separate coding systems, i suppose you could say. the letters, the letter forms, meant different things. not to mention that it was a pain jumping from one case to the other simply to fit into a form. and as i went on in the world earning my living at printing, I got more and more conscious of the "interference" of capital letters.

at the same time, i was getting deeper and deeper into my own writing, and into the work of other poets. one of the earliest influences, or more properly, attractions, had been the world of e. e. cummings, and a great part of that attraction was the magic his use of lowercase imparted. i was drawn into his poems, literally, by it at the same time, i began to learn from william carlos williams, saw how his refusal to use the then standard poetic technique of starting each line with a capital, replacing it by using capitals only in a strictly grammatical manner, at the beginning of sentences, not lines, and for proper nouns only, again made the poem move more solidly.

these two writers gave me the beginnings of a theoretical base for experimenting with the abolition of capitals entirely. i saw the words, and my voice too when reading aloud, as potential dangers to the flow, the integrity, the meaning of the poem. the capital letters were, literally, getting in the way, just as if i got too emotional while reading, my voice would get in the way. and so i started writing poems without capitals, and reading in a flat, uninflected voice. and i felt supported, on a practical level, by what I was learning about printing. after all the usage of capitals had already been modified a good deal from our germanic roots—all those lovely long kraut words with capitals sticking up at odd intervals throughout them—and, indeed, typefaces now were being designed that were meant to work all in lowercase, bauer's futura being the prime example.

i was careful all this time to be precise about punctuation because it was obvious that without tight and accurate punctuation all sense would be lost with no capitals to guide the eye. it's being a continuing cross to bear with this column to hear over and over again, "oh, yeah, you're the guy who doesn't punctuate." in actuality, i probably use more punctuation per piece than anyone in the paper, but people whose eyes tell them something is wrong assume it's a lack of punctuation. and short, recognizable paragraphs become another necessity, for clarity.

i was still using upper and lowercase, then, for whatever prose I wrote—stories, critiques, letters. but then my typewriter shift key broke, and i didn't have the money to get it fixed. from then on everything went lowercase and it's stayed that way since. i liked the flow, and i found that if i put extra space after the periods i could read it as easily as work with capitalization.

unfortunately, i've never been able to convince printers to give me that extra space after the periods, so the prose has at times been difficult to handle. i've felt it myself, reading the stuff aloud. and a typo which replaced a period with a comma could be disastrous as far as sense went.

so now, twenty-five years later, i'm thinking about maybe, just maybe, trying to use upper and lowercase in these pieces. i'm well aware at the same time that of the people who look at this column from week to week, half read me because of the lowercase, and half read me despite it. i'm also well aware that many just turn past it because of the lowercase, but that's never really bothered me. i was doing what i felt i had to do, and what the work needed.

i'm also aware that there have been both economic penalties and benefits from the way I write—i've gotten published some places simply because the editors thought the use of lowercase was a kick or rebellion, or whatever; i've also been denied access to print because of it. the editor of a famous "men's" magazine sent my agent a note saying that when oppenheimer learns to write upper and lowercase he'd read my manuscripts. the only inequity in this last proposition has been that the places i've been given access to have less money than the ones that denied it to me.

so, while i'm down in the old north state, i'm going to rethink my position vis-a-vis upper and lowercase, at least as far as prose is concerned. if it is just too hard to read, if it is getting in the way of the flow, then a new me may come back. we'll have to see.

needless to day, i'd appreciate any feedback from any of you out there who feel strongly one way or the other. decisions like this aren't made by majority vote, but it would be nice to hear if any of you care, and how. i know it's not a matter of earth-shaking importance to anyone but me, but then, nothing much else is, either—for any of us.

and if someone would be kind enough to point out how the shift key works, i'll be able to start the experimental process.

Stop the Presses

Back in the olden days, like my kids say, when I was young, life was simpler because of specialization and bias. My father read the *Herald Tribune* in the morning and the *World Telegram* in the evening; my mother read the *Times*, and Dominic Zaruba read the *News* so he could set up the six-hit pool at school. This was all I knew, and all I needed to know. From these four papers I got a range of information and ideology more than sufficient to the day. I knew there were houses that lived by the *Mirror* and the *Sun*, and even one or two who found their facts in the *PM/Star/Compass* or the *Post*, or God save us, *even The Bronx Home News* or *The Brooklyn Eagle*, but they were other houses, and I could afford to ignore them, and their papers.

It was a lot of papers to have around, but they weren't terribly fat, and it didn't take long to read them. Then came the real glory days for part-time readers, i.e. those who had less than eight or ten hours a day to devote to their pursuit of information. Papers folded and emerged all over town, until we were left with just three. Of those, the *News* needed only to be checked once a month to see what new outrage the editorial page was supporting; the *Post*, under dear old Dolly, having stocked itself with unreadable writers through the middle, guaranteed a fast ten minutes for sports, the first three pages, "Dear Abby," and a couple of comic strips; and the *Times* stayed solid and stolid at two cups of coffee (including the crossword) while I skimmed through in search of the little goodies, like arguments between botanists on whether Venus fly-traps eat each other for food or for religious purposes.

All of a sudden we're into the leaden age again, and with a vengeance. Every Wednesday and Friday morning, I watch sour faces in the greasy spoon turn sourer as they contemplate a four-section *Times*, for God's sake; and, other days, depending on whether they're Breslinites or Hamillians, they may have the *News* with them too. If the truck has arrived on time on Wednesday, they've got *The Voice*. At the same time, the afternoons are getting crowded because there's always the suspicion that there might be something hidden in the *Post* in between page three and sports—although, in fact, the only thing I've discovered on Page Six was an error in the birthdate of Doc Holliday.

The worst offender, by far, is the *Times*. It's not so much that there's more to read in it as that there's more to plough through to get the same stuff. My tendency is to discard the fourth chunk immediately, except that once or twice I discovered later, to my horror, that they'd hidden the sports section back there! Instead of one book review about one book I don't want to read, there are now two or three or even four reviews about two or three or even four books I don't want to read. But I have to give them a glance at least, as one or two of the reviewers might be of interest. Then we've got John Corry, John Leonard, and "Metropolitan Diary" to sweat through, in place of the one lonely "About New York" column the rest of the time, plus enough recipes to feed an army.

In fact, the other day I tried to sell my publisher a cookbook that consisted solely of the Wednesday recipes from the *Times*, the *News*, and the *Post*, but he said it would run twice as big as *The New Joy of Cooking*; so it was rejected. The only hope is that since the world is running out of food perhaps it will soon start to run out of recipes also.

My main objection is not really the bulk of these refurbished papers; it's the disruption of routine. Newspapers, ideally, ought to tell you what's going on, but in a way which supports you by supplying a routine that will carry you through the other routines of your day. One ought to be able to read one's paper and get shocked only by the news, not by trying to find it; and one ought to be able to time things by one's reading and to use the reading as Pavlov used his little bell. For example: The commuter has a decent right to know that if he does the puzzle, the book review, and the editorials in the *Times*, he will arrive at such and such a station; that the sports and entertainment pages will carry him closer to his destination, and that the front page will get him there. It is impossible to do that on Wednesday and Friday. Similarly with timing a second cup of coffee, or a bowel movement, or the start of another creative morning; some set pattern is necessary for most people.

But it gets worse. Saturday's *Times*, which was dependable as the issue which carried the news they didn't want to report during the week, now features something called the "Weekly News Quiz," or some such, which is placed annoyingly enough to bug you if you see it and bug you if you don't. My friend the Realist Painter and I usually meet Saturday mornings for coffee, and jointly we've yet to score better than eighty-three per cent on it. But why are we even paying attention? In any event, what suffers is my ability to get off to a running start on Saturday.

And all this interference is about to be compounded by the magazines since old colleague Carl Tucker just bought himself the *Saturday Review* and Tom Morgan is trying to set up his own bi-weekly journal. I've found myself able to ignore the *Saturday Review* since 1949, but here I go again, out of loyalty.

We're being swallowed by newsprint is what's happening, all because every paper is trying to be all things to all readers and thereby to grab all the readers. In olden days, like I said, it was easier: papers picked their spots, and you went to the ones that made you happy, and they were happy they even had some of us. Those were the good old days, I guess; now, we're just demographics in the business of print.

This Little Phobia
Went to Market

All of a sudden agoraphobia is "in," with a book about how to live
with it being hawked on the talk shows and everybody who's
anybody claiming to have it. It's even been given a popular name:
Housewives' Disease. The word, as you all undoubtedly know by
now, means, literally, fear of the marketplace, from the Greek
agora. The phobia embraces a number of generalized neuroses, but
basically it boils down to a fear of new places.

If you tremble at the thought of doing the weekly shop at
D'ag's, keep putting off the run to Macy's for the kids' summer
wardrobes, really don't want to meet your friend in a strange
restaurant, panic halfway to the information booth at Grand Cen-
tral Station, you've got it.

But it ain't new, and it don't belong to housewives. I've
suffered from agoraphobia for years, and in fact have made use of
it, too, because back when it was exotic, friends would occasion-
ally cater to it. Now I'm afraid that they'll start treating me instead,
or recommending terrific shrinkers. Actually it's probably one of
the healthiest phobias around. I remember a Peanuts cartoon years
back, from a long series in which Linus, after having sweated out
his age requirement, finally got his much-desired library card only
to discover that he froze in terror at the thought of entering the
marble edifice. Charlie Brown, attempting to help, patiently ex-
plained that he had Library Block, that it was not abnormal, and it
would pass. He told Linus everybody had a place they were afraid
of, a place they couldn't even think about without getting the cold
sweats. Where, asked Linus, did Charlie Brown feel that way
about? The World, sighed Charlie.

That's about it with me; if I walk to the Lion's Head via West
4th Street instead of Bleecker, or across Charles instead of tenth,

I'm vaguely uneasy through the whole trip; conversely, coming home, I have to use West fourth and 11th, or things just aren't right. I've drunk at the Lion's Head for twelve years, and gone next door to the fifty-five physically almost identical, only three times— once when the cigarette machine was broken, once for a phone call, and once when a large German shepherd was leashed across the entrance of the Head. I can't even call unfamiliar places without worrying about it. And it all has nothing to do with being a housewife. In fact, now that I've assumed the duties of a house-husband for the last several years, I've noticed that it's wearing off a little—partly because I get out so seldom now that I get bugged if I block myself from a chance to be free; partly because the responsibilities of a single parent demand that I do certain things, there being no one around to trade them off with; and partly because my new financial situation demands certain economies, so that I can't always take a taxi.

The new publicity makes having agoraphobia fashionable. It's like being told that astigmatism is in, or athlete's foot. Here you've gone along for years adjusting to your deformity, only to be told that it's terrific, and everybody wants it.

Fortunately acrophobia remains "out," so far out that the designers of our world are actively pushing to destroy acrophobics. Acrophobics are, of course, deathly afraid of heights. So the powers not only are building higher and higher buildings with more and more window space, but they're putting restaurants on top of them. In February my best friend (what, an enemy would do this to you?) insisted that he had to have his annual feast at Windows on the World. His companion and I, both acrophobes, spent the evening on the inmost banquette, facing the wall. Some-time during dessert I finally managed a quick sideways glance out the windows to see Queens. Incidentally, it was 8:00 P.M., and while I watched, all the lights in Queens went out, and the whole borough evidently went to bed!

They're adding to the terror by making outside elevators, and buildings that move around while you eat, so you can have a choice of where you fall or jump to your demise. Acrophobics in good shape are capable of being terrified by doorsills, and now the world wants them to enjoy the 100th floor!

The fourth member of that birthday party was a woman who not only was not agoraphobic but couldn't believe that any one else was. It turned out she had no phobias at all, to hear her tell it, except, I figured, phobiaphobia, or the unhealthy fear of fear. The birthday boy at least had the decency to confess that bugs and to her creepy-crawlies drove him up the wall, and considering that his favorite vacations are camera safaris in Africa, that would seem to indicate a deep masochistic streak in him.

It's my considered opinion that most phobias, far from being "unhealthy," are reasonable and sane reactions to the world around us, and that they are, probably, exactly what save us from really cracking up.

All my children have managed to live quite well although someone else took them on that horrible boat to the Statue of Liberty, and then up the inside, saving me from the chore and the subsequent trip to the funny farm. And Nathaniel was quite happy watching the famous Rose-Harrelson square-off game in the '73 season from the topmost tier in Shea, while I scrunched around a peephole under the stadium with my feet on the ground. Children accept phobias; it's only adults who have to make them into something to be abhorred or desired.

In any event, I plan to continue being phobic whether it's in fashion or not, just as I plan to continue holding on to my astigmatism. The athlete's foot comes and goes as it likes, without my having much say over it.

Good-bye to
Big John

It would have been a good fall for baseball talk, even with the Yankees running toward another pennant, because we've had a couple of weeks of Yaz bedeviling the Yankees on their way, and John never could handle that—it was a betrayal to have another Polack fighting him. He never quite forgave Bill Mazeroski for hitting the home run that stole the 1960 World Series for Pittsburgh. And now, on top of Yaz, there was Luzinski waiting with the Phillies.

It would have been, and could have been, but it won't. Big John Bodnar, unlikely Villager, owner of the Cedar Tavern, is gone, hit by a massive heart attack on Tuesday, September 13th. He died at home, where he was recovering from an earlier attack last spring.

The Cedar is still there; John's partner and brother-in-law, Sam, will see to that, but it won't be quite the same. Big John was big, physically, and in other ways that count more, too. He was a regular army sergeant who somehow ended running an artists' bar down here and fell in love with the whole thing and brought his whole self to it.

In the early '50s, when the drinking members of what was to be called the Abstract Expressionists began to sell a few paintings and have some money, they moved their nightly hanging out from the cafeteria on Sixth Avenue to the bar on University Place. It was just another neighborhood bar then, unimpressive in decor, certainly not attractive to tourists, and you could sit and drink and talk all night long. It was owned by an old guy named Joe, who sort of took care of everybody.

I dropped by early one Saturday evening in '55, and Joe introduced me to a couple of guys in their thirties and we stood and talked for ten minutes or so and then moved down the bar. Joe whispered to me that he was selling out, and he wanted to make sure all his regulars approved of the new owners. It's hard to believe these rip-off days that there could be that concern, but that was a different age.

We okayed them, they okayed us, and John and Sam moved in, took over. John was big and blond and bluff, Sam, small and dark and almost reticent. It was a perfect mating for the partner-ship. It turned out to be a perfect mating for us, too, and the bar went booming along. Somehow we all became John's bums. Three a.m. Sunday would find him scooping up the leftovers, those of us still sitting at the bar, and we'd go off to Rikers for some eggs. More often than not he'd drop us off on the way home, too. And if you needed ten, you had it, and if you'd been drinking too hard too long, you got coffee and some food—and sometimes, when it was necessary, you got tucked into bed.

But meanwhile the shouting continued. He had been a master sergeant, and he'd fight to prove it. But in it all was the care, for the bar and for us. Sure, the partners made a living, but the place was more than that. It was a home for the homeless, a club whose members had very special privileges. One night in a spurt of madness I interceded in a fight between some stranger who was trying to pick up a woman at the bar, and the woman, who most definitely was not interested. I was kind of boxed, and boring in, when I felt myself grabbed from behind and shot my elbow back, giving whoever it was a good one in the ribs. Thirty seconds later I was cold sober and quaking, aware it was a cop I'd hit. But there was John saying, "It's okay, officer, this here's a friend of the bar." After the cops had gone, I got a night-long lecture on why I shouldn't be a hero, with much guffawing and poking of my ribs.

He was a good man, and a good friend, and a terrible bar-tender. He'd get furious if you ordered something fancy like a martini—his idea of a mixed drink was a shot and a beer. But he always knew when you were hurting, and he was there when you needed someone to share good news with too. When someone hit it with a show, somehow it was John's triumph too, and that was right.

It's not that the bar was an intellectual salon, of course, because what we all were about was drinking and talking and coming on to ladies and arguing about the world and baseball— like any other bar. But it had its touches. In '56, John bet his share of the bar against Franz Kline's studio on the Dodger-Yankee series, John won—but he settled for a painting instead of taking the whole damned thing.

Well, times change, and people too, and I moved over to the West Side, and I got remarried, and Nathaniel came along, and I dried out, and somehow John kept up with it all. I'd walk in every few months or so, and he'd be there, with a dossier on me. He cared what happened to his bums. But when my book on the Mets came out, he greeted me growling. How could a guy who knew as little about baseball as I did write a book about it without consulting him? Who would be dumb enough to publish it? And sure enough, a few years later when I brought in my twenty-one-year-old son, who'd last been in that bar at four, John started in again about the book. But he bragged about me, too, to show the son who the father was.

So he's gone, and it's too bad. He was only fifty-seven, and he should have gone on 'til 90, but the good ones never do. He was homefolks for a lot of people who needed that and couldn't find it anywhere else in their lives. He bought a bar because it seemed the easiest way to earn a living, and he inherited a bunch of bums. I'm sorry he's gone, and I'd like to lift a drink for him. *Ave atque vale,* friend.

Checks and
Balances

Several weeks ago, buried in what passes for the *Post*'s business section, there was an article entitled "Execs see 'burial ground' for careers in Washington." It was about the theories of Professor Eugene Jennings, a management professor at Michigan State University who agrees with the execs. He said, for instance, that "Few chief executives could pass the test put upon Bert Lance . . ."; he said that it's "preposterous that they, whose careers were shaped under the rules of planning, organization, and efficiency, should lend their talent to a behemoth of opposite qualities."

The key was buried, as usual, in the middle of the piece. Jennings spoke of the growing awareness among corporate chairmen and presidents that they "are a crucial element in the remaking of society. They feel the private sector is the productive sector and that more than ever they must be relied upon to produce the goods and services of a better society."

The only remaking of society I've noticed lately is the rich getting richer and the poor getting babies, like we used to say. I mean, if big business really believes itself the revolution's leaders, watch out, because it's gonna be one hell of a revolution.

As far as any thinking person can tell, the real problem with the American government all along is that it's been not the burial ground but the forcing-house for managerial types straight out of the corporations. Every administration in my lifetime has made a big deal out of putting business men in charge to get things done—while the people keep electing lawyers to the legislature to make sure that everything gets brought to a dead stop. It's a perfect setup to keep things at stasis.

If we really wanted change the government would be made up of all the people whose careers weren't shaped under the rules of "planning, organization, and efficiency," like mothers of six or seven, guys who have to hold three jobs to pay their alimony, poets and musicians and actors scuffling to stay alive, and tinhorns waiting for the big triple in the sky. First of all, there'd be solid creative bookkeeping and fiscal management that would put guys like Bert Lance and Abe Beame to shame—and it'd probably work better. After all, most of us make it pretty well, except for a great deal of chronic anxiety, without bouncing six-figure checks.

Professor Jennings said that Washington is no place for talented people, and he may be right, except that we'll need a definition of talent. If talent, in fact, consists of the ability to feather one's nest at the expense of everyone else, okay. But 5000 years of recorded history seems to indicate the opposite. Who ran the military industrial complex during the Trojan War? Which was, incidentally, a pretty damned inefficient operation.

The more I think about it, the more I like the notion of having businessmen drop out of Washington. If we can get rid of the lawyers, too—although every other freak and head under thirty I meet these days is either becoming a lawyer or is one already, so maybe we're getting our guys in to play the law our way. The point is that the way it's worked up 'til now, we've always been in the hands of pimps and whores—there's really no other way to describe businessmen and lawyers. We like to pretend that we're the greatest moral force the world has ever known, but we're run by the world's two oldest professions.

The sad part is the people believe in that "moral force." Everyone, sometimes even me, for God's sake, has a deep-down feeling that entrepreneurs know what they're doing, and that lawyers care about the law, and that the law cares about us, when all the evidence points the other way. The law is an ass, said Mr. Dickens, and Mr. Kennedy added that all businessmen are sons of bitches, and W.C. Fields took care of bankers forever—yet we still believe.

The nation had hoped, of course, that electing a peanut farmer would change things, but of course all it did was substitute a different "old boy" network that operated with the same rules. I think I'm going to start pushing for a more realistic approach, like electing a good saloonkeeper president. He could then name bartenders to the various cabinet posts and get some really creative lushes in as advisers. That way, maybe everyone would get a chance at some of the action—at least until they all began to realize that they were, indeed, in power. At that point, we'd have to start over again with some new segment of society. But it ought to work for a couple of years, anyhow.

In the meantime—until there really is a change—we'll have to settle for the continual stand-off, with the bankers and businessmen using "normal business practice" as an excuse to steal legally, and the lawyers making sure that nothing ever changes unless they're paid enough.

In such a system, we can rest assured that there'll be plenty of goods we don't need and can't afford, coupled with low employment, phony money, and fewer and fewer government services. And we will keep on believing it's because the "bureaucrats" are doing it to us, and because government is interfering with private enterprise, and because the people are immoral. I keep thinking, more and more these days, of how the Tasaday, that most primitive of people, answered when the anthropologists were questioning them and their priorities. If there's not enough food, they said, of course the children eat first. And were amazed that the question would even be asked, or that the answer would be in doubt.

Mix and Mask

Halloween is alive and well and being studied. On October 31st the *Times* ran one of its patented squibs noting that some professor somewhere or other had just discovered that the holiday was descended from an ancient pagan ritual dating back to the seventh century. And on November 2nd, All Souls' Day, my old friend Steve Joseph had an Op-Ed piece about the dangers of filling children with the scary parts of Halloween instead of the constructive ones. It happens that I jumped the gun on this one, having written a column little noted or long remembered several years ago, in which I counted Halloween as one of the major days on my personal calendar. Whether one subscribes to the Old Religion, in which it counted as one of the four major days of the year, or buys the later Christian interpretation or the more recent commercial one, Halloween remains one of the most interesting holidays. It is indeed year's end, the end of the good part, the time to have one last fling before settling in.

Over the last couple years the Halloween Parade through the West Village and the late-evening masquerade party at the Theatre for the New City have been enjoyed with ever-increasing attention by me and my family. The parade starts from Westbeth in the early evening, and I can stand at my living-room window while the crowds begin to gather and Ralph Lee's fantastic and beautiful creations take their places, and then, when things seem ready to start, the kids and I can run down the fire stairs and slip right in. The watching has to be integrated, of course, with steady runs to the door for the hordes of trick-or-treaters availing themselves of Westbeth's soft touches. This year I got dressed a bit myself (tailcoat, top hat, Swiss army all-leather motorcycle jodhpurs, Adidas, rubber glove in handkerchief pocket, wristwatch on bicycle chain draped across chest), to the amusement of my adult neighbors, the scorn of the teenagers, the bemusement of the four-to-ten-year olds, and the complete disinterest of the younger-than-fours, all of whom just said "Hewwo Joel," as if I looked like that every day.

Ralph Lee's creations are of course masks and figures; this year we walked in company with a four-humped camel and a tall Medusa, while some sort of gigantic general strutted, chest covered with medals. Before, behind, and around us, a huge, sectioned snake, supported by bamboo poles in the hands of fifteen or so volunteers, wove its way on a route that ended at Washington Square Park. We were led by a hay wagon for the very little ones and an honest-to-God marching band, which I never saw but kept hearing loud and clear. Along the way we were greeted by ghosts on a Bleecker Street fire escape, the traditional scarecrow riding up and down the flagpole at Seventh Avenue, pumpkin-headed goblins on a low roof on Twelfth Street, windowsful of Victorian grotesques in the brownstone on Charles where two years ago a lifesize Punch and Judy was acted out as we paraded by, and then, predictably, a hail of eggs from one of those lovely high-rises that make the Village what it is today.

Traffic on Seventh Avenue was agreeably stalled; my neighbor said, "God, do they have to wait until the whole parade goes by?" and I answered "I hope so." Once a year it's nice to be able to cross Seventh Avenue in safety. I suppose it's corny, but the parade is the one time all year that the Village feels like we all keep saying it does year 'round: warm and pleasant and small-towny. People yelled hellos all along the route, joined in, dropped out, and generally were there for fun and not hassles. Of course, fame has begun to take its toll—I'd estimate that fully forty-two per cent of the marchers this year were dressed as photographers or video-tapers or filmmakers, but for once they seemed part of the thing, rather than interlopers and disrupters. They tended to converge on a marvelous Dracula, who brought along his own upright rolling coffin, and who later showed up at the Theatre for the New City's party selling the opportunity to be photographed with him as a benefit for this chronically under-funded artistic endeavor.

The Theatre for the New City is the work of Crystal Field and George Bartenieff, with lots of dedicated help, and it goes on, somehow, year to year. Its productions, to my taste, have been spotty—some great, some awful, and some in between; whatever else, it always provides its actors and playwrights and the whole theatre with enthusiasm and élan. I suspect that a million-dollar endowment would ruin it forever, but someone ought to be able to give it something less than that just to keep it with us. The Halloween Ball started a year or two ago as a fund-raiser, and this year it was just splendid. There was a giant swing band and a reggae band and a loud rock band and a quiet jazz trio, and there were singles acts, including that great lady of everything, Rosalyn Drexler, singing. There were jugglers, and small plays, and a graphologist, and a sign for a phrenologist, although I never saw one in action. And there was a parade of costumes with prizes of a year's pass to the theatre and a lottery ticket. I had the honor to be one of the judges, for which I received no remuneration, no bribes, and a great deal of calumny because I picked a woman with terrific breasts as the Most Poetical. Why not?

All in all, the evening seemed a suitable way to say good-bye to the streets for the next six months, and when we hit them again, it'll be in the individual outbursts of spring. This was a huge and good and happy gathering of all of us, grown-ups and children, men and women, straights and gays, blacks and whites, all the dualities out there, holding off the darkness and the ghosts, and saying Goodbye, Sun, see you next year. When I got home the roaches were already at the jack o'lantern, but Lem's Hullmask was glowering at me, so reality had been changed just a little, and bed looked safe and good.

Whither Billiards?

It was billed as "The Match of the Century." Minnesota Fats, who claims to be the world's foremost pool player and who may or may not have been the model for Jackie Gleason's role in *The Hustler*, was playing Willie Mosconi, fifteen times the world champion of pocket billiards, in a $15,000 "grudge Match" at the Starlight Room of the Waldorf Astoria.

It was a grudge match because Willie, the pro's pro, feels that Fats is nothing but a cheap hustler who degrades a high-class sport and because Fats has lost no opportunity to belittle Mosconi and his like for their "airs," such as wearing jackets while playing. Fats's dictum: Chinamen wear jackets to play. He adds that coats are for monkeys. And then he asks, rhetorically, if anyone has ever seen a hockey player or a tennis player in a coat. But then everything Fats says or does is rhetorical.

I was there as the *Voice*'s representative, trying to be a sportswriter—but the other papers seemed to have the right idea, since I spotted several "color" or "human interest" people from the *Post* and the *News,* and only one genuine sportsperson. I say trying to be a sportswriter because pool, or pocket billiards, is something I gave up on early—at fifteen, in fact, having failed to sink a ball except on a scratch in two years of trying. In Yonkers pool was taken seriously by my crowd, so I decided to concentrate on things I could handle, like poker. And I'm not kidding when I say seriously—one of my friends spent his senior year in high school living at the pool parlor, officially. It was the pool parlor's phone number that was entered as his home number, and the guy who answered the phone at Phil's covered for his "son" whenever the school called.

In order to talk knowledgeably about the game, I enlisted the services of one of our esteemed editors, a guy who actually played the woman's champion once, and was drubbed mercilessly. When the cab rolled up to the Waldorf, he said, "Can you take the cab? I only have a C-note. I'll break it later." I knew the evening would be more (or less) than a simple sporting affair. The next hint was the amenities. After all, we were at the Waldorf, puttin' on the Ritz. So the checkroom had a sign up asking for 60 cents in advance. No one walks around all the time with two quarters and a dime in his pocket, and I could hardly ask for change, so there went an ace. Then although the seats were folding chairs ranged around a solitary table, we still got ushered, for another half a buck. I went to get some sodas at the bar after we were seated and was told I'd have to get tickets. The tickets were being sold by a fat lady straight out of every carnival I'd ever seen. And she had three rolls of the same kind of tickets they sell you at those places. One color was $2.25 for hard drinks, one was two bucks for beer, and one was a dollar for soda.

Back in the arena, the full dimensions of the hype became apparent. Howard the Mouth materialized, testing his introductory speech in front of a TV camera cunningly placed to dominate the room. (By now Howard's neck and shoulders bend toward the mike even when he's off.) The voice rolled on and I realized, perhaps belatedly, Howard's true place in the hierachy of entertainment: He's a carny barker.

As the spiel built in intensity, I noticed a smallish, white-haired man checking out the table. I thought he might be Willie, but he was wearing a plaid suit, gray with rust, and I had been sure he'd be in a tux. Then he straightened up, sighting the ball as it rolled, and the way he did it snapped me back to Yonkers in 1945. This was indeed a pool player; it was there in every movement of the eyes and body. Fats appeared, clad more sedately in a dark-gray flannel suit. Both men are in their sixties, and both have bellies. Willie's is the little pot a thin man gets late in life; Fats, on the other hand, was fat—and seemed older, droopier.

Fats took the offensive even before the game began. He told Howard that between the two of them they had the whole thing covered, they didn't need Willie. Willie stayed quiet and grim. The match was to consist of five kinds of pocket billiards: nine ball, eight ball, rotation, one pocket, and straight pool. The first four games would be settled by winning five out of nine; the game of straight would be a single match.

Nine ball established the pattern. Fats talked a lot and occasionally shot pool; Willie talked very little (and very quietly) and played a lot of pool. He was clearly the dominant player, moving with precision and grace. Once in a while, Fats made a great shot, and Mosconi's teeth clenched and he bore down. Those games were super ones for him, and I believed the talk about bad feelings and saw why Willie is a pro.

Both men played in shirt-sleeves, after a long, heated discussion—out of which came Fats's statement about the Chinamen. Willie talked about gentlemen and Fats hahaed him; in the end Willie, with a wry smile, took his jacket off, to immense applause. One might say Willie was trying to play billiards while Fats insisted on pool. Howard, of course, was interested only in war: he spent his time trying to build up conflicts at the expense of the game—but then what else is new?

Meanwhile, my partner was doing a splendid job of keeping me in touch with the finer points of the game, but he got his comeuppance during a verbal altercation between Fats and a spectator. Fats challenged the guy on some point, pulled out a roll of bills to back up the challenge, and peeled it down until he came to the thousands. It made that lousy C-note look pretty puny when it ended up being cashed to pay for our dinner.

The match never went the full course. Willie won nine ball 5–3 (and might have won 5–1 had he not missed a hanger in the sixth game—even the best do it sometimes, kids), took the eight-ball match 5–2, and followed with a 5–2 win in rotation, so the rest of the games could not help Fats. The self-proclaimed king had fallen to the quiet man. Despite the hype, it was a pleasure to watch.

Counting the Measure

Traditionally, Jews haven't been much known for singing and dancing (preferring to brood on the destruction of the Temple), but the Ba'al Shem Tove, founder of Hassidism, prescribed a healthy dose of it for his followers—one version ascribes this to his reading of David's dancing before the ark in praise of the Lord. Lag b'Omer, this month's holiday, was a favorite time for such merry physicality in days gone by, so last Wednesday I decided to celebrate in an appropriate way.

When I was a kid in Hebrew School, Lag b'Omer was called the "Jewish Arbor Day"; it wasn't a terribly important part of my life. But the holiday was a mystic significance because it's involved with the counting of days between Passover and Shayuous, which is when the Law was revealed at Mt. Sinai, and it lends itself to the mathematical games the sages and scribes like to play. It is the thirty-third day of forty-nine, so it's got all sorts of potent numerological powers going. These days, again, it's celebrated both as the feast of the first harvest and as a joyous other-wordly reaching out to God and each other.

I had heard about a Hassidic storyteller and a concert by some Klezmerim—a reincarnation of the traveling musicians of the Eastern European shtetls, who carried news and gaiety with them—at a nearby synagogue. My plans were warped, if not thwarted, from the beginning; Nat announced that he had an overdue assignment to work on, and Lem took it as duty. Then it started to rain. That meant the end of spring—obviously, the next good weather will be summer. But I persevered, and Lem and I took off.

The story-telling turned out to be a sermon with some stories sunk in it, and like all sermons it went on too long. Lem had the good sense to fall asleep in my lap halfway through, muttering about grown-ups and their idea of stories. But like the pregnant lady at the Coronation, I was determined—"I wanted 'im to 'ear the music!" Finally the sermon stopped and the Klezmerim assembled. They turned out to be the Derech Olam Band, four young men with two fiddles, an acoustic guitar, and an electric bass. They were subtitled "New York's famous bluegrass musicians," and that's a fair enough name for Klezmer music, which is heavy on fast, wailing, almost bluesy improvisation over a solid beat. Usually there's a clarinet in there riding around the melody, but it was missing here.

They, too, led off with a sermon, this one on the value and virtue of dancing when the spirit moves you, but when the dancing started it seemed to come straight out of folk-dance classes, and had as much to do with inspiration as the story-telling. It occurs to me that the People of the Book—and most Americans—have become the People of the Book about the Book. But I woke Lem up, we listened for a while, and then I asked him if he wanted to stay or sleep. He opted for sleep; we went home.

I understand that one gets used to dashed dreams—a lost festival isn't the end of the world. But the loss does lead inexorably to down moods, and if bad news comes then it hits even harder. A harsher light is put on everything. In this state, I heard the phone ring. A friend and former student, just checking in. He mentioned the death of Louis Zukofsky; I hadn't heard a word, hadn't seen the obituary which I'm told was in one edition of Sunday's *Times*. Zukofsky was one of the great voices of poetry in this country, what in a more innocent world we called a poet's poet. Difficult verse, sparse, magical, not the stuff that would get him a birthday party hosted by Jimmy Carter.

Ten years ago, Louis and I were on a panel, facing a question on the Function of the Poet in Society. I thought I was pretty smart; fourth in line to answer, I had snapped out, "The function of the poet in society is to write poems." Louis, then in his sixties, smiled

sadly, and said, "The function of the poet in society is to survive."
He understood, as I am just beginning to understand. His poems
survive.

The storyteller had said earlier, "The point of mysticism is
that nothing is serious, except God, and if God is serious, nothing
else can be." But after another of his stories, one that soared to
become a poem, a lady behind me said too loudly, "What's the
point?" And we were off and running, explaining again. As I
explain here, and we spend our lives.

It is the story and the poem and the dance and the song and the
painting that explain it all, or nothing. And the commentary, the
book about the book, has nothing to do with anything. Louis once
described Miss Liberty as a statue in the water. I think that every
Lag b'Omer we will read his poems together, and understand about
seriousness, and try that way to survive.

Who's Counting

The idea was to get me out of the house, cast me adrift as it were. My editors felt I was going stale sitting home with the kids. "Cover things," they said. "See how things are out in the big world." It is neither significant nor earth-shaking, but it's amusing that they are both women, and me a male (as in, "At least you get out of the house, hear some adult conversation, do grown-up things").

I am not one to act hastily, so it seemed wise to begin with a simple task that would get me out but keep me involved in the home. I went shopping for summer supplies. Bathing suits, since the kids seem to have grown. Extra sheets for the sublessees. Camera equipment, so the glories of vacationtide in Maine could be registered forever.

Alas, there is no longer such a thing as a simple shopping trip. It's not the prices; one gets inured to them. It's not the constant hard sell either. I'm a grown person, educated, intelligent, I don't buy impulse items—at least not without convincing myself that they're absolutely necessary, so they're no longer impulse items. Besides, they were all on sale, some for as much as fifty percent off.

What has complicated matters is, as usual, progress. Progress in the form of advanced cash-register design. Would you believe that a beautiful lady and I stood waiting at men's haberdashery in the world's largest store for a full fifteen minutes while the clerk tried to consummate the sale of one (1) pair of men's walking shorts to her? It's true she was paying by personal check, but she had ample identification (even the machine admitted that, finally).

The problem was that the clerk—middle-aged, male, white, bright, educated, etc.—had not been fully trained on this lethal piece of machinery, and it rejected every attempt to register anything. Eventually it printed some numbers on the bill and on her check and then stopped dead again. At this point, a co-worker—

young, female, black, bright, educated, etc.—came over. The machine refused her, too, thus showing that it was absolutely devoid of prejudice. It then developed that a clearing zero (or nought, as the salesman called it) had been forgotten; at last the bill, check, and receipt came out. The only difficulty was that the sales tax was wrong: figuring eight percent of twelve dollars is hard for anyone, no less a machine, and so the process started over. The check looked as if it had been tattooed—policy evidently required that the woman's identifications be stamped on the back, and they now appeared at least four times.

Okay. It was my turn. I was charging on a Macy's card and feeling smug; everyone knows that personal checks cause problems. It took me three tries—one because he thought my card didn't need the clearing zero (nought), and another because he left my pair of walking shorts off.

At the world's largest store's fiercest competitor, the same machine had been placed in the children's department; this time the clerk was disguised as an elderly white female, bright, educated, etc. The machine did everything correctly, but cunningly refused to disclose the location of the button that would serve to indicate shipping charges—unfortunately, I had thought to ship the stuff to Maine rather than carry it. The clerk and I had four pairs of glasses between us, and it still took several minutes to locate the pesky thing. (My receipt indicates that we found COD Delivery Fee instead of Shipping Fee, but the figures are right.) This store had deduced that even if the machine works correctly, they can stall further by forcing the clerk to write down every item— complete with colors, sizes, and other pertinent details. Which actually turned out to be good, since the machine was printing so badly that the receipt is illegible and appears to say things like Boys Furnishings for every item. After we had done all the addressing, the clerk mentioned that it sometimes takes months for things to get shipped out. I hope she was exaggerating—we will be home September 2nd.

Where we are going there are still some stores where the clerk writes things down on a pad with a piece of carbon paper in it. He or she writes the price next to the item, uses a pencil or a pen (wetting the point if it is a pencil) to add the prices up, multiplies by the appropriate sales-tax percentage, enters the result, and reaches a grand total. One hands over one's money, or one's credit card, and receives one's package and a copy of the receipt, handmarked "paid." The entire process takes forty-five seconds—or, with credit card, one minute fifteen seconds. And, if it's groceries, the receipt is usually the brown bag the groceries are in.

But Maine, too, will eventually succumb to progress. I knew there was a reason I was sticking close to the house.

Running True to Form

Now that the first snow of the year has fallen, lain its brief moment in the sun, and melted, it is time to remember Villon. When he lamented, "Where are the snows of yesteryear?" in "The Ballad for Dead Ladies," he was, of course, talking about skin-deep beauty, while we occupy ourselves on more profound levels. But the line has stayed with us for some 500 years now, so it must strike a responsive chord.

It did for me, anyhow, walking toward coffee and the *Times* as that first snow fell. Through the flakes I could make out one faithful runner, one lone sweat-suited fanatic. There is hope, I thought—M'sieu Francois, perhaps you are right again, and these stalwarts, too, are fading. Maybe next summer David Markson will be able to break through the solid ring around Washington Square Park to take the sun. Maybe Ernie Larsen will be able to drive the Interstate without changing lanes to avoid packs of feral joggers. Maybe I will be able to light a stogie without someone telling me how running helped them give up the weed.

Last spring I formed my own club. Attired in colorful matching shirt and pants, and with my Adidas Tobaccos (as far as I know, their only nonrunning model), I would emerge from Westbeth at 5:30 A.M. to seat myself on what passes for our stoop. I would open a collection of essays by Paul Goodman, and as the bodies flashed by I'd smile and say, "My brain is jogging." They all thought I was crazy, which made us even.

Don't get me wrong—some of my best friends are runners. But it's a good thing I don't have a sister. I do have some anti-running friends, God bless them, and two, Vic Ziegel and Lewis Grossberger, have produced the season's saver. It's called *The Non-Runner's Book*, it promises everything you need to know about the virtues of sitting still, and it delivers. The two authors are unclear as to exactly how the collaboration worked, Ziegel claiming he wrote every other line, Grossberger claiming he wrote the bottom half-pages, but the text does not jump around. Although I presume it is intended as a serious study of man's oldest way to Nirvana, it is hilariously funny. It ought to be in every runner's support stocking this $mas.

Ziegel and Grossberger are fanatically committed to nonrunning, as I am; commitment is always solid stuff, even when it's to something you don't want to do yourself. Jim Shapiro's *On the Road—The Marathon* deals with the other side. The book is subtitled "The Joys and Techniques of Marathon Running," and it will tell you everything about that exotic pastime except why. But you can avoid (I almost said skip) those chapters, and concentrate on the parts that talk about, and quote from, some of the better known distance runners. Shorter, Rodgers, Gorman, and the rest speak at length—and interestingly, too—about how it really is. Shapiro still hasn't convinced me that the marathon is an art form (a statement he keeps making and remaking throughout the book), but I believe the professionals.

I also believe Ziegel and Grossberger, who tell us how hardened Bostonians avoid their marathon: "Most of them leave town, taking whatever possessions their flabby arms and legs enable them to carry. Others get sick and throw up. Still others hide behind their accent. Carl Yastrzemski plays baseball. . . . We can't all be lucky enough to live in Venice."

I admire marathoners in much the same way as I do drummers, sculptors, and novelists, which is to say as curiously inarticulate members of an interesting but very different species. Runners, however, are a different matter, and I wait patiently until next spring when the snows are gone to see how many remain upright. I have no doubt that some will, and will have changed their lives, just as there are still some working communes in New Hampshire and New Mexico where people have indeed learned something from the '60s. But I suspect that a lot of running stores will be going out of business pretty soon, as a newer madness takes over with the masses.

In the meantime, I will sit and watch selections from Z&G's list of the nine greatest nonrunning movies, which include *Citizen Kane* ("A publisher builds a big house and nobody comes to visit him . . . contains no running sequences") and *Lifeboat* ("Hitchcock scores again, cleverly setting this entire movie in a lifeboat on the open sea, thus drastically restricting any opportunities for running"). And I will chuckle at the brilliant selection of illustrations accompanying *The Non-Runner's Book*, most particularly the one on page seventy-two, which features an astonishingly attractive woman who has the misfortune to be coupled with a lout in Tree Leaning Doubles.

This Is Your Country

We call it the Whitney, and we forget that it's the Whitney Museum of American Art. *William Carlos Williams and the American Scene*, the new show which runs until February 4th, ought to dispel any questions about that operative word. The full sweep of painting in this country over the two decades from 1920 to 1940 is covered, and it makes a magnificent presentation.

The focus on Williams, the poet-doctor from Rutherford, New Jersey, allows a scope from regionalists to cubists, surrealists to precisionists—because Williams himself was so intimately tied to, and interested in, the possibilities of painting. Committed in his own work to the celebration of the local, the careful image, the development of craft, and the perceptive eye and ear, he is the one poet who could respond fully to this other art, could write about it unself-consciously, and could love it.

His friends are here—notably Charles Sheeler, Charles Demuth, and Marsden Hartley—represented by paintings that hung on the walls of Williams's home. Matisse is here, with *The Blue Nude*, accompanied by Williams's *pense* about it in *Contact II* in 1921: "No man in my country has seen a woman naked and painted her as if he knew anything except that she was naked."

It is in the full sweep that I become aware how much we have changed. This one interested person could find virtue, value, and meaning in as diverse a group of approaches as can be imagined—something not allowed today, when one must pick one's position and stand immovable. In that far country, Georgia O'Keeffe's stark *City Night* shares space with John Marin's dancing *Region of Brooklyn Bridge Fantasy*; Grant Wood's tiny panorama, *Spring Turning*, grabs you in one room, and in the next a startling Jacob Lawrence street scene, done when he was nineteen, pulls you to it.

Throughout the rooms, Williams's poems loom large on central columns and on walls, printed in a handsome large Garamond Italic that lets them sing. On other sides of the columns are displayed the many and various little magazines with which Williams was associated over the years, again in a full range, from purely aesthetic to purely political with every shading in between— William Gropper's fierce cartoons, Picabia's machines, and ads for long-forgotten causes.

In one instructive panel, Williams speaks of a conversation with Walter Arensberg about *Nude Descending a Staircase.* Arensberg presents a philosophy of novelty and chance in art. Williams responds by saying, "I wish Arensberg had my opportunity for prying into jaded households where the paintings of Mama's and Papa's flowertime still hang on the walls. . . " and goes on to suggest a search for, and an exhibition of this art. It is Williams at his purest, when faced with a closed-in aesthetic which will not allow the "real."

And for that real, we see first, coming off the elevator, Demuth's great *I Saw the Figure 5 in Gold* side by side with Williams's poem "The Great Figure" which inspired it. It is the perfect entrance setting for the show—two great artists singing together. In another room Williams's poem "Classic Scene" (A power-house/in the shape of/a red brick chair) bounces off Charles Sheeler's *Classic Landscape*, which is not the same scene but the same sensibility.

There are marvelous bonuses in this show, too. Marsden Hartley's incredible *Mountains in New Mexico* glows in its corner; Henry Billings's *Lehigh Valley* gives us its billboard advertising "Enough or Too Much, sold by W. Blake." Noguchi's sculpture *Death*, here shown for the first time in forty years, since it was condemned as "a little japanese mistake," dominates the room it stands in.

Enough already. See this show. It will stir memories of different days, days when many things were happening at once and not just one. Paintings etched in the recesses of the brain show bright and clear again. And Williams, the most multitalented of any of our writers, shines clearly amongst them. Buy the catalogue, too—or better yet, wait until January and buy *A Recognizable Image*, a collection of WCW's essays on art and artists which New Directions will bring out. It promises to be a magical book, as this show is magical.

Teng and Death

While the rest of the country has been busy assessing the realpoli-
tik of Teng Hsiao-ping's visit, I've been immersed in speculative
pre-history, gamesmanship, and cultural anthropology. My studies
were probably triggered by the curious fact that no one is willing to
spell the Deputy Prime Minister's name the way they pronounce it.

Of course, headlines reading PRESIDENT SEES DUNG
would hardly do in a country where the comedians get laughs
talking about kaka, and where the word harass has had the accent
shifted from the second syllable to the first in our generation. But
language has always been our primary defense, and so one must
look further for the essence of the question. I believe that essence to
be a natural relationship between China and the United States, one
that has been neglected, nay rejected, because of petty differences
in skin color, but that must now assert itself to restore both coun-
tries to their naturally ordained predominance in this world.

Our liaisons with all other areas of the globe pale into insig-
nificance when one considers the data. I am indebted to Henriette
Mertz of Chicago for that data, which is to be found in her book
Pale Ink, published in '53 and revised in '72. Mertz puts her
attention to two ancient Chinese works, one dating from 2250 B.C.,
and one from A.D. 400, both of which seem to indicate the possi-
bility of Chinese exploration of this country. Indeed, the later
work, "Fu Sang," details a visit by a Buddhist monk believed to
have been transformed into Quetzalcoatl by our Mexican neigh-
bors a millenium and a half before they discovered the oil that is
going to save us. We make much of our European heritage, but
that's a mere 500 years; our ties to Africa and South America have
always been purely exploitative; and as for Russia, a continent in
itself, where do you go after John Paul Jones and John Reed?

Mertz's book started the ball rolling for me—obviously our
two countries have been destined since the dawn of recorded

history to co-exist, and more, to help each other. I began to realize that despite the enormous artificial racial hostilities and seeming cultural differences, our children constantly quote Confucius (or Kung Fu-tse, to get rid of the odious latinism) and almost never St. Cryil or Tolstoi; further, that our diet depends in large part on cardboard containers of Chinese food.

Okay, so we've got a base to build on, both historical and cultural. And politically, I believe I have stumbled on a significant fact, through a siege of "Risk." "Risk" is a board game that presents a world divided into forty-two countries and a system for supplying each player with armies; the object of the game is to conquer the world. A grant recently enabled me to spend two weeks engaged in serious combat with a number of dedicated academicians in North Carolina, and the inescapable conclusion was that the game almost always went to the player who had strong bases in North America and Eastern Asia. Africa, Australia, and South America provide safe hideouts for rebuilding strength but are too far from the main arena; Europe and Western Asia are the main arena constantly torn by opposing armies. But the player who presses from North America on the one hand and China on the other stands an excellent chance of taking the world.

In one game I tried a noble experiment: the historical journey of the Mongol Horde. But I made a bad mistake, in that I was not aware of Henriette Mertz's research at the time, and so I sent all my men to Europe instead of splitting them west and east. As a consequence, they were wiped out on the fifth move by Africa, who had no historical perspective to speak of. As a matter of fact no one in the game did—I kept saying things like "Here comes the Khanate of the Golden Horde" as I entered Mother Russia, or "How are the Teutonic Knights today?" as I swept toward Northern Europe, and the only response was "What in hell are you talking about?"

But despite that tragic loss, "Risk" proved a point for me: a political tie-up between China and the United States would be irresistible. I am sending a set to Teng, and another to Jimmy, and I can only hope, for all our sakes, that they play the game studiously. I would send them *Pale Ink* also, but the book has to be specially ordered from Ms. Mertz herself, which takes time.

The title of the book, incidentally, comes from one of those sayings of Kung Fu-tse: "Pale ink is better than the most retentive memory." Which is an awfully good line to remember the next time someone asks "Why do you write?" It has gone up on my wall next to an adage I've carried with me for twenty years: "The way out is via the door, how is it no one will use this method?"

To Sweep,
Perchance
to Dream

There is no believer like a convert, the ancient wisdom tells us.
And, predictably, now that I've learned to keep my own house in
order I find myself casting a jaundiced eye at the world. Sunday
morning Nate was playing baseball; Lem and I took a stroll to
Sheridan Square for waffles and the papers. We walked along
Christopher Street between Bleecker and Seventh in the morning
sun, and it was like wading through the town dump.

Maybe it had to do with the tugboat strike and the concomi-
tant pile-up of garbage as the city sanitation crews went about their
jobs; maybe it was just the aftermath of a good spring night on a
busy street. Whatever it was, it was a mess. The image of aged
Dutch ladies scrubbing the stoops of Amsterdam flashed into
mind—and then, not quite so romantically, I remembered that one
of my duties, years ago, was sweeping a piece of New York.

My father had a small store on forty-fifth Street; the frontage
was perhaps twelve, perhaps sixteen, feet. A couple of times a day,
every day, one of the stock boys, which meant me on Saturdays,
was out there pushing a broom. This wasn't an isolated activity—it
happened up and down the block. I don't know if it was pride, or
civic-mindedness, or the law, or busy work, or anal-compulsion, or
what, but by God, the sidewalk was clean.

At home, in Yonkers, we did the same thing—not several
times a day there, but a couple of times a week. And the streets, in
New York as well as Yonkers, were clean, too—because the
Whitewings were around. I suppose only old gaffers like me
remember the guys with rolling garbage cans, brooms, and dust-
pans. In pining for their return, I join such as Jane Jacobs and Pete

Hamill, and gladly. Jacobs has pointed out that the Whitewings served not only to sweep, but also as unofficial cops on the block, observers of strangers, and the like. Since each had his own territory, he generally knew who lived there, or worked there, and who was new. And Whitewings got the streets clean.

We are so obsessed with machines that we forget how badly they do most of the jobs they are designed for. This past January, in North Carolina, I stopped at a gas station for a refill and saw a guy walking around the tarmac pushing a noisy machine that was raising clouds of dust and whirling them about. I asked my riding partner what the infernal device was. "An automatic broom," was the answer. It was just terrific. It stank, roared, used gasoline, and did nothing but push the dust from one place to another. It also used manpower. It was, in fact, the perfect machine. The fact that the same man with a plain broom might have succeeded in getting rid of some of the dust seems to have escaped everybody's notice in the headlong rush toward automation.

So it is with the big street cleaners which have replaced the Whitewings; aside from forcing car owners to get up before 8:00 A.M., they have no discernible salutary effect on the condition of the city's health, and only add to its discomforts.

Yes, yes, I am suggesting another area in which to try vainly to stem the machine, which will lead to renewed accusations of Ludditism—an accusation to which I proudly plead guilty; I am suggesting that the "Me" generation do something that is at least partly altruistic; and, by calling for the return of men in place of machines, I am risking the creation of another municipal monstrosity.

The first battle, against the Machine, seems to be bred into me. The second can be won, I think. New Yorkers have responded beautifully to the dogshit law; every day I see little old ladies and young kids bedeviling dog owners who aren't doing their duty, so to speak. I would think, eventually, a similar attitude could prevail in terms not only of sweeping, but of yelling at miscreants who litter. As for the third point, we've got a town full of people out of work. Last summer, CETA workers descended on the city with brooms; let's hope they come back. Sweeping the street may not be much of a job, but like the mouse who went up in a rocket said, "It beats the hell out of cancer research."

Also, before conceding on an economic level, I'd like to know some comparative figures on the cost of the bloody machines and the men to run, house, and maintain them as opposed to the cost of wheeled garbage cans, etc., and the men to push them. How you figure in the aesthetic gains I don't know, but I'd be very surprised if the two systems weren't competitive in cost. Ecologically, of course, there's no question that we'd be ahead by saving gas.

I begin to tremble now, because I foresee a committee being established to make that survey. Maybe the way to begin is the way of my father and his neighbors: Let each shopkeeper begin the sweeping; let those who live here, owners, renters, supers alike, begin the sweeping on their blocks. Maybe the bureaucrats will take heart. Maybe the sanitation men will see it not as a threat but as an aid. Maybe the city will actually begin to look like something, and everybody will gain. This is all unlikely, of course, but worth a shot.

No Runes, No Wits, No Airers

The fourth time the Yankee announcers complained about their seats in Tiger Stadium was enough for me. It was the first inning, so I have to conclude that my tolerance for sports announcers has sunk to a new low. Two weeks ago I heard Phil Rizzuto follow up a Tiant spot for Yankee Franks by chuckling, "Boy, that Tiant sure is gettin' them Latins to eat a lot of wieners!" All I could hope was that someone from the advertising agency was listening.

I tend to be a little harsh on Phil, since he works for the club I love to hate, but the Mets's guys aren't any better these days, and they have less to talk about. At least, if I watch the Yanks, I may be able to savor a loss. And now that I've gotten a big color set it's more fun. It's my mother's Zenith, and it's so old it's got a curved screen. But it works. And somehow I feel safer rooting against the Yankees with it; I doubt that Dent would've cleared the green monster if I'd had this set last fall.

I made the mistake of watching ABC's big move into soccer coverage the other week. Jim McKay and Paul Gardner must have been under orders from headquarters to keep talking at any cost. They spewed and respewed facts, figures, theories, and explanations; they were so intent on educating us in the subtleties of the game that we never got a chance to enjoy the subtleties of the game.

But that treatment is nothing new for television. Sometimes, one despairs of even seeing the game, because the screen is constantly cluttered with "visuals." They might more properly be called antivisuals, since a thousand words effectively obliterate any picture.

Channel 9's coverage of the hockey play-offs was, conversely, a pleasure. Maybe it's just that I'm not used to Chadwick and Gordon, so that I haven't learned to be annoyed by them yet. But I doubt that's the story. After all, I came to the Ranger-Islander series a novice at the game. I've been to one in my whole life, and at that one I dropped a pint of bourbon as I sat down. This was clearly a sign from above and so I've ignored the game ever since. But this year the fever caught me as it did so many other New Yorkers—helped no doubt by a young neighbor who'd asked if he could watch at my house. I let him and I got hooked, at least through the final game at Montreal. Next year, I expect I'll be able to ignore it again.

But for now I had the sense that I was being allowed to share the sport, not being conned into loving it. The coverage was sometimes corny, sometimes too frenetic for me to understand, and always partisan, but by god it let the game go on. We have to be thankful that the series ended with the fifth game, since ABC had the contract for the seventh. The thought of Howard explaining the fine points of the game rouses approximately the same sensations in me that dropping the bottle of bourbon did.

Hockey seems to have adjusted to the fact that it failed as a network sport; it's expanding again next year, and as far as I know the fans keep coming. They may be few, as Vic Ziegel pointed out last week, but they certainly are loyal. Maybe soccer ought to reconsider its push toward acceptance. It seems to me that the way you build fans is through a local outlet, with your announcers; you don't worry about sweeping the nation. The problem with sweeping the nation, as we keep discovering over and over, is that there's always a new broom coming after.

The reason baseball has held, and increased its audience, despite the competition of football, and its inherent weaknesses as a video spectacle, has been precisely because it grew its home audiences. I may dislike a Rizzuto, or sneer at a Bob Murphy, but at least I know that channels 9 and 11 are interested in the team. I don't mean to sound romantic, I simply mean that they understand that they have to serve their local fans. They're not using the game as a shill for the next sporting event—that ridiculous notion the networks have that we live panting for anything they call sport.

What we do pant for is competition, skill, and letting us watch the game at hand. It's nice if there's some magic involved, too; the Rangers gave us that for a couple of weeks. That's why I was watching, even though I have trouble believing hockey is a game. The big old set helps here, too, since it's the first time I've ever been able to see the puck. That includes that first game of mine, when I was too busy worrying about dropping lit matches into the spilled bourbon to see anything.

I haven't said a word about the basketball play-offs. That's because no one I know is willing to admit they're still going on. If indeed they are. There were twenty kids outside in the Westbeth courtyard today and half of them were playing baseball, six were frisbee-ing, and four were playing roller hockey without skates. Nobody was dribbling. Of course that's unfair, since there aren't any baskets in the Westbeth courtyard, but there isn't a hockey net either, or a home plate, for that matter.

While I've been working on this, Richie Hebner has driven in his eleventh run in three games, and I'm beginning to find Bob Murphy interesting. On the other hand, the Yankees scored eight, which has made Rizzuto even more intolerable.

A Thousand Flowers

"Enough, or too much!" screamed William Blake. My contemporaries have made their choice, and so have I. Enough is what I crave, and what I hope I've learned to see. On the other hand, everybody else wants more. Until they're glutted with it, whatever the it is, and they drop it and run. This applies to sex, energy, material possessions, and all forms of self-improvement.

I have found, however, that I'm happiest letting things come little by little, and learning to enjoy, use, or otherwise benefit by them slowly. So I remember each first contact, each new cherry lost to the pricks of time, if you'll pardon the expression. It's an old-fashioned feeling, of course, and my only excuse is that I was born in 1930. That was not only a long time ago, it was also the heart of the Great Depression, when everybody had to do without whether they wanted to or not. It also means that I had passed through the early formative years by the time the great cultural changes brought about by World War II started to sweep the world.

So I bumble along, falling into pleasures now and then: my first stereo in 1976; color TV just a month ago; the pleasures of dressing up in my early forties; haircuts in my late forties. Sexually, unlike so many others, I have come to each variation slowly, and with awe and wonder and fear and trembling, and so retain each separate pleasure, and relive it again and again. Of course I've missed a lot this way, too, but it's a trade-off we make. Other people have burned themselves out on each pleasure by too much too soon. Like the lady used to say. "It's six dozen of one and half of another."

It even took twenty-three years for me to become a full-fledged alcoholic; others have done it in five or six. And a conversation with a twelve-year-old the other day featured him saying,

"My folks told me they expect me to try everything." We were talking about dope. I was horrified. I didn't stop to question whether they were being realists and meant that they assumed he would try everything, because that was the nature of the world, or that they wanted him to try everything, because that was how it should be.

I threw my oar in, saying that there were several things I had not found it necessary to try, in a lifetime of getting high. I said that sitting with a bunch of guys who stuck needles in their arms and then puked in order to achieve nirvana had convinced me heroin wasn't a thing I had to do. In the same way, conversations with acidheads which featured all the paranoid visions I had when straight had kept me from that particular heaven. I also suggested that twelve was perhaps a little early to feel you had to fuck yourself up.

This is all very reactionary, and I know it. But "this above all, to thine own self be true," etc., and so I continue, missing out on lots of goodies.

I consider these things every Saturday as I make my stroll and buy cut flowers. This is new for me, and it took only forty-nine years to get here. For six weeks now, I've browsed the flower stores, coming home with seven or ten dollars' worth to distribute throughout the house. It started from some vases I picked up. There's a classic Chinese number, with dark blue-purple leaves swashed on a yellow background, a slender brass one with a constricted waist, and a garish, white glass number from the '40s encrusted with even more garish glass buds.

Then the kids wanted flowers for their rooms too, so I hauled out some pitchers that had accumulated. The last step was to say that I was allowed to have some in my very own bedroom and by my very own chair. So now seven vases, pitchers, bowls hold flowers all week long.

The increase in the budget was excused by inflation. Hell, seven to ten bucks a week when they're forecasting $100,000 annual wages? And when the average price of a house has gone up to $70,000? It is to laugh, like we used to say. So I stroll out, with the kids or without, and I pick some peonies (too lush, I don't really like them—but they are magical) and some irises (invented for watercolor, or watercolor for them, I can't decide which) and sweet williams and daisies, statice, whatever grabs me.

The Village isn't Amsterdam or Paris, where I understand you can buy a houseful for practically nothing, but once you begin to look, you discover that there are a lot of flower stores around. I can hit five or six in a ten block walk, and even D'Agostino's sometimes features bright red carnations. Once home, the sorting and arranging can begin. The kids hover, to see that neither gets cheated—that's sort of a pleasure, too, to see them concerned about flowers rather than attention or presents or food. I can't pretend to any expertise in the arrangements, since I still make mistakes like putting the peonies in the Chinese vase, where the shapes and colors war in the old battle of romance and classicism, but there is a pleasure in seeing them all out, displayed.

I don't know how long this will last, but I'm glad it's happening now. In a spring which, like all New York springs, has disappeared, it brings spring into the house, and it gentles us. It's even possible to get Lem to stop playing ball inside because he might hit the flowers, so it has a utilitarian side as well. And the side benefits have been that I've started bringing flowers to other people's houses, with discretion of course, because not everybody wants them, and I've started getting flowers too. Recent dinner guests have come in with posies, which I flutter over just as any Victorian maiden might have.

To turn a case-hardened child of the '30s into a Victorian maiden is enough of a bonus, I should think. And perhaps now I can put TM and est and jogging off 'til next year.

Other Places

Rochester is a blur. In my innocence, I assumed that the Ninth Annual Writers Workshop at the University of Rochester would call for occasional genteel discussions of verse in pleasant surroundings. The surroundings were pleasant, but it were work! I was able to investigate only one feature of this notable city to the northwest: the grave of Adelaide Crapsey.

The distinguished American poet lies buried in Mount Hope Cemetery, across from a large hospital and medical school complex—perhaps the most efficient set-up in America. Miss Crapsey's grave is part of the family plot; her father's headstone is marked with his Civil War unit, her brother's with his unit in the Great War, but Adelaide's has only her name.

I'm afraid that I took advantage of a talk-show appearance, boosting the workshop, to call for a subscription for funds for identifying Adelaide as a poet. I believe we were bleeped every time I said her name. Joined by Bill Stafford, the distinguished poet from the Pacific Northwest, I took advantage of the rather befuddled, but helpful, public relations person from the University to avail ourselves of photographs at the grave. We did not go to Susan B. Anthony's grave several sites away; presumably that is marked suitably.

Rochester is a rich city, and the University is rich also—it bills itself, I was told, as the Harvard of the Midwest. This is for scholastic reasons, of course, but the money shows also in a rather neat campus with some interesting buildings and good vistas. The vistas come from the original design, based on Jefferson's plans for the University of Virginia, so that sometimes the newer additions jostle the quieter older buildings, but the Quadrangle still manages to hold its own. The Workshop, as I've said, did demand work, but it was filled with good people, both "students" and "faculty," and all I really missed was my afternoon nap, so I shouldn't complain.

Buffalo was next on the itinerary. The kids were with me by now, and I had a workshop and a reading scheduled as part of the Summerfest programmed by the Niagara-Erie Writers. Ed Sanders, Charlie Morrow, and Penny Kemp from Canada were there this weekend, and a heavy schedule of poetic activities continues through July 29th, happening all over the city. It's an ambitious undertaking and I have a button reading "Poetry City USA" to prove it.

My first visit was some twelve years ago, and the memory is of unrelieved gray; but now Buffalo seems to be emerging with a great number of live young people. The city has built a swell marina on Lake Erie, and we picnicked there Sunday afternoon, and watched a rich boat from Toronto bully a poor boat from Buffalo out of its docking space. We also tramped about a light cruiser and a destroyer (The Sullivans, for those who remember 1942). Lem was astonished to discover that there are johns in destroyers, but I found myself bemused by the tiny barbershop. It really was a different war, I guess.

The reading was given in a bar which has just started holding such things. My name was in lights outside. There was a pool table in the front room, and the mike wouldn't work—which is fine by me since I can never decide whether to read to the mike or the people. After the reading, I was inveigled into a long session at the table where, by virtue of good partners, I swept the contenders, for the first time in my life. I actually sank three balls in the course of five games.

Monday morning's paper had a headline which read "Carter Calls for NEW American Spirit." I was so detached by now that I thought he was alienating his last remaining pocket of strength by calling for vodka instead of bourbon; I did not read the story, so I could maintain the delusion.

Subsequent events seem to prove I took the wiser course since it is clear by now that he meant cosmetic change only and there was no sense getting excited about it. There was sense, however, in getting excited about Niagara Falls. We stopped there because Nathaniel requested it; I figured I'd be a terrible excuse for a parent if I let us just drive past it. But once again his instincts were right, and mine, those of expected boredom, were wrong. The Falls are a wonderful and dramatic sight, far better in the flesh than all the photographs and movies lead one to expect. And if the mystics and seismologists are right, we may soon lose this too. Later on the way back, we stopped at the American side, and as we stood on Luna Island looking at the Bridal Veil it occurred to me that perhaps the answer to broken marriages lies in the decline of the Falls as a honeymoon spot. No one I know has gone there for a honeymoon, and no one I know is still married.

From the Falls we went on to Toronto and spent a glorious four days in this wondrously clean and modern metropolis. Except that we stayed with our friends on Ward's Island, discrete from the mainland, and dependent on an honest-to-God ferry for egress. Toronto, which blossomed into hugeness after the war, has been planned in a way that's been impossible in New York, and visually (and in terms of transit, too) it's a genuine pleasure. The kids loved this place, and we found a well-planned amusement park and an exciting Science Centre to play in.

We also watched the All-Star game from the Island. Our Canadian friends were astonished at the number of people who had voted for the teams; I pointed out that the candidates were more qualified, more attractive, and more reliable than the candidates in any recent presidential election. I wish I could report a spontaneous outpouring of joy over Mazzilli's derring-do, but Toronto is, after all, an American League city, so the celebration was limited to a great deal of jumping and shouting by Lem and myself, Nathaniel and the other sitting dourly by the set.

Crossing the border, we declared some used books; the customs man went racing to the trunk, looking for who knows what. We showed him two by Robert Duncan, and he said, "Oh! Poetry. . . " and waved us on disgustedly. I had smoked up my allotment of Havanas by then, of course, and we cruised back into the U.S. of A. Something will have to be done about this situation, however. It's terrible to be able to kill one's self in class over there, and to have to do it tattily here.

Speaking of which, as we flew down from Buffalo, Nathaniel spotted some cooling stacks perking merrily away. He thought it was Three-Mile Island, but the pilot informed us, "Oh no, that's just another one, on the Susquehanna." Terrific.

Shifting Gears

See, they return; ah, see the tentative
Movements, and the slow feet
The trouble in the pace and the uncertain
Wavering!
—Ezra Pound, "The Return"

The kids back in school, blankets at night, the social whirl spinning again—it doesn't matter whether you've been away or not, summer is now over and the world is different.

I know autumn won't officially arrive until later this month, and I know there'll be plenty of hot weather to come. I know Labor Day is just an artificial holiday, and yet it ends playtime just as surely as my alarm ended that sweet dream this morning. The alarm is part of it. Now it's set not for personal needs so much as for the world's: the kids have gotten off on time no matter how I feel or what I have to do. All summer I used the alarm when and how I wanted to; there was some choice in it.

There are things to do, is what the clock says now. My notebook is filled with words like "stationery," "haircuts," "clothes"; my checkbook is filled with stubs with similar notations; my head is filled with formless dread.

THERE ARE THINGS TO DO!

Yesterday was clothes, or some of them. Tomorrow is shoes to go with the clothes. This morning, as a breather, I suggested the barber after school. Screams and moans: "Just my bangs! Just my bangs!" "Only a trim, it's short enough!" Only by assuring them that I will submit to whatever they have to can we make it through the meal.

Meanwhile they are both disturbed by another evidence of the world. Each of them had homework to do from the first day of school, and somehow that seemed a breach of good manners, as if it should have been eased into. The first night of that first day the basic local units on the phone were all used up by a series of panic calls to friends trying to remember what was learned just ten weeks ago. French is a foreign language once again, arithmetic an arcane science, spelling a lost art.

They are buoyed only by the thirty or forty dollars worth of supplies it now seems necessary to start out with: notebooks, magic markers, unblemished pencils and erasers.

I have nothing to buoy me so. Faulty planning leaves me half way through a ream of paper; the typewriter's due for an overhaul but I forgot to put it in last month so it just growls at me instead of purring. And there is a stack of mail—and of assignments—that's growling too. There are letters that tell you in June there's no sense answering them until September, but then September comes.

I spent the week between Labor Day and the first day of school frozen in terror and sapped by depression. I could have used that gap to catch up, but it all seemed insurmountable, so I pushed papers around instead. Now it has to be done, all of it, and quickly.

One useful piece of busywork to get me in the spirit is deciding where to put the books I didn't read this summer. *Plagues and Peoples* will do nicely by the bed. McNeill's brilliant history qualifies as the most exciting depressant I've ever found. But what of *Water Margin*? One of the world's first novels, this work by Shih Nai-An first presented itself to me in an abridged translation by Pearl Buck years ago, as "All Men Are Brothers." I loved it, and when I found the new version in June I snapped it up. I carried it with me to Rochester, Buffalo, Toronto, Oneonta, and home, and have read the preface and the first two chapters. Can one get accepted to Yaddo or MacDowell in order to read a Chinese novel?

Meanwhile, the nights that might be used to do that reading have already started to disappear. Three gallery openings, two publication parties, a friend's fortyth birthday, a big wedding anniversary for two other friends, the imminent arrival of six different people from six different places at six different times, all dot the next three weeks. And that doesn't include Rosh Hashonah, with Long Island, the Brotherhood Synagogue, and Yahweh all beckoning. Two hours after I got back in town I was visited by a one-man delegation armed with the latest pressing problems at Westbeth, and his account was interrupted by two former students who each needed advice about their new jobs.

I believe this is all called life.

This is beginning to sound like a plea to abolish summer. Perhaps it is. Everything else is being abolished, so why not that? Perhaps we were not meant, really, to have that couple of months when we feel free, relaxed, even when we're working. More discipline! That's the answer—no time in the sun, or out of it, over long tall drinks. No time to feel relaxed in, to say, "Gee, thanks, no. I think I'll just relax."

Pound was talking about soldiers, back from an expedition, but coming back to the wars from vacation is just as unsettling, just as defeating. There's no easy way to shift gears; those friends of mine still desperately clutching their house in the Hamptons, or one last day at the beach, are no better off. In fact they'll pay more dearly as they try to give up summer slowly, because the agony is long, drawn-out. It's like an affair which must be ended quickly, so your poor broken heart can begin to mend.

By October I will have found a rhythm to this winter drudgery and may even be happy in that rhythm. But now the alarm goes off screaming, and the kids are sullen at breakfast, rebellious when I send them to bed. I wonder who they learned those feelings from, as I grumble over my coffee, as I snap the light off at midnight, as I push the papers on the desk, wondering where in all that mess to begin.

Once More
with Ceiling

In a special pile among the piles on my desk are all the requests for apartments I've received in the last four weeks. September and October is the big season, of course; people making the big move like to take the summer off to let it settle in.

There are students who want "anything," and mid-life crises victims who want the "right one," and they all call and ask if I've heard of anything here in Westbeth, or in the Village, or anywhere. Like any other old settler in these here parts, once in awhile I do hear, and once in awhile someone actually gets an apartment through my intercession. The others find something on their own, or they give up and leave. In any event, eventually I get a phone call or postcard telling me the new address and phone number.

Two more called while I was watching the last game of the Baltimore-California play-offs. I forgave them the interruptions because I understand that there are rare occasions when baseball has to take second place, and not having a place to watch baseball is one of those. But since this particular game was devoted to showing us pictures of Richard M. Nixon stuffing his face while watching from Gene Autry's box, there was an added poignancy to the calls.

After all, I've got it made. I live in what is, for me, a perfect place. Here at Westbeth, I have great space, a reasonable rent—at least until the next rise—and even a little eclat. It ain't the Dakota, but once in a while people's heads snap, and they say "Oh, yeah. That's where all the artists live . . ." Of course that implies "How come you . . ." but I ignore that.

But it's not only the apartment and the building, it's that it is in the Village, and I've always wanted that, or at least have wanted it since I was sixteen, which is almost always. That was when my father described the Village as Bohemia, and then defined Bohemia as the place where "you're at a party and a man goes over and puts his hand on the hostess's breast while her husband watches." At sixteen that seemed reasonably exciting, although in practice, of course, it turns out to be the same old shit—and it also turns out to happen everywhere else these days.

It's also New York City. I came here from Yonkers but it might as well have been Dubuque for all the couth I had when I came. I couldn't wait to get here. So I suppose I ought to understand Nixon's yen.

But I don't. I don't want him in my city. In fact, I can't think of anywhere I want him, but least of all here. People of my generation know we've been eternally saddled with this monstrous man. But to see him now, starring in the game I love, and about to move into the city I love, is too much of a cross to bear.

The fact that he could buy a house for three-quarters of a million bucks of our money is abominable enough. That it should be a house once owned by Learned Hand is even more atrocious. It's as if Eichmann had been allowed to buy a condo in Tel Aviv. But then, condo people could have filed lawsuits like they did here, while there's nothing to be done about a private house.

It's a difficult thing for a writer to admit to inarticulate rage, since articulation is what we're about but I'm filled with it. Bad enough he lived sucking on the public tit out there, bad enough he broke his word again and sold the San Clemente palace for personal profit; unbearable that he should be here in my city on those monies.

There is, of course, a great surge of revisionism swirling about him now, helped no end by Carter's death in office and the never-ending sniping at Kennedy and Johnson. The fact remains that Nixon did more and worse and almost pulled it off, almost stole the country. It's not, it's never been, a mere question of degree. Aaron Burr, after all, wanted his own country, not this one.

So I sat and watched the Orioles dismantle the Angels and

whatever feelings I had for those yearning southern Californians were dissipated every time I saw that mawkish face pouring another drink into itself. It was fitting perhaps that it sat next to a fat, rich, old man. I thought how when Buck Jones died in the Cocoanut Grove fire he was still a cowboy, or at least looked the part, and I was glad that he had been my man. I understand Autry's ache—any Red Sox, Dodger, or Phillie fan has that same ache multiplied by ten. But we can't buy a championship. And we can't buy a four-story townhouse in the midst of people we have abused— or anywhere else for that matter.

I wonder if the people of the city can't, like the co-op owners and the condo board, take action against an undesirable neighbor. I wonder why we can't up and say, "Go. Go away. Go back to southern California where they love you." But we always have been too generous, too liberal. We will let him stay, I suppose, and we will get to see his face in his old friend Steinbrenner's box rooting for the Yankees and we will hear how he is their "number one fan."

The friends who call me might conceivably give this city something, and in addition are neither liars nor thieves. I suppose that's why we have no space for them.

Careless Love

Much of the malaise in modern-day America can be attributed to
the recent sexual revolution. This is not news to anybody, of
course—but it occurs to me that we have been misreading the data.
It is not a question of morality, as such, or some re-shuffling of the
surface order, but a much deeper problem of structure.

At the height of the '60s, whatever else was brewing there
was no question that a genuine sense of cooperation, of sharing,
imbued the young revolutionaries. There was a place for every-
body, and if everybody wasn't in their place, well, that was okay
too. There was room for those who marched to a different drum-
mer; not only that, but, to continue the metaphor, there was enough
money around to pay the piper when you danced.

These days the money has dried up, the pipers are all playing
disco, and the orderly progression of loving sexual encounters has
turned into a free-for-all. The melee which ensued from the break-
ing down of sexual barriers has swallowed all but a few of us. Only
those in Delaware seem untouched. Herewith, a few examples:

My friend, with whom I have shared the romp through life
since the early '50s, used to be a gay poet. He was not only out of
the closet, he had never been in it. At party after party he steered me
to available young woman poets while I steered him to available
young men poets in a symbiotic relationship as pure as the driven
snow. The women trusted him because he was safe, the men trusted
me because I was too. If **X** recommended me to an acolyte, she
could be sure she was getting straight goods, and the reverse was,
of course, true for anyone I introduced to him. Now **X** is bisexual.
No longer can we happily co-exist; now parties are a continual
struggle as **X** and I face each other across the crowded room.

Y, on the other hand, was a straight woman painter. But she
was not only straight, she was lusty. Pick and choose and use and
dump was her motto, and for a good number of years she bestowed

her favors freely, and reaped varying rewards, as she cut a swath through the serried ranks of stalwarts young and old, who eddied about her dimpled knees.

Her sisters convinced her this behavior was promiscuous; further, that only in sisterhood could true love lie. Now she is adamantly gay, and worse, is a proselytizer, proclaiming the true religion. She pounces if she sees a suspect heterosexual conversation developing, and one more channel of communication is closed.

Z has fallen into a different trap. A tall, handsome, young black man, he arrived from a small college in the deep South innocent but open, and within a few weeks was satisfying both his own and others' fantasies in classic fashion. Wasp, Celtic, Nordic, Oriental, Semitic, they all flocked to him, choosing to ignore, or never even noticing, that he had no rhythm. He and I also shared a symbiotic relationship, since his slave name, which came from an Anglo-Irish-Scottish family, meant that he gave Wasps and Celts the lowest priorities and was more than willing to trade off phone numbers for those of southern European extractions.

In the late '60s Z discovered (a) nationalism, which reduced his choices to black; (b) religion, which seemed to him to call for monogamy; and (c) revolutionary politics, which demanded celibacy. When Z and I meet now, infrequent as it is, we share a drink and drum our fingers nervously as we try to find some ground on which to talk. Not even baseball is allowed, children are obviously taboo, except in the abstract, and nostalgia for "the good old days" suffers so much from revisionism that I am almost happy to be living now.

These are but three cases in a myriad. All over the Village, all through the city, all over the nation, people who once were friends are now antagonists, or at best idly aloof. We talk about a breakdown in communication, and we wonder why and how.

Again, I suppose, I'm asking us to turn back the clock to happier days, or at least that's what it sounds like. But not so fast—certainly I don't want a revival of the rampant chauvinism of those days, the ghetto-ing of the sexes, because those things were as destructive to me as to "them." I just want a little more structure I suppose, so that I know where I'm going, and so that we can all talk to each other again.

It's conversation that's suffered most, and when that stops we get the closed-off screwed-up place we're living in right now. **X,Y,Z**, and I used to be friends; now, willingly, we're antagonists, not only sexually, but as full human beings. A lot of energy gets wasted maintaining the defenses which used to get spent in happier ways. And the work has suffered too, for whatever that's worth. **X**'s poetry, **Y**'s paintings, **Z**'s stories, my own stuff, they all come in fits and starts, and with lots of false starts too. It's like we're all searching for what we used to know without looking.

If it seems too easy to tie this all to the sexual revolution, what I have to say is "why not"? The ideology has, as usual, swallowed us up, all we're left holding is the rhetoric. Somewhere up ahead there must be a better ground. But, like we used to say, I've seen the light at the end of the tunnel, and it's heading right for me.

Rites of Passage

Growing up is hard to do. It also keeps happening, or should. Every culture has one particular marker, a rite of passage, that clearly defines status as an adult. But then one discovers that the markers keep looming ahead, step by step, no matter how old one gets.

My bar mitzvah, the traditional rite for a Jewish boy, was not particularly successful as such. For one thing, I sang so badly that I became the first youth in the history of Congregation Ohab Zedek to read his haftorah, the passage from the minor books of the Bible with which every candidate demonstrates his proficiency with the language and the religion. I droned it in a monotone while the old men near the reading table stared. Later, at the party at our house (since this was before the era of the safari-type bar mitzvah), my father introduced me to the Irish bartender hired for the occasion and told him to give me all the ginger ale I wanted. This did not seem an auspicious beginning of manhood.

So when Nathaniel asked me two years ago if he could be bar mitzvahed, I was both nonplussed and pleased. While I had made some effort to let my boys know they were Jewish, I'd never taken them to shul, never pushed the religion, or any religion, at them. A classic child of the thirties, I had my doubts, and I was not about to lay something I doubted on my kids. But Nathaniel, for whatever reason, decided he did want the ceremony—and as a ritualist, if not a good Jew, I understood that.

So we joined a synagogue, and he went to Hebrew School and finally, a date was set. Then, this fall, the studying began in earnest—and my anxieties began also. I wanted it to be right for him, but it couldn't be a parodic bar mitzvah either. And I was going to have to face, once again, the reality of my relationship to my own family, which is atrophied at best. As always, I leaned on my friends, the people I've learned to look for in trouble and in joy. This is a column about friendship.

Friends filled the synagogue. People who hadn't been up before noon in years were there at 9:30. Lapsed Catholics, Protestants, representatives from Islam and the East, even apostate Jews. Bob Smith, raised in Chicago by a Jewish Socialist Atheist, and now Nathaniel's godfather, opened the Ark. Al Koblin, in his crocheted yarmulke, did too. My oldest son, Nicholas, raised nondenominationally by his once-Catholic mother, shared another turn with his youngest half-brother Lem.

Every time I turned from my seat on the side of the reading table to look out I spotted a different friend—and when I tottered under the weight of the Torah (terrified as I was as a kid, because the legend was that if you dropped it, you and the shul would be destroyed), I felt them with me.

Sharifa, Nick's beautiful wife, sat patiently with my mother, putting up with her eighty-four-year-old barbs ("Is he going to talk forever?") And finally Nathaniel himself shone—reading, speaking, acting like a man, a mensch.

We had a small family lunch at Northwest Corner. Joe Early, another old friend, came through, so that my mother and Nathaniel's mother's family could spend some time with him. For once my mother didn't yell at me, because she had my son Dan to do it to. There are some mantles you hate to see your children inherit, but maybe he can handle this one.

And that night we had the party I'd hoped for. David and Jeanie—The Anarchist Printer and The Lady Photographer of earlier columns—gave their loft. Annie and Roberta led a battalion of determined cooks into the fray. Food spilled over the tables, and people tore through the food. It was such a good party that I've had a hangover since, without having had a drink. We had music; Dan brought his partners Sonny Boy, Tommie, and Cary, aka The Lords. We had stars. Ron and Cecilia Swoboda came in from Milwaukee and Nathaniel's friends lined up for autographs, while the twenty-five-year-olds stared and muttered "I can't tell her I had the hots for her when I was twelve." The forty-year-olds stared and muttered "I can't tell her I had the hots for her when I was twelve." The forty-year-olds did tell her, and she smiled.

There were the friends from City College and the friends from the *Voice,* and the Head, and the print shops of twenty years ago, and even some from Black Mountain days. And the cousins I love all showed, with their kids. I've lived in so many worlds, while never budging, but they all came. And Joe Flaherty delivered the toast to Nathaniel and ripped and praised and was funny and I loved it. I think I'm growing up. Marty Shaer said that next year I'd vote Republican after a bar mitzvah like this. I told him I would if Stassen ran. Lenny Kriegel took one look at the poem I'd written for Nathaniel, and that Dan Haberman had printed for me, and said "You'll do anything to get published." He was right, I told him, and smiled.

Sometimes you have to have your children grow up before you find out what you have. That's what happened here, I think. Today I am a fountain pen, I could say. But I feel like a grown-up, and I thank my friends for showing me how.

Wring Out the Old

I thought the last ten years would never leave. They exhibited the same lack of timing as the joke-mangler at a party, the same bad taste as the office clown. And, like both those bores, they went on and on. Whatever else you want to say about the '60s, they moved.

Consider how each decade began. On New Year's Eve of 1960 we were all toeing the line, waiting for Camelot to begin. We'd had it up to here with Ike, with the Silent Generation—and we weren't disappointed, because the first report we got was that JFK had danced until four at the Inaugural Ball. Not since Andy Jackson fell out the window at his Inaugural Ball had we seen a live president installed. When the '70s began, we'd had two years of Nixon—and the thing I remember most is that nobody had had an extra ten in those two years.

Everybody had started to clam up, too. Okay, things had gotten a little extreme, toward the end of the '60s, and there was still a lot of yelling and shouting and dying to come vis a vis Vietnam. But the antiwar movement was about to turn into a majority and all the rest of the agitation, civil rights, student anger, and the rest, was turning off. Even now the antinuke people suffer from the lack of the very real energy that bubbled fifteen years ago. It's like the demonstrations now are trying to follow the script from then, but no one's quite sure how.

About all we really did in the '70s was to grow older. All of us. This is, of course, customary. But these last ten years everybody was terribly aware of it, whereas in the '60s we all felt like we were getting younger, so it's more noticeable. In the '30s and '40s anybody who stayed alive and got older felt like they were ahead, and in the '50s we just sort of expected it.

The other big discovery of the '70s was the self, the "Me." This turned out to be a discovery with a joy factor of about four minutes, and then we were stuck with the other 5,255,996 minutes to be bored. And when you consider that everybody made the same discovery, individually, and everybody else, individually, was stuck with everybody else's discovery, you've got a lot of agonizing minutes. The people who didn't discover their selves were engaged in finding their selves. There was a difference, in that discovering yourself involved forgetting there was anybody else in the world, whereas finding yourself meant leaving your husband, or in a few perverse cases, your wife.

Those who could neither discover nor find themselves, changed. Sometimes this involved a job, sometimes the genitals. In any event, usually, after a few years, they were back where they started, trying either to find themselves or discover themselves. It was sort of a circular decade, with the mouth swallowing the tail constantly, and getting sick.

Progress continued. Having perfected television, the engineers now made it possible to record the things you hadn't wanted to see in the first place, rerun them at your convenience, and throw them on a wall-size screen, instead of a set which required you to focus your eyes. Perhaps the archetypical man of the decade was the hotshot the *Times* featured in its Home Section who built his loft so he'd never be without TV, and without anything else in the damn place.

It was a decade in which we managed to make pornography pornographic. After all, humans had been turning on to dirty pictures for thousands of years, maybe even tens of thousands if you look at the cave paintings in the right light. But somehow this time, after the seventeenth book and the fiftieth picture and the third movie, boredom moved in. Maybe it was Ugly George. Anyhow, suddenly, nobody could get it up any more over simple things, and we moved on to five year olds, golden showers, lactating mothers, and the like.

The United States spent half the decade trying to destroy Southeast Asia, the rest of the world spent a good deal of it trying to destroy other places. The birthrate went down and the deathrate went up, but not under the happiest of circumstances. Government exhibited the same decline, both in style, and personality. Just last night, in the dying light of this decade, I watched Thatcher and Carter trade encomiums—although that was a gain from some of the pairings featuring Ford and Tricky Dick.

Inflation and recession, starvation and glut. It was a decade of enigmas, exacerbated by the experts who kept tripping over their expertise. It was a decade in which we fought to stop an unnecessary dam, which incidentally also threatened one little species of fish. The experts found someplace else for the fish to live, they hoped, and then to prove something, the dam was built anyhow at a huge cost overrun, and at the expense of homesteads and sacred Indian grounds. The Cherokees say the world will now end. It probably did already.

If I seem to be getting heavy-handed here, it's because I've never had to write a sum up of a decade before—when the last one started I'd just done three or so pieces for the *Voice*. It's an awesome responsibility. And it's just my lousy luck to get this one to break in on. And I can't even get drunk to welcome in the '80s, since August will make my first decade on the wagon. Oh well, easy come, easy go.

In the Gold Old Summertime

The results are in, and the Duke finally made the Hall of Fame. I hoist a glass of seltzer to the Brooks who were, and particularly to the only Californian I ever took to. You can talk all you want about Mantle and Mays—and I'll even grant that their lifetime numbers are better—but for the five years they all played each other here in the Big Apple, I'll take the Duke. I don't think any town has ever been blessed with a better argument, and it went on everywhere. Willie was incredible, and Mickey was a monster, but the Duke was just beautiful.

I tried to peddle an article a couple of years ago, proving he was the best, but all the editors told me nobody cared. Enough people care so that the letters will start piling in unless I modify that "best"—I mean just for the five seasons they played head to head, '51 and '54 through '57. And you could look it up!

Another thing you could look up is Rex Barney, while you're in the encyclopedia. He's going to be this year's recipient of the Casey Stengel "You Could Look It Up" Award, which is given each year to a ballplayer who had one moment of glory. Barney's came on September 9, 1948, when he no-hit the Giants—but for any loyal Brooklyn fan, the glory was more than momentary. This was a guy who could throw the ball through a stone wall—or over it. We died with him for five years, watching the steam, and watching the bases fill up on walks. And we dreamed about the no-hitter we knew he could pitch.

That was his best year, and even that one wasn't spectacular, with a 15–13 record and a 3.10 E.R.A. I was away at school in Chicago then, so I had to read about it in the papers, and little they cared about Brooklyn or Barney. But it had never been easy: I was the only Dodger fan in Yonkers, where the natives rooted for the

Yankees or the Giants. I lost a lot of money on damn fool bets, let me tell you.

But despite my distance from my idols, I kept in touch. And in the spring of 1951, down at Black Mountain, I noticed a squib in the Asheville paper announcing the imminent arrival of the Brooks for their annual exhibition game with their farm club. They were on their way North from spring training; in those days, clubs took it slowly, working their way up through the Carolinas and Virginia, playing minor league affiliates, and didn't arrive in New York until the middle of April, when you could go to the ball park without your thermies.

There'd been a steady stream of reports out of spring training camp about Barney; Leo Durocher, who'd kept faith with him for five years, was willing to give it another try. With each new showing, Leo'd announce that Barney was still on the club, but it was said that one bad outing would be the end. The year before his record had been a measly 2 and 1, his E.R.A. 6.42, and worst of all he'd given up forty-eight walks while garnering only twenty-three K's.

So when the paper said that Barney would pitch, I grabbed Fee Dawson and Tim LaFarge and we began devising ways to con Harvey Harmon into driving over for the ballgame. This was necessary because there was no other way to get there; Harvey had the only available car on campus. This was after all, Black Mountain College, and it was 1951. The age of affluence, the mobile American—neither had been discovered yet—and if they had been, they wouldn't have pertained to Black Mountain anyway.

By pooling our resources, we managed to come up with enough gas and beer money to lure Harvey in. Nobody else at the college much understood why we even wanted to go to a ballgame, although Olson tried. I've often wondered how much of Charles Olson's insistence on getting poetry out of its ivory tower developed before his time at Black Mountain—I know a lot of it did, of course, but I like to think that a little of it came from trying to understand callow youths like Fee and me.

The ballpark was green and wonderful in the April evening. They always are. But Fielding hadn't been to one since St. Louis three years earlier, and for me it had been as long since I'd seen Ebbets Field. It was a ballpark, with deep fences, hotdogs, and the North Carolina Hills for background.

I don't remember the score of the game, because that wasn't what was important. What I do remember is Barney warming up, then zipping through the batting order, the first time round. For three innings he was just terrific.

In the fourth, the Asheville lead-off batter came up for his second try, and he scratched a hit. Barney must have eased up a little then, because the next guy lined one into left center, and the next guy hit a huge triple out against the far left field wall. Barney was still in there though when the clean-up hitter came to bat. Durocher was calm on the bench; there was a guy throwing in the bullpen, but nothing hard. The first pitch to the batter went about fifteen feet above the plate. The runner on third came home. Barney took off his glove, put it on the mound and walked to the bench. As far as I know he never wore a Dodger uniform again.

So that's what I'll be thinking of when Rex gets his plaque — just as, next August, when the Duke gets inducted, I'll be seeing that perfect swing as the ball arches into Bedford Avenue.

Going out in style—I guess that matters most. Rex picked a good way. Duke was glorious, but Barney was a Dodger!

Fate of Grace

A poem ought to be interesting. Sometimes it might even be expected to tell us something, or amuse us, or move us, or, at the form's best, make more real the connection between ourselves and the world. But first of all it ought to be interesting, so that we want to read it. In simplest terms we have a right to expect that a poem, which can tell us more about the universe than any other form of art, tell us at least as much as a story, a novel, a newspaper article. And that it do this with a fidelity to craft that allows the language to sing—which is what those other things cannot do.

But most people are afraid of poems, so they ascribe some mystical power to them and to their writers that absolves the need for mundane considerations like interest or use or craft. When poems that have nothing to say are praised and honored the gulf between poetry and its audience is made wider.

These reflections are prompted by Anthony Hecht's new collection, *The Venetian Vespers*, which appeared accompanied by a front page review in *The New York Times Book Review*, and a nomination for the National Book Critics Circle award. Despite these encomia, the book is arid.

Hecht has a way, even when dealing with what ought to be interesting material, of losing everything in description, as if that is what makes "poetry":

> She turned her gaze deliberately
>   away
> From the road, the cars, the little
>   clustered knot
> Of humankind around that sheet of
>   glass,
> Like flies around a dish of sweetened
>   water,
> And focused intently on what lay

before her.
A grizzled landscape, burdock and
    thistle-choked,
A snarled barbed-wire barricade of
    brambles,
All thorn and needle-sharp hostility.
The dead weeds wicker-brittle, raf
    fia-pale,
The curled oak leaves a deep tobacco brown,
The sad rouge of old bricks . . .

—and so on for another ten and a half lines, to say what could have been said in one or two. There is a spurious use of particulars that are not needed, either to tell the story or hold our interest. They are there to fill space, to make it sound like writing. But writing, good writing, depends on precision and economy as well as grace.

When the poems use particulars that aren't needed, they seem diminished. Incidents, accidents, found items—all exist neither with their own dignity, nor the dignity engendered by careful juxtaposition (so that we see them new!), but merely as ephemera given momentary grace by Hecht, for which they ought to be thankful. Hecht's language and his use of it do not help. A dedicatory poem, "For Helen," ends with the following quatrain:

But all the joys and forces of invention
That can transmute to true
Gold these base matters floated in
    suspension
Are due alone to you.

One could build a text for beginning writers on what is wrong with these four lines, but the most glaring problem, the one that bears on our interest, is that the function and the meaning of "true" doesn't come clear until the third reading, and won't sing correctly ever.

There are some nice poems in *The Venetian Vespers*—but one is an adaptation of an ode by Horace, and two are "versions" of

Joseph Brodsky poems, in which the material manages to outweigh the handling of it. A fourth is the curious "Invective Against Denise, a Witch." This rhyming piece works, because Hecht is interested—he is angry. It is a small and old hinge, but it suffices:

> And yet that punishment is slight
> Compared to what is yours by right;
> Just Heaven must not bestow
> Its mercy on so foul a thing
> But rather by its whirlwind bring
> Such proud excesses low.

This is a solid rant, and as such succeeds. While no credit is ascribed with the poem itself, a note in the back reads "RONSARD, BOOK II, ODE XIV"—so this material is also presumably borrowed. Poems ought to carry news to us. And ought to carry it better than the news itself does. This book does neither.

Points

Sometimes it all comes together, it fits, it makes sense. More often, of course, it just lies there disconnected, and the only thing to do is write about disconnection and hope that the juxtaposition is what makes sense.

This spring's been one of those for me: one step forward, fall back two. And not just for me, but for everyone I've talked to. Perhaps it's the madness we're living through, prices, houses, jobs, candidates, Iran. It's one of those times when everything conspires.

At Westbeth, where I live, we've been threatened with everything from a forty percent rent increase to the outright sale of the building to private speculators, so the general level of paranoia has risen even higher than usual. But, feeling a little like the band on the Titantic, we set about making a tenth anniversary party, partly to say "Hey, we survived!" and partly to try to focus some attention on just what this strange building full of artist-folk is, in hopes that HUD might pay attention and lay off.

The party — billed as "our gift to the city" — went off on May 3rd and 4th; I'm writing this a few days later. For a frantic forty-eight hours I watched and took part in a wonderful thing, which indeed turned out to be a gift, to the city and to ourselves. It ranged from jazz to opera, poetry to painting, theatre to tightrope walking. The tightrope belonged to Phillipe Petit, who doesn't even live here. He walked in, drew a chalk circle in the courtyard, and gave an inspired performance within it. Then he gave the money he collected to the Residents' Council.

Most of the events were free; concerts by David del Tredici, fresh from his Pulitzer, and Joseph Fennimore and Richard Hundley; pieces of operas by Peter Salvator Tomas and the Camerata Singers; dance performances, piano recitals, folksings, a slide show, an exhibition of paintings, prints, and photographs, readings by Spencer Holst, Lynda Schor, Hugh Seidman, Helen Duberstein,

Hilda Morley, Harry Roskolenko; as well as readings of Muriel
Rukeyser and Edward Hoagland. After the politicos spoke to open
the party, Billy Harper and Freddie Waits backed Patti Bown as she
sang a Westbeth theme song she'd written for the occasion.

There was a bookstall full of books by Westbeth authors, and
a silent auction where I won Lem a free drum lesson and lost
chances at meals at the Black Sheep and Le Petit Robert and
Trattoria da Alfredo—and somehow forgot to get a bid in for a
lesson in French Cuisine from Anne Dobbs. There were ten or so
hours of jazz, and I discovered I'd better start listening again
instead of playing my Sonny Rollins over and over. Waits and
Harper jammed with Stanley Cowell and Bob Cunningham, and
Gil Evans drove a big band beautifully. I didn't get to hear Chuck
Israels or Patti Bown perform with their groups, but I did catch a
thirty-minute duet by Waits and his son Nashid, all of nine years
old, and it wasn't kid stuff, let me tell you.

The tourists were here, and the neighbors, and general good
spirits all around. There were a few walkouts from an outrageously
dirty play, but then we started issuing parental guidance warnings
and that solved that. It was the first time I could look out my
second-story window and see our "public" spaces filled with
people, instead of stick figures in an architect's drawing.

Sunday night finally came, and I was in the middle of hosting
a cast party for all those people who'd broken their backs putting
my play together in less than three weeks. Mark Roth, the director,
had just arrived after striking the set, when the phone rang. My
sons Dan and Nat and Lem began whoopin' and hollerin'—how
they could know what the call was about had me puzzled. It was my
oldest son, Nick, calling from Virginia. His wife Sharifa had given
birth to Loren Gabriel Oppenheimer. I was a grandfather. Nick had
called at three with the word and had sworn his brothers to secrecy
so he could tell me himself, and they'd kept the secret—from me,
anyhow. It turned out everybody else already knew, because Lem

just had to tell somebody every five minutes that he was an uncle at eight, but it never got back to me.

I have friends who plunged into depression as soon as I mentioned that my daughter-in-law was pregnant—to them it was incontrovertible evidence of their approaching senility. But for me, in my perverse manner, it was nothing but joy, and further evidence that we do win out in the end. And with a young kid very much in evidence in my own house it's hard for me to feel old—tired, yes, but not old. So Loren is here, another boy in this damned male line, when I had hoped to have a little girl, finally, to dandle on my knee, but big and healthy and happy, and loved.

This was, then, a coming together. To have friends who killed themselves to put a play on, to have neighbors who put something wonderful together out of nothing but their own talent and energy and time, and to have children who understand what life is about.

There is no poem for this occasion. There is this statement itself, and the occasion itself. It is enough. Or maybe the poem was there, in one particular moment in the middle of the party. During the Waitses' duet, Freddie had left his drums while Nashid soloed, so he could stand in the audience and watch. The little boy got a little lost, floundered for a few seconds, and Freddie cupped his hands around his mouth and called, "It's okay! Forget that figure, go on to the next!" and Nashid heard, and did, and got right back into it. It was art, and it was what fathers are, and it was beautiful. And it wasn't patronizing either, when the crowd gave Nashid the standing O, because he'd earned it.

Yesterday he was outside my window playing baseball, and Billy Harper was standing at the elevator in his running suit, and John Dobbs was in his studio painting. That's what this place is all about. And I was out buying the new mother a pretty blouse, because a new grandpa ought to do things like that. And soon I'll have my grandson on my knee, and tell him how things were the day he joined us.

Keep Your Bags Packed

Nathaniel came home from ninth grade the day after the election and said, "Some of my friends want to give Reagan a chance." This is obviously an opinion passed on by parents, since no thirteen year old I ever heard of was willing to give anybody a chance. And since the school he goes to is on the border between Chelsea and Greenwich Village, it's in good old liberal territory.

I guess I haven't grown much past my own early teens, because I can't see "giving him a chance." It seems to me that the one thing the left, the liberals, the progressives have to do these days is to dig in for the long siege. And a long siege it will be. I'm not so much worried about Ronnie as about the Senate. And the Moral Majority. Four years of Reagan can't be insupportable after the last several prexies, but a three-to-one ratio of right to left in the upper house means twelve or eighteen years of reaction. And with the loonies finally figuring out how to use their money and their righteous indignation, the House of Representatives should keep sliding backward too, at least for a couple of years.

It looks, in fact, like it will take another McCarthy era for the media to wake up, and to wake the people. Keep your bags packed, like we used to say. That three-to-one majority I mentioned is a rough estimate of what it looks like to me, if you add up the conservatives and reactionaries in both parties—and I'm giving the other side the dubious benefit of people like Lowell Weicker, God save him. But there he was last week, one of the few defenders of busing, while the majority of the Senate was voting against it. Strom Thurmond's straight face staring into the camera while he intoned that no racism was meant, but just that children ought to be able to get to the school nearest to them, is a taste of things to come.

At the same time, same day, the jury in Greensboro was

deciding that the Klan and the Nazis were firing in self-defense while being attacked by the Godless Commies. The lesson of this, children, is that nothing changes. The old libertarian strain in America is now split between those who want to unleash the Private Sector, and those who see salvation in the State, and the few honest people interested in the redress of grievances and the correction of inequities—i.e., the restoration of balance in our lives—will be ground between them, while the mass, interested in security and profit, will stay happy with scapegoats.

There's an interesting piece by Russell Means in the December issue of *Mother Jones*—so interesting that Adam Hochschild has to insert an editorial disclaimer before it. Means talks about the commonality of purpose of all European thought, right or left, and of its dependence on Rationality. He says, "Rationality is a curse since it can cause humans to forget the natural order of things in ways other creatures do not. A wolf never forgets his or her place in the natural order. American Indians can. Europeans almost always do." What the piece is saying, really, is that Capitalism and Marxism both end up the same place. If he's right, and I tend to think he is, then we really do have no choice, since those are the lines that are drawn. One falls back then on the one which hurts the least—which is precisely how the blue-collar workers, the suburbanites, and the Moral Majority thought they were voting this time. But they will see, as we all will.

It's always nice to dream, like the old Jewish anarchists pictured in Channel 13's showing of *The Free Voice of Labor*, and like Russell Means, of a more perfect world. But that more perfect world won't ever be allowed in our European culture because the payoff takes too long and people want a quick one. Reagan promises that, even at the expense of the natural order.

My problem, despite this lack of difference between the choices, is with the nature of the winners. Reactionaries and conservatives, by definition, don't want change, and no change means the same old shit, the rich getting richer, and the poor getting (specifically in this case!) children. The Democrats, at least, spread the thieving around a little. This line of reasoning is known as the "Hoffa principle" based on the fact that while the Teamsters officials got fat, the rank and file put a little meat on too, while earlier only the bosses had profited.

Anyway, I told Nathaniel that I thought we mustn't allow ourselves to "give him a chance"; we must act just as obdurately as the right had acted for the last fifty years for the pendulum to swing back. Otherwise I'm afraid there won't be much for it to swing back to. Make no mistake about it, whether it's a bar joke about all of us being forced back to the missionary position, or a cosmic joke about atomic power, we are threatened.

Lem, at nine, took a much more pragmatic view of the results. Almost in tears, he asked on that Wednesday morning if he'd now have to pray in school. I promised that he wouldn't and I intend to see that he doesn't have to. But that effort may cost more than we think, because those folk are serious, while we, this loose configuration of Democrats, liberals, socialists, anarchists, libertarians, humanists, what have you, still think it's a game with rules we understand.

The rules are, on the other hand, partly the Ayatollah's, i.e., no negotiations (read: ideological purity, or "litmus tests"), and partly the ruling classes', i.e., bread and circuses. It will indeed be a long haul back.

And it will all matter a hundred years from now, I'm afraid. There's a case now progressing which attempts to prove that trees are the prime cause of hydrocarbon pollution, and it's beginning to look good. Perhaps we should remind the loonies that "Only God can make a tree." Except that they seem to be very selective in their ideas of what is godly.

Thieves Like Us

The Brits have been claiming Ireland as a fiefdom since the twelfth century. And for the intervening eight centuries, the Irish have been saying "no" in one way or another. Bobby Sands becomes then another name on a long list of freedom fighters.

This fact keeps getting obscured in all the blather about "terrorism," "guerrilla warfare," the "will of the people," and the other governmental language spewed out whenever the people get restive. According to Her Majesty's Government, Bobby Sands was a common criminal and thus not entitled to any special status. But criminals are like weeds, in that their naming depends on outside definition, not their own intrinsic state. The government says who is and isn't, just as the gardener decides this plant is useful and this one misplaced.

I tend to prefer the German word for weed which makes it all perfectly clear: *unkraut*, not cabbage! i.e., anything which I say don't belong is dead.

That's how the rules have been set up, so we can discount Mrs. Thatcher's pious maunderings, or the nonsense from her spokesman about how Bobby Sands "just finally starved to death." I find it interesting—and disgusting—that the Bobby Sandses have had to endure and die for 800 years solely because of theirs and others' governments. The first Brits in Ireland were invited by the deposed King of Leinster to help him restore his throne. In the way of such helpmeets, they stayed.

And, since then, the words "terror" and "rebellion," and the related ones like "anarchy," have been tossed about to keep us all in line. Most of the time they do, too. The majority of American colonists were "against" the terror and anarchy fomented by the Adamses and their Southern co-conspirators. Most Russians thought that the czar was bad, but "anarchy" was worse.

Rebellion is interesting because it's usually meant to stand for a revolution that didn't make it. The Brits, for example, use it to refer to a nineteenth-century war in what is now Western Canada, in which they defeated a free and independent nation of Metis and Indians. They then passed retroactive laws to justify the takeover of territory, named the war the "Riel Rebellion," and hanged the leaders as "traitors" to the queen. It's a way of handling history that Hitler liked too.

But don't misunderstand me. I don't think that the IRA would be any better at this nonsense than the governments we already have. I'm fairly certain it won't, in fact, and I use as evidence a statement from a leader of the Spanish Basques, who have also been fighting governments for a long time: "No political entity can live without a coercive apparatus." So governments coerce, and what else is new. I understand that. But there comes a point in that coercing where they have outstayed any freedom to continue, and where somebody else has to get a chance at the coercing.

Since I despair as much of anarchism ever being given a fair chance as I do of the Luddites winning their battle, all I can ask is for the new Bosses to be allowed in. At least for a while the people—what we used to call the masses—might get a break. In the meantime throw out those who have proven themselves bastards.

This is a view of history that I don't expect Mme Thatcher or President Haigan or General Reag to be much convinced by, but it's all I have. I take a very simplistic view of the universe. Bobby Sands was a political prisoner murdered by the state; the "terrorists" in Central America, whether it be El Salvador, Nicaragua, or Guatemala, are poor people fighting to get the damned rich off their backs.

They are being murdered and will continue to be murdered as surely as Bobby Sands was. And until Americans understand this, and understand our own complicity in these murders—despite our anger about Sands—we will continue to be on the wrong side. Not in some political alignment, but in life.

But in the meantime, before that heavenly day comes that we become truly pro-life, let us at least hope for clean language. While I listen to the president and prime ministers lie, I keep thinking of those fights in grade school. The bully kept pushing and pushing and finally the mouse would pick up a rock or a stick or a chair or something—and then be accused of "bad sportsmanship" or "foul play." There are times when one's only defense is "foul play," and when "fair play" only benefits the leader. But I suppose it is destructive to the democratic system to suggest such heresies.

By and large, fairness exists only in baseball and such—which is why I like it. Those who don't understand such affection on my part are continually sniping at my involvement with things that don't "matter" while they go on vainly hoping for fairness in life.

Okay. Brits out of Ireland, Spain off the Basques, U.S. out of Central America. Let everything break down small enough and we won't need Bobby Sands to die for us. We'll be able to do it for ourselves. I mean that. The whole idea of government calls for people to be bigger than life, to be symbols. The more we can scale our symbols to ourselves the more chance we have of being human.

There is no manifest destiny or epic dream. Life itself is glory enough if we let it be. Let it be.

That is the lesson of Bobby Sands. The minute a government finds that a human being "just finally starved to death," it ought to crawl out of office in shame—or, lacking that, be driven out. Governments, I am saying, are always, and by nature, cowards. Only human beings can be brave.

The Lourdes of Baseball

I thought about all of us fans marching up to Yankee and Shea stadiums and taking over. We could send word to the Players Association that we were ready to go, alert the TV and radio stations, get the umpires back, and start playing.

The stadiums do, in fact, belong to us, and the owners lease them for the purpose of playing ball. They are no longer allowing that to happen. Perhaps the two clubs—or the league—own the team names. Oh well, we'll use different names; the players'll still be recognizable. It might even take a few weeks to get the bugs ironed out, but I'm sure we could figure out a way to have these guys, who already know how to play, play.

How this would sit with the current mood of Reaganism, I have no idea. I mean you could think of this as rampant individualism, or you could think of it as grassroots collectivism, depending on whom you wanted to scare.

I'm afraid that the current mood will force this to be an impossible dream. We don't want anything to interfere with the proper business of business, which is generally conceded to mean "give the boss his way" or "it's his baseball."

An administration which has embarked on the destruction of public lands, public safety, and public morals, is about, in the guise of Hatch and Helms, to take on public health by allowing for "some degree of risk" in our food supply. All this is in the name of free enterprise for the few, so they would never let *people* run baseball teams.

Well, it's all kidding anyhow, because the next thing you know Ed Koch would be in the dugout asking "How'm I doin'?" instead of watching the pitcher for signs of tiring. And the fans may not deserve the team, anyhow. I'm almost convinced we don't deserve baseball at all.

The evening after the strike began, Art Rust Jr. had Lee Lowenfish and a poet on his call-in show. Lee wrote *Imperfect Diamond* with Tony Lupien, the old Red Sox first baseman. The book is a sordid and, I'm afraid, depressing study of the history of labor-management wars in baseball, so Lee qualifies as the expert on such negotiations, at least as far as I'm concerned.

Ninety percent of the calls we got began, "Those guys make an average of . . ." and went on from there. Neither reason, logic, the difference between average and median, nor irony served to stem this flow of calumny from a bunch of yo-yos—even as you and I! —none of whom can go into the hole and throw someone out, or pound one over the fence, or strike out someone who can.

Nor do any of them object to the fact that Warner Wolf, for one, makes two or three times that average, just for talking about the guys who can do that stuff!

We tried talking about market value, but none of these free enterprisers wanted to hear that. Only owners, evidently, are allowed to make a lot of money. To most Americans it seems unseemly, if not Marxist, for workers to make it.

And the basic point, that it is not money which is the bone of contention, seems never to have occurred to my fellow rooters. The notion that a worker has to be protected from his boss seems to have disappeared from the American consciousness.

So, perhaps, we do deserve to lose baseball, just as we probably deserve supply-side Reaganomics, to toughen us all up after all those "easy" years. I don't know how I'm going to explain to my kids that part of the toughening process is to stay virgins, especially when they won't have bread or circuses to keep their minds off puberty, but I guess I'll have to work that out somehow.

Whatever is involved in that solution, I intend to investigate it in a place where there is baseball. I will be spending the next several weeks watching my beloved Oneonta Yanks battle my beloved Little Falls Mets. There are them who snicker and talk about Little League ball, but they can settle in and read old boxscores if they want. I'll take it live.

A quick glance at my pocket schedule tells me I'll get to see about thirty home games, with maybe another ten away if I can work out the traveling arrangements. After all, following a team in the New York-Penn league isn't quite like flying to San Diego for the Padres.

I'll have my choice of seats in a stadium where you really can see all the field from any seat, and I'll also be able to walk home from the games. I can meet the manager for breakfast at the local coffeepot and rehash victories. Rehashing defeats is frowned upon in small towns.

I think this is what the pols like to refer to as grassroots America. My only question is whether they had me in mind as part of it, and I suspect they didn't. There are, in conservative eyes, no grass roots in Jews or city people. Or as one conservative said recently, grass wouldn't listen to a Jewish prayer, because the Jews don't believe in chemical fertilizers.

What I am looking forward to most is a few weeks spent away from the nefarious influence of the New York City media. The problem here is—despite our bitching about the *Times* and its brethren—that we keep hearing more than is good for us. Upstate and in other small towns, the national and local news is kept as it should be, in separate, avoidable, columns. Each item of the four covered is limited to three or four lines, so there can't be anything to alarm anyone.

So I'll be in the woods, happy with baseball and a couple of books and no news. It will, I hope, be most restorative. And then I can come back and continue complaining—and, if they let me, watch young blood keep swinging. And I can keep on making metaphors which use baseball and life interchangeably. That, after all, is what human beings do best.

Mobility

I am fully aware that the great majority of my fellow citizens are not only capable of, but in favor of, picking up and flying off to other places whenever possible. They believe in their hearts that "getting there is half the fun." I have long held an opposite and mostly irrational opinion.

A recent trip has convinced me that the feeling is not irrational, and has, in fact, a sound basis. Lafayette, Louisiana, beckoned—further there was cash involved, and ego-gratification too. Mindful that Paul Goodman once instructed young men to "budge only for folding money," I prepared carefully. I arranged the flight to New Orleans—some two or more hours from Lafayette—early enough to qualify for some sort of rate break. This was fortunate, since the full fare would have eaten up most of my substantial fee for going. The flight I selected fulfilled most of my criteria for plane travel: it was nonstop, thus limiting the take-off panic attacks to one; it left in mid-afternoon, thus saving me an early morning arrival after the expected sleepless night, plus allowing for a full breakfast which would enable me to avoid the airline food; and it left from Newark, which would cut considerably the time and expense involved in getting to the airport. A Newark departure also meant that some fifteen minutes or so would be deducted from flight time, a not-inconsiderable saving for a man who has, by sheer force of will, been able to stretch his emotional capacity for the terrors of flight to two hours.

That flight selection took place in August. By September, after three calls with apologies from the airline, I was booked on a flight which left LaGuardia at 9:15 A.M. Somehow, also, the flying time had been stretched from two and a half hours to three.

Oh well. I was committed to the trip—and more, I really did want to see both Lafayette and New Orleans. Not only had A.J. Liebling told us all that New Orleans was one of the three places in

America where one could eat real food, but also, Ron and Cecilia Swoboda were now down there and I hadn't seen them in a year or so. Lafayette had its own charms, since it is the major metropolis of Acadiana, home of the Cajuns, and I was looking forward to that cuisine.

So I stocked up with the newest Nicholas Freeling, an Amanda Cross I hadn't yet read, and Jerome Charyn's *Blue Eyes*, as well as with the latest issue of *Games* and two summer issues of its offspring, *The Four Star Puzzler.* That seemed a sufficient quantity of words to read and words to find to carry me through safely.

I did not take the air controllers' strike into consideration because I did not have enough nervous energy left to handle it, and that was, of course, the fatal flaw. We entered our plane at 9:00, and started to taxi on schedule at 9:15. Then we stopped. The captain informed us that there were twenty-five planes ahead of us and it might take a little time, so he was going to let us smoke.

One hour and twenty-five minutes later, we took off. I had read one chapter in each book by then, and done a little of seven puzzles. I was also hacking furiously, from one hour and fourteen minutes worth of smoking, and exhibiting every sign of incipient breakdown possible. All I could think was that we should have been halfway there already.

I played white-knuckle for the next three hours, drawing strange glances from fellow passengers as I raced back and forth amongst the three books and all the puzzles. A page here, three words there, a page, two more words. I felt as if completion of anything, puzzle or book, would doom me, and as a result I have no idea as to whom Kate Fansler, Castange, or Manfred Coen were chasing, or why, or if in fact it was Kate Castange, Manfred Fansler, and Coen.

In any event, we arrived. The Swobodas were wonderful, I loved the French Quarter, probably because it looked just like MacDougal Street, and also because R.J. and Brian, the Swoboda boys, knew just which topless bars and strip joints had the best open doors to gawk through.

The next day, after my first-ever promo talk show for *Marilyn Lives!*, I reentered the Quarter to meet my lift to Lafayette. This gentleman turned out to be a gentleman indeed, and the ride, which crossed the southern end of Lake Pontchartrain, the mighty Mo, and the Atchafalaya Basin, was both scenic and speedy. Unfortunately we had had a passenger foisted on us. The passenger was the eighty-year-old mother of a deceased novelist. Said novelist having completed his book, and having waited long enough for it to be rejected by almost everyone, had then committed suicide. His mother, not to be daunted, had engaged in a ten-year campaign to have it published, had succeeded, and was now a famous literary person. She was also a monomaniacal bore, and since the car was a two-door coupe, and she was afflicted by a walker, guess who got to sit locked in the back seat? The first words out of the lady, after establishing herself, her daisy-covered hat, and her white gloved hands, in the comfort of the death seat, were, "My son was a genius, and was so from birth." These words were, of course, delivered straight out of the Tennessee Williams school of Southern diction. The voice continued for two-and-one-half hours, but the only other phrase I recall in all its astonishing clarity was, "I have always loved Dickens, of course. He was a truly great writer. But my son had a far better vocabulary."

I spent a good deal of this trip amusing myself with questions like, "Why didn't he kill you instead of himself?" and avoiding giving my address, since she kept threatening to send me three manuscript poems of his which she had "discovered" and which were, she kept assuring me, "very profound."

Eventually this trip also ended, and I discovered Lafayette to be a place of beauty, joy, and inordinately good cooking. But the question of how I am ever going to be able to get back there keeps raising its ugly head. I suspect that buckboard to Lancaster, Pennsylvania, stagecoach to the Ohio, and packet to New Orleans may be the answer. I'll walk from there to Lafayette.

The Descent

Once again, the gloom. This Sunday they changed the clock, and we are faced with the annual countdown. Eight weeks 'til the sun starts coming back, four or five months, depending on the fiat of Congress, 'til we have evening light, two months 'til Christmas, fifteen weeks until the pitchers go to Florida and we can be saved from football, basketball, hockey, indoor soccer.

I intend, as usual, to spend the time musing. I don't go into full hibernation until Thanksgiving, but already the process has started, the slowing down, the thickening of the blood. Musing, or wall-staring, which comes to the same thing, allows me to think that I am thinking.

I intend to muse on the curious fact that on the same day Sadat was killed, a man in North Carolina killed his wife and daughter because he was toothless and had been served pork chops for dinner. I see the connection dimly now; in the depths of winter I will understand it better. There is a rage against what we cannot control. In better times, we find other ways to handle that rage. Now, we kill. Sadat is an unbeliever or a traitor or a Yankee lackey; it doesn't much matter which, he's got to die. The wife, who presumably has noticed her husband's lack of teeth somewhere along the way, decides pork chops would be good for dinner, and she must die.

I've been without teeth, myself, although now, thanks to progress and dental coverage, I've got them when I want them. That poor bastard didn't, evidently. I would like to know what the wife'd been cooking all these years. I don't want this to sound like I'm making light of murder—in fact it's precisely because I don't see much difference between the one act and the other that I'll muse on both of them. You've changed, we might say to the world, you're not the lover you once were.

I intend to muse on the coming confrontation between the

technocrats and the Luddites, and the confusion between that confrontation and the one between the humanists and the Moral Majority. There are people who can't seem to see that these are two separate wars, and my own program as a humanist Luddite seems to outrage them.

But I get just as upset over the archaeologists who think they have a "right" to desecrate graves in Jerusalem as I do over the fundamentalists who support Israel so that the Jews can be gathered together and killed, thus fulfilling the biblical conditions for the Second Coming.

I'd like to sit and think and come to an understanding of why the opposite of technology is ignorance, as so many liberals seem to think. Preserving the graves of the long dead isn't antiscience, it's just human decency. On the other hand, supporting killer bombs and man's dangerous ability to change his environment while denying life's innate aversion to standing still, as the Creationists insist on doing, is just as dangerous.

There is a truth to Myth which science will never supplant. But Myth and science are both, or can be, knowledge. Technology denies both, because it keeps telling us things get easier. Knowledge tells us just the opposite, and it should. Musing leads to that knowledge, while busywork destroys it. We all know that, yet we keep busy, either making things, or searching to be amused.

The cycle of the year ought to be enough. It has confounded us since before the ice came down and taught us how to improvise. One of nature's mistakes, those Ice Ages. They forced movement, and adaptation, and fire, and clothing and machines. It seemed like a good idea, the gods might have said, and then it was too late to stop the snowball, so to speak.

The problem is that we think the answers are within our grasp, and that the answers involve a black and white choice. Either believe the Book—whichever book, from wherever, as long as some demagogue tells us it is the Book—or keep messing with where we live to make it easier.

But the answer has to lie somewhere between. There are received truths, and there are also things to learn; neither precludes the other. Balance, balance in all things, is what is needed. Musing can help here: let everything come together, and be there when it happens, is a good rule to live by, as well as to make poems.

If one can find a good spot to sit in the winter sunshine one can last out the night; and if one can last out the night the spring will come. But it's lasting out the night that is so hard, that leads to all the frantic partying from now until the spring, that leads to all the frantic inventing—of things, of ideas, of amusements. We have to learn again to sit and muse. The Muses do come if you let them, but they run when you pursue them.

They gave us knowledge, in the old days. They still can. I've learned to accept winter as a boon—like Peter Sellers in *Being There*, quoting Scripture. There is a time to murder and create; there is a time the snow covers us and a time we bloom.

So the clock will change, and right behind that change comes Hallowe'en, an even older way of laying the ghosts to let the musing begin. Whichever, move your chair to the spot the winter sun falls on. Let the walls be bare, or covered with that which lets your mind begin to wander. Two winters ago I found a thing by G. Spencer Brown called "The Laws of Form"; in it he says, "To arrive at the simplest truth requires years of contemplation. Not activity. Not reasoning. Not calculating. Not busy behavior of any kind. Not reading. Not talking. Not making an effort. Not thinking. Simply bearing in mind what it is one needs to know."

He was talking about the fact that at a cocktail party a psychiatrist had told him that these days any competent shrink would clap Sir Isaac Newton in the booby hatch. While I hold no brief for what the technocrats have done with Isaac's Laws, I find the musing which led to them perfectly acceptable. And you'll notice that since he arrived at them from an apple falling on his head, it must have been mid-autumn while he mused.

Moves

I may have gone too far this time. I am writing this ensconced in a converted barn 3.2 miles from civilization. Civilization, in this case, is Henniker, New Hampshire. The last time I was here, in 1975, Henniker had some 900 inhabitants; now, it's up to about 1500, so it's a little larger than Westbeth, my home in the city.

Lem is here with me, prepared to enter the fifth grade as that most feared of outlanders, the New York City kid. Nat is back in the city continuing his advanced studies at Bronx Science. So for the first time in a number of years, despite short stays in places like Oneonta and North Carolina, I've really changed my way of living. Of course, it's only for four months or so—the length of the spring semester at New England College, where I'll be teaching—but it certainly is different.

First of all, there doesn't seem to be a greasy spoon or a newspaper kiosk anywhere in sight. In fact, the only things in sight are trees and snow. There seems to be a good deal of snow. Back in the city, people kept asking, "Winter in New Hampshire?" and I kept smiling and answering, "It's the Spring semester." Now, I'm not sure.

The general attitude around here seems to be that spring may arrive around May 14, if we're lucky. And they all do keep reassuring me that "the worst is past." The "worst" included an ice storm the day before we arrived which immobilized the town and the countryside, but bright sun and temperatures in the high fortys on the day we drove up seemed to ease a lot of those problems. However, the garage was almost totally blocked by the earlier passage of the snowplow, and it took our van about eight slow turns to slide in so we could unpack. By the time we came back from dinner, one of the local contractors had cleared the rest away, and life was a bit easier.

We're living in a house that was converted, years ago, out of

a barn and some sheds by two ladies named Mary Potter and
Tempest Johnson. They were members of the old Round Table at
the Algonquin, so the place is replete with literary vibes. We have
the barn and shed part and another couple has the original farm-
house, with what amounts to a minuscule apartment. Nancy runs
the college bookstore and Kevin is a writer, and there's a baby due
in May. I'm hoping he or she'll come early so I can practice my
dandling, but Lem would just as soon be gone by then. He doesn't
like babies ever since he discovered that they're generally more
interesting to adults than ten year olds.

The vista from my living room window is wonderful. The
living room is the barn part, and it's huge. It has a full loft which is
occupied by Ken, one of the students. Ken and I have a deal—he'll
pay no rent, but he'll help if I need someone to stay with Lem, and
he has a car (since I don't drive, that's crucial), and most important
of all, he's going to keep the roof clear of snow. Evidently, horrible
things happen if you don't keep the snow off the roof, and my
landlords—there are two of them, husband and wife—quite prop-
erly refuse to believe that I am capable of, or would want to,
clamber about up there pushing the snow off.

The place isn't primitive—I have, for the first time in my life,
a dishwasher, a washer and a dryer, a kitchen big enough to swing
a cat in, and lots of nice accoutrements. The only thing I don't have
is the aforementioned greasy spoon and kiosk, and a few amenities
like a neighborhood bar and people. Ken, Kevin, Nancy, Lem, and
me. That's it. Each morning I'll get a lift to school, each afternoon
I'll get a lift back. In that eight hours or so I shall have to get all my
talking done, all my impulse-buying, all the things we city folk
take for granted.

The one thing that sustains me is that my landlords are both
transplanted New Yorkers who have evidently let memory mag-
nify their own adjustment period, and so they are convinced I can't
handle this life. I'll show them! At least until mud season, that is.
I'm told that mud season, which should start in a couple of weeks,

can break anybody. I'm also told that our particular road is good for mud to the thighs. To offset this possibility I have brought part of my war game collection, and shall fight World War I in its entirety through March, and all of Napoleon's campaigns through April. I will warm up with assorted Civil War battles these first couple of weeks, and finish the term with a flourish doing World War II.

I also hope to read a lot and even write some. Kevin says there's nothing else to do, and that manuscript piles just grow and grow, even if you're not typing. I certainly hope so. After all, I keep telling myself, I've been wanting to try something like this precisely because I'd gotten in a rut back in the city. Everything was turning into a *tsimmis*. Writing, reading, teaching, laundry, shopping, socializing, everything kept knocking into everything else. Here there's not much possibility of that happening.

I'm even determined to break the morning *Times* habit. Kevin gets it every day; I am going to take the third section each night, do the crossword puzzle after dinner, and give it back to him for his wood stove. If I need a fix in the morning it will be the *Manchester Union-Leader*, so I can see how the rest of America feels.

Of course, I do have television—but I don't have Ugly George. I've seen frozen bagels, but no rye bread. On the other hand, fellow down the road has fresh eggs cheap, fellow up the road has real milk with cream on the top cheap. And I've located the Concord radio station on my clock radio so we can tell if Lem's school is open every morning. Can it be all bad?

This, then, is by way of introduction to myself as temporary country squire and reclusive writer, both roles clearly new to me. We shall see how suited I am. After all, it's only for a couple of months, I keep telling myself. And it hasn't yet quite registered that Russell Banks, whose courses I've taken over while he's on leave, got himself a sublet on the Upper East Side. But then Russell's been here a long time, and he's probably as frightened of the city and all it stands for as I am of this lonely road.

I'll tell you one thing, though. Last night the snow was falling quietly when I went to bed, and this morning it was still lying there white and undisturbed. It hadn't fallen much, so there weren't any problems, and it sure looked nice not turning black.

Leading the Union

A letter entitled "Claims Reagan Hasn't Done Anything" ends, "The prices are running away with us and what have you done to stop it nothing. A nurse at the hospital where Mrs. Von Bulow was given an injection which the paper said cost forty-five dollars, but was charged ninety dollars. . . . No wonder this country is falling apart."

From a letter written in response to another letter espousing gun control: "As the Joyce Brothers philosophy (as with many others) continues, where a child is never disciplined or punished but deviously nudged away from their wrongs and never recognizes them as such, there is no instilled guidelines that give subconscious warnings of deviations from righteous thought and action, in the child or the adult. If the trend continues, a large part of our income will be spent to repair (person and property). And anyone in their home who is physically inferior, to the unconscionable invader who has seen years of Mutual of Omaha's killings, bull fights, cock fights, dog fights (in the news, maybe), and TV murder as a daily diet, is in a sad state of affairs. Also when you soft-heads get America disarmed the Russians can send their leaders into the air with re-fueling tankers and lob a few nuclear bombs on us and have their choice of landing sites while their troops mop up U.S.A., with no citizen opposition. THEIR = the, them, they, he, her, etc."

Or, "If you give the federal government enough time, they'll ruin everything. Take the once enjoyable hobby of stamp collecting, for instance."

Starting the morning with the *Manchester Union-Leader* certainly does set the pulse beating. The editorials and columns are predictably irritation, although occasionally outrageous as well, but the letters pages—two or three an issue—are wonderful and frightening. Each page, every day, announces to the readers that "this newspaper publishes more Letters to the Editor than any other newspaper in the United States. . . . It is our policy to publish every letter to the Editors received by us from New Hampshire residents, unless obscene or blasphemous. . . ."

The notice is signed by Nackey S. Loeb, publisher. The infamous William Loeb is dead now, so the tradition is carried on by family and disciples. The editorials are mostly written by Jim Finnegan, who seems to have inherited the mantle. But I confess to a little sadness over having missed the glory days. I'm told that big bad Bill used to run front page headlines during the Nixon years like "Kike Goes To Mideast."

Don't get the notion that the paper ignores people outside the state; a decent percentage of letters come from faraway places, and there are some regulars who evidently have found a home here. There's a guy from Ozone Park who appears once a week or so with news of Sodom and Gomorrah. And a man from Pepeekeo, Hawaii, writes, in part, "I must again warn tourists of the danger on this island. The 'liberal' maggot menagerie has stirred up the dark-skinned types here to where many of them will murder 'haoles' (Caucasians) indiscriminately if they get a chance! Do not go into secluded areas by yourself. Do not ride bicycles along the roads. None of the roads here have adequate shoulders. Above all do not attempt to make illegal drug buys!. . . . it is getting harder and harder to tell the good guys from the bad guys. 'High' schools are well named nowadays. The wicked walk on every side when the vilest men are exalted. Psalm Twelve."

I don't want to make light of this. All the letters are funny and mad—the people are bonkers!—and certainly they're not representative of all of New Hampshire, or the nation. It's clear that the nuts have found a comfortable, accepting home in this paper. But what is one to make of a culture which spews out this kind of madness—the continual quoting of scripture and the Communist Manifesto and what Mr. Loeb "used to tell us" to support everything from kindness to animals to nuclear warfare. I won't even mention the non sequiturs.

Sometimes—often—two ends come together. One will find a letter complaining about dogs killing deer which ends in a dire warning of the Commie plot, and next to it a letter complaining about the Commie plot ending in a complaint about dogs killing deer.

There is also an alarming amount of bad grammar—from people who are continually bemoaning the decline of the good old values—but bad grammar mixed with misused big words. It's a lesson in a little knowledge being a dangerous thing. I suppose I'm hypersensitive to such things just because I'm a writer, and particularly since my writing (or at least the poems) outrages people like these with my refusal to use syntax. Nevertheless, as has been pointed out since Confucius, a culture which can't use its language properly is in serious trouble.

The other problem with the paper is a familiar one to anyone who's lived outside New York or Washington or one or two other large cities. Most of the national and foreign news is jammed into a page or two, and edited down from the wire service reports. It's no wonder these people believe as they do, since they get almost no input on what's happening in the big world. It's fashionable, and probably accurate, for us to laugh at the *Times*, but, damn it, at least it makes an attempt to notice that there is someplace else on the globe besides one's own particular home.

Even the fringe material is curiously dated. Alley Oop still runs here—and we all thought he was dead. Major Hoople graces the newspaper, and "They'll Do It Every Time." It's as if we're still in 1946.

But before you get the idea that this is just another New Yorker bitching provincially about the provinces, let me assure you that I've spent my life going to the local newspapers wherever I've been. I like local newspapers—they tell you where the people are in that locality, and quite often where the best people are. *The*

Charlotte Observer is one such. The Bangor paper I used to read in Maine is another. They don't carry as much out-of-state news as I want, but they keep a careful eye on what's really happening around them, and by and large they write it up well. The *Union-Leader*, which bills itself as the state newspaper of New Hampshire, sees itself as the determinant of what's happening. That's the scary part—that, and the fact that it's found a constituency of delusionists to agree with it.

Little Wars

There are two interesting sidenotes about the Great Falklands War. One is the absence of any real coverage by the media, and the other is the "safe" sense the rest of the world seems to have about it. Contemplate the character played by Sean Connery in *Wrong Is Right* faced by this war. What could he do? Short of hiring his own task force, and steaming down to the action surrounded by ships, planes, and missile cover, he'd be reduced to interpreting communiques just like his real-life brothers and sisters. Here we are, ensconced over our morning coffee with the papers, or settling down in front of the evening news, and there's nothing to read or watch. We've been spoiled by all the action captured on videotape, all the first-person exposés, and now we're reduced to moving pins around a map, or totting up claimed losses, just like in World War II. What happened to progress? How dare they do this to the consumer? Can't a spy satellite beam down and pick up details of the action, ships sinking, planes disappearing in clouds of smoke, men dying on the ground? How do they expect anyone to believe there's really a war down there?

Balancing this sense of loss is the wonderful knowledge that the war is not likely to spread very far, nor lead to nuclear catastrophe, nor, in the end, matter very much. It's true that the *Post* and the *Union-Leader* keep trying to drum up some apprehension about the Russkies coming in, but even those two papers seem to be doing it out of a sense of duty rather than really believing it. It's also true that the Tories are now calling for bombing of the Argentine mainland—at least of the air bases there—and this is more likely to happen, simply because the Brits can't afford to keep losing ships. But the rate at which the Argentines are losing airplanes may preclude this drastic step, and even if it happened, again what would follow? Does anyone believe that the OAS would send out a combined fleet and airforce to attack Britain? The more likely supposition would be that the UN would pass a host of resolutions condemning Britain, which would have the usual effect.

I think this is why this war is so appealing to so many—the fact that the horrors of it are not being stuffed down people's throats, and that no one (except the families of those involved) need lose any sleep over it.

Unlike Poland or Afghanistan or the Middle East or Central America or Indochina, the Falklands exist in a dream. The other places could trigger all sorts of nightmares.

The British company that erred in taste by pushing its war game over subscription TV was actually on the right track. This is a war that most people feel they can play at. Just as the TV networks can wheel old generals out of mothballs to hold their pointers and pontificate in front of maps, the ordinary man or woman can carefully delineate all the ways one side or the other should behave in order to "win."

Of course, this is ignoring the fact that there can't be any victory in this war. If Britain does take the island back, the Argentines have already threatened a war of attrition to make it too costly a foothold to maintain. And no one can believe, with four ships sunk, that the British will allow the islands to go unconquered.

There's also a feeling that one's watching the kids fight. Let 'em get it out of their system, and so what if they get a bloody nose or a couple of teeth marks. They can't kill each other, and they may learn something about growing up.

There are a couple of history professors at New England College who've been teaching a course in the rise of the modern nation-state and the development of nuclear weapons. One third of the term's work consists of a game called "Nuke," which is one of those newfangled roleplaying things with flexible rules. Paul Daum and Alan Moberly, who run the course, have worked out the thing so that each student gets a country or a bloc of countries, or the UN, or a group of terrorists. The nations have each to (a) protect themselves, and (b) feed their people. The terrorists are trying to disrupt things to make way for the better tomorrow, and the UN is trying to hold it all down and together. Biology and physics (what the bomb is and does) and world conditions (an oil glut, for example, or a dry wheat-growing season) get worked in by Paul, who serves as the control.

Technological advances have to be preplanned and carefully worked out. He tells with delight of the student who managed to move Bulgaria lock, stock, and barrel under the Mediterranean. But there is a luck factor as well as skill and ingenuity. A country's natural resources are determined by combining the results of a test score and a poker game, on the theory that luck can put you on top of a lake of oil, but skill is needed to get it out and market it.

The other interesting thing about the game is that there's no cut-and-dried definition of victory. The game just ends. Sometimes it ends in the holocaust, sometimes it ends in One World, and there have been results anywhere in between. Equally, those pacifist students who have chosen to leave themselves unarmed have been blown away, but so have those who've chosen a strong defense.

I want to sit in on the course next year. I hope I don't get Bulgaria. Of course everybody else will be learning about human behavior and geopolitics, while I'll just be playing a game. But I know all about all that stuff, since I'm old. And when the course is over I'm going to call out the students I think I can beat, and I'm going to design a game based on the Falklands. It will have a wonderfully huge board, so the fleet can steam on day by day, and the students can learn how much fun war used to be, before the bomb and the media.

The State of the Rest

Back in the late '60s, when some of us were pushing for the fifty-first state as a solution to New York City's economic woes, Pete Hamill had a ready answer for those worried about a name for the area. "It'll be New York, of course," he said. "Let the rest of the place call itself Buffalo!"

Now it's the '80s. The last piece of Pete's I've read presented itself to me the other morning in a greasy spoon on Elmwood Avenue in Buffalo. Things do come full circle. And the *Buffalo Courier-Express* carries Pete's syndicated column, so I guess the city has forgiven him.

It, Buffalo, seems to have come up in the world, as a matter of fact. The good citizens are celebrating their 150th anniversary this summer, so the place is certainly starting to mature.

Tony Randall appeared at a big birthday do here last week and lauded the Buffalo Philharmonic. "Without it we would be Troy" is what I'm told he said. I take it he meant Troy, New York, because there sure ain't any topless towers around here.

I went to an outdoor concert by the orchestra the other night. The *Buffalo Evening News* had sponsored an evening of music and fireworks, and the only problem was they held it in a parking lot under an elevated highway. That's not entirely fair, since some of the audience, and the orchestra itself, were in Naval Memorial Park under the guns of a couple of retired WWII ships, but most of us were in the lot.

The paper said there were 80,000 of us there, and at least 40,000 were busy looking for better seats, the rest rooms, refreshments, or friends. When any of them found what they were looking for, they were immediately replaced from the pool of the heretofore seated.

The concert was predictable; of course, I didn't expect Cage, Feldman, Bartok, or Berg, but Rossini, Sousa, Strauss, and the inevitable "1812" fell a little to the other side of my hopes. The only really good thing about the music was that when they played the medley of service anthems they included "Semper Paratus" and I was the only one in my area who knew it was for the coast guard.

It all turned into a nice sort of Charles Ives piece. Stationed about ten feet behind us was a wheelchair-bound vendor who shouted "Peanuts! Popcorn!" at irregular ten to fifteen second intervals throughout the whole thing. He threw the stress in "peanuts" on the second syllable, and gave the "popcorn" sort of a dying fall, so it was a class rendition. Like most merchants, he was capable of totally ignoring the angry glares of his neighbors, including a fierce blue-haired lady, which they still have in Buffalo! But he was so laden down with things to sell—balloons attached to one wrist as well as clutched by the fist, while a cord in the other hand held onto a menagerie of plastic animals—that it was almost impossible for him to actually consummate a sale. I believe he was hired by the organizers to lend verbal panache.

Ives would have loved, also, the rumble from traffic overhead, as the rest of Buffalo kept about its business; there really is something frightening about sitting under a massive construction of steel and concrete that sounds for all the world like a two-plank bridge whenever anything goes over it.

I was there with good friends, though, and we'd eaten richly on the grass at the marina a half-mile away, so I was able to relax and enjoy it. I was also incapable of moving very much because I'd played nine holes of golf—my first ever—earlier that afternoon. Never has one person walked so much to so little purpose in such a confused state.

Despite the parking lot and the condition of my legs, it was a splendid evening. I'd like to think that the fact that it happened at all is a sign that Buffalo—and by extension, all the Northeast—is fighting back. Fighting the depression and Reagan and the Sunbelt, and saying "Damn it, we do exist!" There's talk up here that the steel mills are gone forever, just won't reopen at all. Unemployment figures are dreadful, and still the city seems to be pulling itself together, at least (and if only) on a neighborhood to neighborhood basis. New malls are still opening outside of town and further decimating downtown, but voices are being raised in protest and may yet stop that insanity. It seems universally agreed upon here that the further madness which moved the state university out to the suburbs was indeed just that, madness. SUNY Buffalo now sits moated on a prairie, with the dorms so far from the classroom areas that it's impossible to walk, and the whole thing looks like some strange NASA installation. Meanwhile, the Erie waterfront which might have been its new home fills with condos instead.

I shouldn't complain about the university, since I'm here for a few weeks to do some courses for Black Mountain College II, which is a part of the school. But since everybody else who works for the place is unhappy, and vocally so, about it, I suppose I'm allowed to be, too.

Despite grand errors like this, Buffalo survives. And it may even begin to thrive again, if it can develop its own little silicon valley as Arizona runs out of water and Florida turns into sinkholes and California slides toward the sea.

I think it's time to stop making fun of the place, and to realize it really is a piece of New York, as we are a piece of Buffalo. A good line in '68 ain't necessarily so good in '82.

The Operative Phrase

Watching Harvey Kuenn limp slowly out to the mound yet again, and hearing Joe and Tony once again discussing what the poor man's been through the last several years, it comes to me once again: nobody really wants to hear about an operation.

Everybody asks, sure. And depending on who they are, and what their relationship is, they want an answer. But nobody really wants to hear about the operation. In fact nobody wants to talk about an operation after they've had one, really. All there is to say is, "If someone tells you they want to put their hands inside you and take some pieces away, say 'No!' as emphatically as you can."

That doesn't help at all, of course, because one usually doesn't get told that unless somebody thinks there's a compelling reason to do it, so one can't usually work up the courage to say no. One goes along.

In fact, there's nothing much to say about the operation itself, it turns out. Modern anesthesia really works. I had visions of General Herkimer in *Drums Along the Mohawk*, propped against his tree, the shattered leg extended for the surgeon to work on, while the doughty little Dutchman slugged whiskey, smoked his pipe, bit the bullet, and plotzed.

Almost forty-five years after watching this scene I visited Herkimer's house and discovered that the good general was not operated on at the battle field, but was shlepped back to the house, worked on there, and took a week or so to die from blood poisoning, rather than just going off ka-boom. I also discovered that the reason he was a general was that his daddy or his granddaddy had copped a prime piece of turf, the bank of the Mohawk where the portage ended, so the family got a piece of change for every boat that went back in the water, and that made them the biggest folks in the county. So much for the Battle of Oriskany, the defeat of Gentleman Johnny Burgoyne, and eighteenth-century surgery.

But I don't want to sound like I'm wandering or ungrateful. Although six hours of anesthesia left me with the concentration of a flea for several weeks, I'm back to handling the puzzles in *Atlantic* and *Harper's*—although I now show a disquieting tendency to read the articles as well.

And I'm genuinely grateful for all the people who cared and do care about how I'm doing. The point I'm making is not that I'm unloved, it's simply that writers and other human beings need to talk, to tell stories, and as I keep telling my Introductory Creative Writing Class, usually you tell a story about what you know, and usually that's what will interest an audience.

That rule holds true from Homer down to the work those students are wrestling with right now, but the exception that proves is what you know about your operation. People ask, and you forget, and start to answer about what it really feels like, and, even on the telephone, you can feel their eyes glaze over. You can hear their brains shut off. And why not? They're just as terrified as you are—and it might yet happen to them!

It's like the way drunks get scared when they hear somebody's gone on the wagon—even if the wagoner isn't talking to them. Hell, I get scared myself and push the thoughts away unless I'm talking about them (i.e., getting rid of them to someone else). And one of the few people I've been able to talk to, a lady who went through it five years ago, says, "A year 'til you're physically all there—and then the emotional bullshit starts. You spend three years worrying about what happened during that six hours you weren't there, and had no control!"

I can't wait.

Meanwhile, I try to learn to control the lying. When my family asks, if they're older than me, or my age, I tend to ask for sympathy; if they're younger, I try to act strong. If my colleagues ask, I have to walk a fine line between "Gettin' stronger!" and "Not ready for faculty meetings quite yet. . . ." If the doctor asks, then I have to sound bad enough that he'll still pay attention, but well enough that he won't want to do any more to me. With friends I just plain tend to babble, in the hope that they can forgive me. That's the thing with friends, that perhaps you've listened to enough babble from them that they can listen to yours one more time.

It occurs to me now that perhaps the reason I rooted for Milwaukee—for the American League for the first time in my life!—was simply because Harvey's been through it all. Maybe I figured we could just talk about baseball, and not operations . . . although I suspect we'd have talked about Rollie Fingers's medical problems instead of our own.

But this camaraderie that seems possible between people who've been to see the elephant, as it were—a phrase I've always heard came out of the War of 1812—doesn't want to come too close to home. About five days after the doctor had his hands in me, one friend called and while commiserating, mentioned another acquaintance who'd just had a triple bypass. Boy was I pissed! I mean, you put your life on the line, for real, and you find out someone else has too! I've forgiven John now, of course, but it took a couple of weeks.

The one positive benefit of all the whoop-de-do was the chance to try out for twenty years from now. The first couple of weeks of recuperation I really needed a cane, so Nat went out and bought me a wonderful hazelwood shillelagh—I know, I know, it's supposed to be blackthorn, but the blackthorn ones were all sanded smooth!—and I could sit with it planted firmly as I leaned my crossed hands on it, and think about lashing out with it whenever I disagreed with anyone. That felt wonderful. I didn't actually lash out, because it seemed to me one can only do that with impunity after seventy, but it sure felt good thinking about it.

In fact, I may just read *Atlantic* and *Harper's* while holding the cane; it certainly would have helped while ABC broadcast the playoffs, too. I wouldn't mind telling Howard about my operation, except it'd probably turn out he went to medical school with my surgeon, and remembers the time Branch Rickey looked at both of them and said they'd never make it.

Phobophilia

I started this morning like any other morning, little realizing that it would turn out to be my bath of Archimedes', my nap of Newton's, my tea kettle of James Watt's. For Lem and my editor I hasten to note that Archimedes is said to have discovered in his bathtub the principle that makes a ship float. Newton grasped gravity by being hit on the head by an apple while dozing under a tree on a spring afternoon, or perhaps it was fall; and Watt invented the steam engine, damn him, sitting in his mother's kitchen.

Of course Robert the Bruce was emboldened to regain the throne of Scotland by watching a spider fail six times in its attempt to make a web, and then succeed on the seventh, but that example has nothing to do with my story as I'm inclined to be noncompetitive, and certainly not for the throne of Scotland.

No, I just went about my business, waking, starting the furnace, starting the coffee water, freaking when I realized I hadn't put on the radio for the weather before putting on the water for the coffee, freaking when I remembered I hadn't checked the water level in the boiler before putting on the heat, and like that. I freak a lot in the morning, particularly when it's a morning I have to do something specific, like write.

I freak if I don't do the appropriate puzzle (crossword in the *Times*, Jumble in the *News*, Scrabble in the *Post*), if the eggs come easy-over instead of sunny-side-up, and if there's no pitcher of cream on the table.

When I get back home and am ready to settle down to work, I have to run through seven quick games of solitaire to see how I would have made out at fifty-two dollars a deck, five dollars back for every one up on top, and then I do one or three of the big layouts with only three cards left to save me. Sometimes I do twenty-one games. Sometimes it's a matter of waiting until the mail comes, or cleaning the coffee table off, or organizing the unanswered mail, or even (G-d forbid!) doing the dishes. I don't mind doing new dishes. I hate doing leftover dishes. In fact I dread, literally dread, doing old dishes.

I am convinced old dishes have some strange kind of differ-ent germs on them and I will get a loathsome disease from them. I feel the same way about old laundry, only there it takes about a week for the change to take place. I mean I can pick up dirty laundry that's been lying around for a week but after that I feel like I should use tongs.

All this behavior is, of course, obsessive, compulsive, and terribly neurotic. It is, however, not at all deviant, since everybody pretty much does it or something like it. Well, all writers anyhow, and from the looks of my mail and the registration in introductory creative writing and the burgeoning of summer writing festivals, it seems like everybody is a writer. And every writer I mention my strange actions to nods in agreement. Some used to sharpen pen-cils, but that's passé with VDTs all over the place. Some vacuum. Some even find themselves driven to answer their mail before writing. I myself have never been that freaky.

All this behavior has generally been considered either warm-up or classic stage fright translated for writers. I believe instead that it is in fact phobophilia, the love of fear. I believe, as of 10:17 this morning, when the solitaire didn't come out for the seventh time, leaving me a theoretical eighty-two dollars in the hole for the day's action, that we need to have fears, we love our fears, we couldn't do anything without our fears, and so we construct an elaborate system of behavior which automatically builds in phobias.

Anyone who has ever rooted for his or her team in a key game has used innumerable obsessive magics to bring the team home, trembling each time a rule is broken, and convinced that's why the game was lost. The Jets, for example, lost because—and only because—Lem stood up in front of the TV set just as Miami was scoring. If he'd stayed seated we would have held, and obviously eventually won 3–0.

As it was, the whole thing turned around and I was forced a week later to hear people thanking G-d, Jack Kent Cooke, and the Redskin fans, while talking to Ronald McDonald or somebody. I mean, they ought to know that G-d really doesn't have time for football games. He's worrying about Seaver and Torrez.

But not to digress, as much as I'd like to—since the Torrez trade has me convinced that the Mets, under whatever management, should never be allowed to trade anyone for anyone under any circumstances again. Nevertheless, back to phobophilia. The simple fact is, we love our fears—and probably should, too. It seems eminently reasonable to me that I should be afraid of heights, new places, open spaces, closed spaces, traveling, food poisoning, etc. etc. etc., since all these things are likely to cause harm, or at least are capable of doing so.

But even more important is the wonderful rush having a fear gives you. The heart starts pumping, the blood rushes to the surface, the stomach quivers. You know you're alive. Without fears there'd be nothing to write about and no way to get the juices flowing to allow you to write. So I, as most of my colleagues, have devised all unknowing a fool-proof system to get myself to work dirtying that white piece of paper in the typewriter. I scare myself to write. I run through so many rituals that I'm afraid not to write.

I suspect this may be the prime principle of life itself, as well as of creative behavior. Of course, I've had women friends in the past who've accused me of living by philophobia, or the fear of loving, but I don't think that's relevant here, and it's certainly not true, or at least any more. Now I take it wherever I can get it, no longer being young and handsome.

I propose a convention of phobophiliacs, so we can set up ground rules, procedures, and other obsessions and compulsions to keep us all happy. Obviously our motto will be Fear and Trembling and Sickness unto Death, and our tree the quaking aspen, and we can go on from there. Phobophilia forever, and long may we waver!

Good News
Tonight

I see the president is yelling again. He's upset that we press folk don't report the good news but only the bad. I would be delighted to report good news about the economy or anything else if I had any, but it is the end of winter in the North country, which means Mud Season, which means there ain't any news at all. Although it will be news to some folks that I consider myself a press folk, but I will not worry about them.

I did go down to the Mall of New Hampshire last week and I saw some old news, so I'll report on it. The Mall is a big one in Manchester; I think the notion is that them that make it in Massachusetts will come spend it in New Hampshire—which is an idea I stole from the Mad Maltese, so I'll credit him—thus saving the sales tax.

It's usually a bustling place, in any event, and if one avoids the eating alley (Chinese, Italian, Mickey, Mexican, Old-Fashioned Saloon, etc., etc., etc., and where one *does* pay sales tax!) one might even have fun. The Legal Eagless needed some rose blush by Lancome, and Jaqueline of Wales (I'm not making that name up, she really does sell *les cosmetiques* on Concord's Main Street!) doesn't carry Lancome, so off we went to check out the Mall's goodies. My own plan, of course, was to sneak into the Games Shop and see if "Tito" was still on sale. "Tito" allows you to be a Yugoslav partisan and hide in the mountains while the Germans and Italians huddle in the cities, and while I have one set for myself, there are several closet Titoists I want to get one for, not to mention one forlorn Mikhailovitcher. And it's no use checking back to *Winds of War* on these names because Ali McGraw didn't mention them.

But as Bobbie Burns (a noted Scots Titoist) once said, there's many a slip between Filene's cosmetic counter and the war games, and so as I was passing a small fashion shoppe, I noticed a crowd gathered about the window. This is New Hampshire, and New Hampshire is right next to Maine, where my friend The Merchant Prince once saw three guys filming *Deep Throat* in 8mm through the windshield of their pickup at a drive-in in the rain, so I suspected the fashion shoppe probably had some pretty jazzy undies in the window. However, in fact, the window held a true depression memory: a live person acting like a dead mannequin.

She was good. There was a real mannequin in the window, facing us, and the live one faced three-quarters away, wearing a bright red dress, made up in a weird mannequinlike color (a little too waxy for my taste but perfect for necrophiliacs) and perfectly still. Oh, once in a while a finger would move a bit, or a breath would give itself away, but basically she stood as still as plastic. (That's actually an oxymoron since plastic means moving, but what the hell, it's a depression.)

I hadn't seen a live mannequin since 1940 when such things were a regular feature of the better stores around Getty square in Yonkers. I mean, when nobody's got any work, and they're willing to do anything, why not pay somebody to make believe they're a statue? Then all the people with nothing to do can be amused watching to see if the human statue screws up and moves. That seems to be the theory, anyhow. I suppose the store owner figures that anybody watching the window at least won't be shoplifting.

Well, every ten minutes or so she'd take a break or change her stance. Facing the audience was harder, of course, since the eyes blinked, and also she seemed to tremble every once in a while, but facing away she was great. Little boys kept squirming their way up to the window and tapping and making faces, but she didn't budge for them. Neither did the fish in the pet shop at the other end of the Mall, where I saw the same kids doing the same thing, but I don't know what the lesson from this is.

But the lesson for us is, I think, that when you can get people to do anything, and for not much money, the economy can start to improve. That is to say, business can do better for less outlay, and everybody knows that's just wonderful for all of us. It worked in the '30s when it only took ten years and a world war to snap us back into the era of good news, and I guess it's started working now.

The president ought to know, then, that this particular member of the press, even though I'm just a once every four weeks kind of guy, and I write a despised column for a weekly commie or fascist rag (depending on which view you incline to) and I'm stationed in New Hampshire, well, I'm certainly not ignoring good news, Mr. President. I haven't seen any apple sellers yet, which I guess would be another sign of individual initiative, but then it's March and apples don't come into season or out of cold storage until September or October.

The economic weather up here is generally pretty fierce, of course. The state is divided between, basically, absentee rich folk who own lots of vistas and lakes and things and come up and eat once in awhile (we sat next to two of these couples the other night in what passes for Concord's best restaurant; the dominant male was a Harvard and the other a Dartmouth. The Harvard was pissed because his wife's new twenty gee-a-year job was going to cost him eight gees in taxes, but if it kept her happy . . . the Dartmouth agreed, because he was in a lower bracket, and the wives giggled, oh you menfolk!) and, on the other side of it, the poor but honest New Hampshire yeopeople (yeomen and yeowomen equal yeopeople).

The yeopeople, having been sold a bill of goods about independence, work long hours for little pay and believe they are living free. My own feeling is that the New Hampshire license plate ought to read "Live Relatively Free If You've Got Nice Lakefront Acreage But Die in the End Anyhow," but I can't seem to get any grassroots movement in favor of the change. We've elected a Republican governor whose name backwards is un-un-us, which must mean something, and I hear varying stories about his lineage, which seems to combine Lebanese and Greek with a touch of guzano, since his family is supposed to have come here from Cuba. Sununu's basic economic plan so far seems to be to close the University and build a new jail, things which may or may not be related. Fortunately, the legislature meets only once every two years, and that's right now before he's really had a chance to make a program, so a new governor can't do a whole lot of damage. It's a good method and ought to be tried in the rest of the Republic.

And that's all the good news I can give you. I'll save the bad until after Mud Season, when we can all handle it better, or at least not get stuck in it.

Semper Illegitimati

The forsythia are out, finally, as is the sun. Both took a long time—the forsythia its usual year, the sun a more depressing week or so. Last evening Lem and the Legal Eagless gave an ooh and an aah simultaneously and pointed out the window. There were two robins on the little patch of lawn outside. And when Lem went out later to test the new baseball cleats, he found new-piled anthills riddling the same lawn.

So if spring is here, even in the frozen North, why am I so angry? Let me count the ways. Well, for one thing because "The Great Communicator struck again" in the wonderful phrasing of "one happy White House official." Or, in other words, what goes around, comes around, and what goes around once will most certainly get another come-around no matter what happened the first time, and even if the first time and the second aren't related.

So the kids better pack their bags again, either for Fort Dix or Canada. Ranger Ron has managed to do it, just as the infamous "they" always do. You keep slipping and sliding and lying just a little and telling half-truths a lot, and then finally you've built a case the great American public will buy. It's no matter that we have used them as our chattel countries for a century and a half. It's no matter that we're only in favor of democracy (here to there) if the "right folks" get elected.

So, once again, we're to believe that only money, then only advisers, then only a few troops for stiffening, then only, then only. And once again the great American public is going to buy it, because them damn monkeys down there are agoin' to invade us if we don't! I'm starting a movement up hereabouts to let the monkeys invade Texas, so the Texans'll have to stay down thataways pertectin' their borders instead of coming up here invading ours.

But it won't work, because everybody knows that if Texas falls, the dominos will reach right up to North Dakota.

What we keep learning is that the bastards keep winning. War, anti-Communism, nuclear power, whatever, they just keep grinding away and eventually, usually when the rest of us have deluded ourselves that we've "won," they slip right back in. Sometimes it's the money folks, sometimes it's the power folks, sometimes it's the ideologues. But they all share one virtue the good guys don't have, and that's the paranoia of persistence. Oh, we've got our paranoia, sure, but it's more a reactive paranoia, we jump when we're pushed. Those guys just keep pushing all the time.

Here's another: "We can picket, demonstrate, curse and take God's name in vain, but we can't voluntarily get together and talk about God at school. I can decide if I want an abortion or use contraceptives, but I can't decide if I want to come to a meeting to talk about religious matters before or after school. To me, that just isn't fair."

That's a quote, cited in the *Daily News,* from a teenager testifying at a Senate hearing on school prayers. The story doesn't say whether anybody asked her a few basic questions, like how all those things turn out to be comparable activities, or whether, in fact, she can get abortions in her school, either before, during, or after school hours, or whether her teachers really let her curse in class. As for picketing and demonstrating, I'd have thought her civics teacher or history teacher or social science teacher—or maybe even, God forbid, her parents—would have told her that those were rights guaranteed to every American citizen, just like the right to practice or not practice religion on one's own time is guaranteed.

But, eventually, one way or another, she'll win. My kids or my grandkids will have the wonderful choice of being hypocrites or lepers and she or her kids will have their prayers. We had a self-inspection kind of meeting here at my college a couple of weeks ago and one of the questions raised then was the lack of courses in "moral underpinning"! This is at a school where the philosophy department has barely managed to hang on by offering "professional" ethics courses for business, science, law, etc. But it's also a school where a great deal of moral unpinning goes on at night, so I suspect the kids are safe from their saviors.

In fact, I don't object at all to moral underpinning. I just object to what it usually means. If moral underpinning means the strength to stand up to the president when he lies—as he and his spokespeople do about the CIA guerilla war against the duly constituted government of Nicaragua—then moral underpinning is great. If moral underpinning means the sense to see that nuclear energy is not only dangerous and cancerous but costly as well, or if it means working to stop a nuclear holocaust, or if it means trying to feed children rather than to convert them, or if it means having the strength to practice your religion without the need to lay it on anyone else, then moral underpinning ought to be taught everywhere.

Since it isn't, spring is a little harder to respond to every year. The forsythias and the robins keep coming but I've got less and less elasticity—and it ain't age I'm talking about either. It's this long run of liars, it's this long run of blood and morality dripping down our hands, it's this long line of kids being murdered or going off to do the murdering.

I don't want any more of it. Damn it, they either laugh or turn away when I look for the baseball scores—and that doesn't work so well any more either, though I keep doing it—but I want that in my spring. Homers and K's and the look of the green grass on a diamond is what ought to go with the robins and the forsythia. And instead they keep giving us the other kind of red breasts and yellow politicians, and KIA's, and green kids dying.

This is no country for young men, since the old men run it, and decide who dies.

Friends

There's a story Myron Cohen used to tell about the guy who comes home and smells cigar smoke and goes on a frantic search through the house, looking for his wife's lover. He ends up in the bathroom in front of the closed shower curtain which he rips open. There's the culprit, standing in the tub, the cigar still in his mouth. "What are you doing here?" the guy screams. The intruder says,"Nu, everybody's got to be somewhere. . . ."

When you're young and eager and looking to conquer this city of dreams, that somewhere usually turns out to be a saloon. It ain't only a place to get loaded, or even to score. It's also your home away from home, an extension of your living room, your answering service and maybe even your bank.

I've been lucky. I've had three winners. I started out in the Cedar Tavern, waiting there one afternoon in late spring in 1953, because Franz Kline had said a year earlier, "Kid, when you get to the city, go to the Cedars and sit there and nurse a beer. I'll get there eventually." I sat from one until four, slowly working on fifteen cent beers, and by God, he did show up. "Hi kid," he said, "Whyn't you tell them you were looking for me?" And by the end of the evening I knew the bartenders, the owner, the waiter, and a dozen people who would be my family for the next ten years.

And for the last fifteen years I've had the Lions Head, even though I've not had a real drink for thirteen of those years. Still that was the place I lived a great deal of my life—and there were times when I considered giving its phone number to P.S. 3 or I.S. 70 as Nat and Lem's emergency number, because it was and is that second home.

In between those two places there was a man, not a place. I knew Mickey Ruskin from back in his coffeehouse days, but it wasn't till the Cedars closed temporarily and drove us all out in the street that I began drinking at the Ninth Circle and found Mickey as a friend. Then he left there and we stayed friends, so that a year or so later when he called and asked me over to his house for dinner it wasn't a special occasion, but just friends eating together. He said, after the meal, that he was opening a new joint and asked did I have any ideas for a name. That night—despite his misgivings about my choice—Max's Kansas City was born.

When I got married, Mickey gave us the upstairs at Max's for the ceremony in the afternoon and a hell of a good party that night. He even conned the Sangria salesman into donating a barrel of the stuff, because "There's this famous poet getting married and the elite of New York's drinkers will be there, and you'll get 200 new customers"!

Mickey was an entrepreneur, clear and simple. He loved to take places that had never been successful, or were in some location no one'd ever gone, and he'd make them work. Max's was a dismal Chinese restaurant that I never would've taken a chance on, and the Ninth Circle had had a new owner every week before he got to it. The Locale, which came after Max's, was downstairs and dark and the two times I'd been in it before Ruskin got it had been enough for a lifetime as far as I was concerned. Then there was the Lower Manhattan Ocean Club, again breaking new ground, and, finally, Chinese Chance, at One University. In between there'd even been a stab at uptown with Max's Terre Haute.

The one thing all the places had was Mickey, yelling at the waitresses, a bitch to work for but an angel with his friends. Painters and writers, layabouts and scoundrels all, there was a home for us. I walked in one night with a date, and Mickey bounced Huntington Hartford from a table so we could sit down. You could love a guy like that, and I did.

The only problem with Mick was that he got bored as soon as a place caught on. He wanted the risk, the dare of opening up where everybody said you couldn't. He wanted to see could he make it work—no, that's wrong, because he knew he could make it work. And he liked to try things out. A couple of years before the state legislature passed the law about making legal jargon readable, Mickey called me and asked me if I'd take a stab at rewriting his legal documents in real English. When the banks started offering "scenic" checks, Mickey had Max's checks underprinted with a faint but discernible shot of John Chamberlain, Neal Williams, Frosty Myers, and me lounging at the bar. He paid us each a fee of ninety-nine cents, made out on the first four checks, and mine still hangs on my wall at Westbeth, framed. I often meant to ask him if the accountant had gone crazy over the uncashed check but I never got around to it.

Now I can't any more. He's gone. I got the call a couple of weeks ago, from my son Dan, who'd worked for Mickey at Chinese Chance a couple of years ago. He was the day waiter then, and Angus Chamberlain, John's son, was there at the same time, behind the bar. John and I said it was the least Mickey could do for us after we'd supported him for so long.

I couldn't get down from New Hampshire for the funeral. I couldn't hear John and Neal eulogize him. I spoke to John the night before the funeral and he was outraged that he'd have to say something. John's like his sculpture, big and rough, and he keeps thinking words are alien materials. "What the hell is a eulogy anyhow, damn it?" he screamed. "Beautiful words," I said. "Just say some beautiful words about the good times, and let the bad times go." And I hear he did just that. Well, that's what it's about, the good times, and you keep the bad times quiet, and just think about how somebody like Mickey bailed you out of so many of them, of the loans, and the time he bought a gen-u-wine manuscript poem because he knew you were broke, and the times he paid for a meal or bought you a drink because you needed it.

The one thing I wish he'd been able to do was to prevail on the Cornell Alumni magazine to do a cover of Max's with him (a real graduate) and the dozen or so of us who were all Cornell failures lined up in front of the joint. He thought it would have made a pretty good shot.

Colding Up

One of the problems I face whenever I find myself in a new situation is that of determining how to act like I belong. Sometimes the problem is so insurmountable I avoid the new situation forever. In the '50s, for example, I had a lot of friends, some black and some white (although in those days we referred to ourselves as Negro, Jewish, or "those other people") who used to want to take me along to the Apollo or Small's or some such. I figured that the last thing a Harlem theater or nightclub needed was me trying to figure out whether I could tap my feet to the music, or more likely, against it, so I never went.

But the one I face now can't be avoided without freezing. We're living, the Legal Eagless and I, in this charming house which turns out by some error in the universal setup to be charming. It's heated by electric baseboards, which I have been assured will cost us no more than a thousand or two a month to keep us toasty, and by two woodstoves: one, a beautiful but inefficient Franklin stove, and the other, a not-so-beautiful but terribly efficient square black clunker of a thing, guaranteed to heat the whole house in seconds.

So what's the problem? I spent the last week freezing, because I was damned if I was going to use some heat (of either variety) before it was time to, by community standards. Ever since the heat wave disappeared, New Hampshire has been a mite chilly—WEVO, our local PBS station, keeps reporting discouraging numbers like forty degrees from places just a few miles northwest of here. And getting into the shower at 7:15 A.M. under those conditions can take a lot of courage, which is a commodity I have never had in any large quantity.

I was so blocked on this mini-macho point of surviving September that I had to conduct a furtive hunt to locate the flannel shirts—no, don't start screaming at me, because I was unpacking the kitchen while she unpacked the clothes—so that the Eagless wouldn't consider me unmanly, and leave with one of the guys in the cutoffs loping around the landscape with a healthy glow on.

But, finally, all was resolved yesterday morning. Half frozen, but holding my teeth still by not putting them in until the sun was up a bit, say 11 A.M., I went about my business: buying the *Post,* trying to read the textbook for Beginning Journalism, solving three scheduling problems for lost advisees, and the like. In the course of all this frenetic activity I overheard two real downhome all-fired New Hampshirites talking about how good the fire had felt that morning, and how nice the plume of smoke coming out the chimney had looked after that dreadful hot summer.

I understood that I had misjudged my people here. It's okay to light a fire in New Hampshire; in fact not having a fire may be an unnatural act to some. One of the people talking, I realized, was the guy I'd noticed wearing his wool knit watch cap all summer even when it was close to 100 degrees. Folks up here take cold as the natural state—they like the story about the old farmer who lived right next to the Vermont border until a surveying error was discovered and he was told he was now a Vermonter. "Thank God," he's reported to have said, "I don't know if I could've handled another New Hampshire winter."

So last night we lit our first fire. We decided that the real stove would be overkill, and that all we needed was the emotional boost of the fire as fire, so we used the Franklin. Since, unlike three months from now when all the wood will be green and damp, the wood was seasoned and dry, we had a merry blaze roaring in minutes. I guess it's like a bicycle—having built my only fire forty-one years ago to move from tenderfoot to first class, I'd in fact never forgotten!

Curled on the couch, the fire blazing, warm for the first time in four days, we looked at each other and the Eagless said, "It's not a bad life, is it? You can almost forget all the bullshit. . . ." It was true. A House vote okaying not only the once and future B-1 and the never-to-be-killed MX, but nerve gas and assorted other mal-feasances as well, could be ignored. The flaming rhetoric could be forgotten. It was almost possible to understand why a great many Americans just can't be bothered with the world.

"But the world is out there," I want to scream every day up here! The notion that Korean airliners could only have been shot down by Russkies, and never by Murricans, is an article of faith in these parts. When you ask them what we would do if a strange plane flew around "our" airspace for two and a half hours and didn't respond to signals, they say, "But we wouldn't shoot it down!" I think they believe we have smarter generals or some-thing . . . that's even more depressing than the belief that "It can't happen here."

When you point out that the reason generals like weapons is because they want to see them work, and that this is indispu-table—that just like actors want the play to go on and poets want to appear in print, generals have ego needs too—they ignore you and start discussing the Red Sox.

I tell you it's chilling, and that's not meant to be a pun, to hear the cold war rhetoric being spouted again by both sides. And no one talks about the kind of mutual paranoia which was bound to lead to this kind of a conclusion. If I keep threatening you and stockpiling weapons, while you keep threatening me and stockpil-ing weapons sooner or later someone is going to pull some trigger. At least, this time, it wasn't the big panic button. I suppose that's our blessing for the day. But my God, an unarmed civilian passen-ger liner is down, and all the people in it are dead, and what the two protagonists do is rattle more sabers—and build more. That, and fulminate against those who would like to live in a world where there are fewer weapons. The level of vitriol expressed against all us peaceniks by letter writers up here is incredible. I begin to feel like I pulled the trigger that shot the plane down . . . or at least that I sent it straying over somebody else's pea patch. And meanwhile, a man who devoted his life, or the most recent part of it, to hate and death, is eulogized as a martyr to my sick lust for peace!

I think I will stay curled up on the sofa with the fire going for a while. It's a lot more reasonable universe here than outside.

Peace in Our Time

For Armistice Day, in my childhood, all the stores ran sales of lead soldiers. They were loss leaders, so to speak, and I would eye the ads hungrily as I looked through the *World Telegram* my father brought home every night. I hoped those looks would somehow—whether through telepathy or empathy—tell my father how desperately I wanted one, just one, of those metal warriors. All my friends had some; when we played outside and built our cities and our wars all I could contribute were my cars and trucks.

Perhaps the whiff of mustard that had touched his lung in 1918, or the tuberculosis that followed it, damped his enthusiasm for such things, or perhaps I romanticize. Maybe it was just that he didn't know I wanted them, or maybe it was more simply just the Depression and there were better things to spend money on.

Finally, in '38, I got my few infantrymen. I was a third grader and all my friends had had theirs since first grade, but at last I was an equal. Maybe by then there was enough distance between my father's service and the present, or maybe the faces of my mother's relatives arriving month by month from middle Europe told him that another generation was going to have to go to war.

He never talked much about his fight to make the world safe for democracy; once he bragged that he had learned to make omelets in France, and could make any kind. I asked for banana and to my ever-lasting regret he made me one. Aaaaagh!

I heard a few of his fellow vets on the radio this Armistice Day morning. He never knew them, nor they he, since they were English, but they were still alive, and he's dead now. They were talking about the battle of the Somme, where they charged the machine guns for four months to gain a couple of yards. One said, "We went over the top that first day 230 strong. Eleven came back."

They were bright and cheery as they talked, except when one or another lapsed into tears. They're in their eighties now; they've survived not only the Somme but life itself. They were "the boys" who went to war after the enlistments dried up and conscription began. In other words, they were not *professionals.*

I know it's not Armistice Day any more, it's Veterans' Day, the Armistice long gone and useless—and the notion I had during the Vietnam years when the government decided to ignore November 11 and swung the celebration to the third Monday after the fourth Tuesday before the first Wednesday to accommodate leaf-peaking tours or some such—one year it fell on October 25th, which was *tres amusante* since it coincided with one or another of those pesky Red Russky Revolutions as one of my faithful readers informed me when I first discussed the notion which I started to mention before this interjection began—this notion of stealing November 11th for the Peace Movement and making it Peace Day, since the warmongers had all moved over to the travel bureaus' Veterans' Day.

Now it's back on November 11 and it's Veterans' Day and Armistice Day all wrapped up together, and we still have "boys" to mourn. The problem is we mourn boys while our peerless leader exploits an army.

Once upon a time, around 1790 or so, the notion of a democratic army, a people's army, a great national army, hit the world. No more would wars be fought by small groups of professionals, doing the leader's bidding without let or hindrance—aside from the other leader's small group of professionals. Now armies would move in masses, and would stand for national dreams, national defense, national expansion, or whatever. The whole nation would be involved, and serving in such a force would be a patriotic duty.

Napoleon's armies marched then, and the great armies of our Civil War marched, and on and on they marched through World War II. And now there are still people who believe that such a force exists; such as my neighbor from New Hampshire who wrote

Ronald Reagan a letter telling him how pleased he was his son could be in the Marines and in Lebanon. And then the President used the letter to sell his war!

My God, can anyone imagine the father of a Hessian gushing on about how pleased he was his son could go to America and fight. Can any one imagine the father of a longbowman at Crecy or Agincourt sending a thank-you note to the King?

But we go on believing we have a democratic army devoted to democracy while the President sends it as he wills and where he wills and despite the laws enacted to prevent this. He is above the law, as Jefferson warned, and the young congressman Lincoln warned, and Eisenhower himself warned.

And the people do keep believing, not only in the myth of the army, but in the magic of this leader. Honest, it's not only the editorials in the *New York Post*, or the hysterical ravings of the whoring columnists who are paid—PAID!—to be independent and to think; it's the great American public. It's the voices around me who say "It's good to keep the press out of things, because all they do is snoop around for details like how many got killed! Who cares?" Another voice chimes in, "It's too confusing. The press makes all that propaganda and then we can't hear what the President says!"

Then the junket comes back from Grenada and reports that our invasion must have been justified because (a) it's politically popular, and (b) the Grenadians all seem happy and rhythmic, and (c) our soldiers are behaving nicely. Of course the two black members of the junket turn in a minority report which says it looks like we would have invaded whether there were Americans to save or not, but who cares what those guys say anyhow? Why don't they just keep smiling and dancing is the feeling—much as Reagan was scared of all those other black men with guns, and ideas too!

And then we hear that our allies in Central America can't prosecute the right-wing death squads for fear they'll be blown away themselves. Some of us wonder why we don't invade if there's such a worry about nondemocratic countries in the Western Hemisphere and if "bloody anarchy" really worries Reagan or the Pentagon.

The last thing I watched this past Veterans' Day was a television show called "Our Time In Hell." It was a montage of footage from combat cameramen and artists covering the island-hopping of the World War II marines: Guadalcanal, Tarawa, Iwo Jima, all of them. The footage was fierce and incredible, almost, except that we know men did die like that, live like that, were brave and selfless like that.

The producers turned it into a paean to killing and buddyship side by side; how glorious it is to have a fellowship of blood and guts; how stupid and evil the Japs are; how good we are; and look, when we've beaten them, even Japs are human beings; and finally, as expected: look how wonderful we are, we dropped two little bombs to make them stop instead of killing the two million who would have died if we'd invaded them, not to mention the other millions who would've committed suicide because that's the kind of people that country is, blindly following its militaristic leaders.

Let the lead soldiers of my childhood be the only ones we buy and sell.

Breakfast Reading

The Nook is what passes for my greasy spoon up here, and every morning I have conversations with the more or less regular attendees abut the weather. Of course, conversation in New Hampshire is always about the weather, but we do touch on politics, sex, humor, and the progress of higher education, since we're all involved to some extent with those fields.

I sit in the middle of a long table, with the smokers to my left and the nonsmokers to my right, so I can sniff what life used to be like while seeing what life is. Tuffy, the power volleyball coach and cellist, and Mad Joe, the librarian, lead the nonsmokers. Tuffy is retiring this year, so she can finally learn to play the cello instead of just looking at it, but Mad Joe is still waiting to mature and settle down.

I presume it's part of that process which led him to get on the mailing list for one of those companies that offers sexual aids of various disgusting natures; he showed up for breakfast Friday grinning from ear to ear and presented me with its latest catalogue. The grin was because *Marilyn Lives!* was featured on page four. This was a book I did three or some years ago, consisting of interviews with people who'd fallen in love with Marilyn's image; the point was, to write about what people perceived about Marilyn, as opposed to all the books about who the "real" Marilyn was.

I was happy with the book, and it got some nice notices like they say, and it even sold a few copies. I've heard that now it's showing up as a remainder item in some stores, and I wasn't terribly surprised. Oh sure, my editor and I both had dreams that it would take off and sell 200,000 copies, but we also knew those were probably just dreams. So we settled for the 20,000 or 25,000 copies that did sell. And I remember, too, that poetry books just get pulped, instead of being remaindered.

I never imagined in my wildest dreams that I'd make it onto

the same page as Hot Babes Masturbating (. . . busy fingers,
pulsating vibrators, streams of water . . . writhing climaxes . . .),
Pleasure Sheepskin (. . . soft sensual wool left unclipped so you and
your lover can revel . . . adds special pleasure to lovemaking),
Touch of Silk (. . . silk and lace barely hiding mouthwatering
breasts and plump bottoms . . . will keep you busy for months), and
Inside (. . . how delicate feminine sisters discover wild lust in each
other's arms . . . no-holds-barred color).

The first thing that occurred to me was to ask William Safire
and Jim Quinn whether breasts can mouthwater, and the second
was that I ought to read what they wrote about my book. They said
it wasn't just another MM book, it was the best, and they thought
we'd "be fascinated." They said it was the real Marilyn—without
Tinseltown puffery. Compared to the blurbs for the other books
they were positively subtle, and I began to be sorry they hadn't
mentioned my name. In fact, if you have very good eyesight you
can almost make it out on the inch-deep reproduction of the cover.
They're selling it at list price, so I suppose I ought to be happy.

To make it into a sex catalogue when all about me only get
reviewed in the *Times* is, I suppose, a mark of honor. And if I order
a copy, I'll get on the mailing list, and there are some terrific
pictures in the booklet, as well as a host of absolutely frightening
apparati, including the Dip Stick, the Public Cube, and the Reliever—
"the ultimate tension reliever of all time": a probable fellatio-machine
that pumps you with pleasure.

I want to tell you, too, that we haven't had so much fun at
breakfast since we discovered one of the professors serving as a
model in a drawing of the "lady riding" position in a textbook on
human sexuality. I told you, we do discuss higher education too.

Mad Joe understood that I would want the catalogue for my
publicity file, but I really needed it so I could pick out items like the
brand new fellatio flashcards (coursework never off my mind)
which promise to be great for the beginner and a fine refresher for
the more advanced. He traded it to me for a copy of the Marilyn

book, but then returned that when he found out it had words as well as pictures. His position seems to be that he's paid to order books, not read them.

Catalogues, it occurred to me around this time, really serve an important function when you're out of town. A good portion of my books these days comes from the mailing pieces sent out by Barnes & Noble; a good portion of the housewares comes from the endless succession of chain and department store flyers sent either directly to me, or to occupant. I get Penney's catalogue, Sears', Zayre's, Osco Drug's, Filene's, Jordan Marsh's, even Herman's, which has somehow found its way from downtown to Manchester!

This is part of country living we never get to see in the city. It would be much better if the damned things burned well, but they don't. My local woodstove mentor tells me that the dyes that make the colors have a damaging effect on the walls of the stove, so you have to be careful to throw them all away at the dump. I believe him, of course, since how would I know?

Now the catalogues are full of bathing suits and seersucker suits, so I presume summer will come, despite the battering by winter which we all took the last week in March. I'm writing this column on April Fool's Day, and the baseball season is supposed to start tomorrow. I certainly hope the snow's melted in Cincinnati, so the Mets can get off to a running start, whichever way they're going.

I like to believe that this year I'll be able to follow baseball, and that the Mets will do well and the Yankees'll collapse, but if not I intend to bury myself in mail order. A month or so ago I clipped one of those coupons in the *Times* magazine section and circled about twenty of the things to ensure a steady supply. I've got kitchen catalogues, lingerie catalogues, tool catalogues, outdoor catalogues, sports catalogues, and toy catalogues all set to appear in my mailbox.

The hell with nature; I'll take art. I get enough nature on my morning walks to the Nook, thinking of what to discuss each morning.

The Long View

Your reporter finally got a chance to see his Mets play—albeit on the tube—and is here to add his voice to the chorus. In the first place, they're for real, at least temporarily, and in the second, which is where they are this morning, they're not the '69 Amazons.

If this opening seems unnecessarily overstated, it's because one of the games I watched was on *Monday Night Baseball*, which meant that I had to listen to Cosell. Why a man who neither likes nor understands the game wants to broadcast it is beyond me, but rather than add to the myth that people watch him to hate him, I'll just mention that there was a two-inning stretch where not one pitch or play was called, while we heard about an interminable golf game, and that he kept ascribing the Mets' current success to New York hype and their similarity to the '69 club.

The '84 Mets are by-and-large homegrown, or at least home-developed, with only Foster and Hernandez having made it big somewhere else. That Hernandez is a wonderful acquisition who makes up for a lot of bad trades is beside the point. The '69 Mets featured only Cleon Jones and Bud Harrelson, aside from the pitchers, as legitimate major leaguers brewed on the farm. This club has Wilson, Strawberry, and Brooks, who seem already pros, while Fitzgerald, Backman, Oquendo, Chapman, and Gardenhire certainly offer stronger possibilities than Garrett and Boswell did then; the pitching staff is stronger than '69, as well as deeper.

As for New York hype, I'm delighted to see that the power of the press is now strong enough to keep a club in contention in July! I'd submit that the boys have to be playing ball to be seven games over .500 this late in the season.

Understand, there are no dreams of glory here, because I realize that it's a young team, and the dog days of August are almost upon us. We will see how the pups do then, and I won't make any World Series reservations until the middle of September.

But it is certainly nice to be able to root for a winning team, and to see pitchers like Gooden and Darling and Sisk and Orosco perform with at least a little bit behind them.

I saw the first two of that sterling group the weekend we came in to watch Nathaniel graduate from high school. It was nice of Bronx Science to work things out with Johnson so we got the right part of the rotation. Now if only one of the speakers had mentioned the arts as part of the makeup of a complete human being, all would have been perfect—but I'll settle for Nat graduating and the Mets winning.

We didn't get a chance to get to Shea because the weekend was short and busy, and I'm sorry about that. On the good side, though, is the fact that the Mets always lose when I go out to watch them, and they only lose some of the time when I follow them via TV. Radio seems to give me the best winning percentage, and, this year, the few games I've been able to pick up late at night, drifting in from WHN, have all been winners.

But it's damned hard rooting from afar. We get Cable Network News up here, with its little sports squibs every half hour, but they always give tennis and golf and for God's sakes USFL football and Olympic basketball first, so half the time they don't have time for baseball, and when they do they give the American League first, which is only bearable because the Georges keep losing.

ESPN is devoted to USFL even more, now that they've got a deal, and the Boston stations treat the National League like the minors. So I was even willing to put up with Monday Night Baseball to see the club, and then, lo and behold, the same week, the club makes the Saturday national hookup! Of course, that's when the game and the city were flooded out, but only because they knew I was trying to watch.

I've taken to swinging the dial around a lot in the evenings, because the ball I can get up here is intriguing. The softball leagues in Concord are on one local channel, and the Nashua Pirates, a double-A club, are on another occasionally. I saw them get whupped by the Vermont Reds the other night. I like the Reds, because they play out of Burlington, and Burlington has the only socialist mayor in the country, and the name fits.

We were talking about that the other day, and someone recalled the period during the '50s when the Reds became the Redlegs. Remember why? So they wouldn't give sustenance and support to the godless enemy. I seem to recall someone else telling me that Macy's had made a major policy decision then also, that they had decided that Macy's had used its red star logo longer than the damned commies, so they weren't going to change it!

I'm writing this column two days before the Fourth, when there will be even more patriotism, and more baseball. In fact, the Mets may be back in first by then. I can't allow myself to think of that possibility because that would lead to the adage about clubs that are in first on the Fourth, and that way lies madness. How do you pitch to the Detroit outfield?

The few Yankee fans around here seem to have lost all spirit. The rumor that George may move the club to Jersey is what did it, I believe, and several of them have slunk (slinked? slank?) up to me to admit grudging admiration for the boys of Flushing. One told me just this morning that when a friend mentioned he'd flown over a full stadium in New York, he'd said, "Must've been Shea, then." I suppose it must've been, and I hope it keeps up.

Meanwhile, the Henniker Little League season just ended, but the fifteen-to-eighteen-year-old boys are in contention for a statewide tournament berth, having won a squeaker last night 11–10. Even without late box scores in the papers, I get the baseball news somehow.

Selling the Gold

Mad Joe the Librarian greeted me the Monday after the Olympics began by hurtling into the Nook and raving about how wonderful opening night was and didn't I agree? When I paused ten seconds he said, "It's just a simple yes or no, for God's sake!" and I had to confess I had reservations.

Mad Joe has good taste in many areas, such as the value of Spandex in making woman-watching at poolside more worthwhile, so I really ought to reconsider my feelings about that Saturday evening extravaganza. I know that if I sound negative I'll be echoing the Moscow line, but I have to say I felt much embarrassment and some of anger.

There were the little things. Peter Jennings saying, "Peking, or Beijing as the Chinese like to call it . . ." Or telling us Chile is working its way toward democracy, without mentioning that the last time Chile tried that the CIA wouldn't allow it. And that wonderful line about how Lesotho had never won anything but keeps sending athletes. How long has Lesotho been a member of the IOC? How long has it been an "official nation" for that matter? Not to mention Jennings's line about their having "great precision at Moscow, but here there's precision and spirit too." Does he really believe there was no spirit in Moscow?

Jennings does deserve credit for trying to shut that ceaseless commentator McKay up so we could hear the world's biggest or best or most recently formed or whatever band playing—beautifully, I must add. Jennings said, "Maybe we ought to keep quiet and listen to them for a while." The silence lasted all of five seconds.

ABC's promos kept promising us the most complete coverage ever for these games, but "coverage" seemed to mean making sure there was something for everyone, and nothing done completely, or without outside distractions. Television is incapable of just letting an event happen—there have to be visuals, chatter, color, interviews, crowd shots, and all the rest of the technical and psycholgical gimmicks. All this and Cosell as well.

And while I understand that the Olympics are a commercial venture, I got a little upset when we lost twenty-five countries to the hucksters. We were told over and over again that there were 140 teams competing, for the greatest total ever, but when the delegations of athletes walked in the grand parade, we only saw 115. I know because I wrote them all down. I think it's wonderful that there are countries who "keep sending teams even though they've never won a medal"—and I want to see them. And that there are countries in the midst of war who send teams, and that Rumania broke with the Soviet Union and showed up, and that there were Nicaraguan baseball players, and that Bangladesh and Burma sent their one competitor each. But I want to know whom we didn't see. Surely we could have met those guys too.

It was that damned self-satisfied, patronizing attitude running throughout the games that got to me. The biggest. The best. And the too frequent assumption that biggest means best. When the band swung into "Sing Sing Sing" and all those drummers recreated the solo that one man had made, I wondered if the incongruity had struck anyone involved in the production. The performance in Los Angeles was fantastic, but wouldn't you rather have been at Carnegie Hall the first time?

I won't even mention the eighty-four George Gershwins, except to say that I missed Jose Iturbi. Hazel Scott at the organ would have been nice too. And one or two black faces jitterbugging to "One O'Clock Jump" might have fit in, no?

This is all merely carping, I know that. And, yes, I do judge my own country by standards different from those I use to judge the rest of the world. It's my sincere patriotic belief that that's the proper thing to do. When Reagan speaks of "a great patriotism sweeping this country" I like to feel I'm doing my share, even if I disagree with his syntax. Damn it, there was enough emotion, genuine emotion, that night without hype, without superlatives, without any adjectives at all. And there was enough genuine American greatness. I seem to have missed the card show by the audience, but that typically American performance is just the kind of corn that should be encouraged, even praised—not, however, by commentators drunk on modifiers blown out of proportion. It's enough just to see a crowd turn into a picture. It doesn't need embellishment.

Later events were handled better, because there was something real to cover. Of course, again, the extras got in the way, and sometimes didn't even do their job. For example, I'm still wondering what a "rotation" is in gymnastics, and how the Americans managed to come out on top after the compulsories. It's that sort of information that ABC's people should have supplied.

I also wish that in all the hours of coverage there'd been a few minutes for the sports we usually don't hear much about. The first medal went to the Chinese in pistol shooting. Show us five minutes of it, and explain how it's scored. I mean, we know how the 100-meter dash works. But I had a dreadful feeling that we'd spend a significant portion of our Olympic hours being subjected to the condition of fruit at the farmer's market, and the laid-back crowd at Malibu, and I turned out to be right.

In preparation for the arduous two weeks of viewing such things, I had spent Friday lying-back at a Henniker, New Hampshire, pool. I've managed to avoid going swimming with Lem and the Eagless, under the pretext of cleaning up loose ends, but it's become obvious I've been doing nothing but reading Lem's fantasy sci-fi books and drawing yet another set of dream-house plans. The thing is that they like swimming and I seem to have grown to hate it. Nevertheless, I figured I ought to accompany them once during the summer. Besides, the Eagless had gotten a new bathing suit, and I wanted to (1) check it out, and (2) make sure Mad Joe wasn't watching her—not out of jealousy but because he's aging and I don't want him subjected to sudden shocks. The new suit makes good use of Spandex.

I got into the pool itself for five minutes; stood at the shallow end for two of them; ducked under and swam the narrow way across, and stood at the other side for the remaining two. As usual everyone kept saying the water was wonderful once you were in and only cold before you got wet. I was cold both times. But the four strokes I took served at least to attune me to the strenuous training of the athletes.

Dogged Days

August is a terrible month. In New Hampshire, as in the rest of the Northeast, we sweltered in heat and humidity, while it refused to rain. The rivers, which a few months ago had flooded the state, were running low, way below the normal depth, and the ponds and smaller lakes were covered with green scum.

The only real relief from the heat was psychological. A few hardy folks ventured up from the Apple to visit. As each arrived at the Manchester airport to find us ready to apologize for the weather, he or she would breathe a sigh of relief and say, "Oh, thank God, it's so cool and dry!" Since everything is relative, this statement immediately made us feel better.

As usual, the weather forecasts were no help at all. The Boston stations have discovered the dew point, and have abandoned relative humidity, the T.H.I., and the "discomfort index" as indicators of how miserable the day is. I didn't understand the dew point in high school and I don't understand it now—nor do I understand why it should tell me when I feel better or worse. In fact, my poetical nature had led me to think of dew as God's pearly gift to us all, so the notion that it could make me feel bad makes me feel bad.

Then the weather would break and everyone would get a cold, waking in the middle of the night chilled, and stumbling in the dark for the damned blanket.

But after the swelter and then the break and the chilly weather, we were blessed with a few perfect days, sunny and warm and clear and dry, followed by cool but not cold evenings. This coincided with the move to Rochester that the Eagless and I had to make. Map in hand, the Eagless's plants in the back seat, and colds in our heads, we took off on a perfect day for driving—just enough cloud cover and breeze to make the long drive bearable. And as we crossed New Hampshire, dipped into Massachusetts, and then

picked up the Dewey Threwey (Duway Thruway?) into the Mo-
hawk Valley, oh damn! there were the red and yellow leaves
beginning to show amidst all the green! There weren't a lot of
them, but there were some, and they kept saying, "It's over, it's
over, fall is comin' in. . . ."

Moving a household is bad enough without that refrain in
your ears. As always, there is first of all, the astonishment at
discovering how much we don't need we've managed to collect in
two years in the Granite State. It seems to me that I arrived in
Henniker with some ten or twelve cartons of books, papers, clothes,
and kitchenware. We left with sixty.

Then there's the emotional side—like a dog, I need to turn
around in my space, but for three weeks rather than just three times,
before I can lie down comfortably. Balancing that, however, is the
fact that this move is dictated by a wonderful title-bearing appoint-
ment at Rochester Institute of Technology, where I'll be the
Caroline Werner Gannett Distinguished Visiting Professor in the
Humanities for the coming year. The title is so impressive that I
think I'll get a long narrow rubber stamp bearing it so I can put my
imprimatur on everything that crosses my desk.

But school doesn't start until after Labor Day, so I've been
able to concentrate on the other good things August brings, like the
Republican Convention, and the Mets's record for the month. While
all is not lost yet, it has been a desperate time, searching out the scores
while the Cubbies win and win and the Mets lose and win.

I have no doubt that the flag-waving jingoism which started
with the Olympics and turned into Hitler Youth rallies at Dallas is
a prime cause of this turnaround in the standings, since Chicago is
Amurrican and New York is New York. After all, neither Carl
Lewis nor Ronald Reagan would ever share a broadcasting booth
with Tim McCarver—or be able to define a palindrome. As it all
turned out this August, the basic Mets palindrome went "Able was
I ere I saw Wrigley Field."

To have my other main area of attention be the Republican

Convention made life doubly difficult. To hear our representative to the United Nations call me and millions more traitors because we believe historical facts—it is historical fact that the debacles in Central America and in Lebanon were caused by our leadership's policies, past and present—and to hear the crowd chant its approval is more than disheartening, it's scary.

To hear speaker after speaker praise state and family and damn dissent is scarier still. I had a momentary life of hope when Reagan seemed embarrassed by the "yew ess ay" and the "four more years" after each phrase of his acceptance speech, but then I realized it was merely his old showman self worrying that the show would run too long, and my temporary optimism fled.

I can't remember any candidate who draws the kind of personal negative reaction that Mondale does since Thomas E. Dewey, who was referred to as "the man on the wedding cake." I mean, people hated McGovern because he was a damned commie, or Stevenson because he was an intellectual, or Goldwater because he was a warmonger, but they were seen as real people. Mondale is not, and I can't see any way we'll be saved from four more years of naps, Nancy's policy-making, and "tough talk," not to mention deficit disaster. It'll be a long four years.

Nathaniel, who was all of two years old when I started writing this column, will spend those four years in college. He arrives here in Rochester in a week on his way to northern New York. I will have the mingled emotions of elation and jealousy as he folds his now six-feet-one-inch frame into the back seat of the car. Somehow, I've shrunk an inch and he's caught up to me, and we stand eye to eye when we speak. If he continues to grow I expect he will fight me for the front seat and its legroom, but fatherhood does carry some perks even in this benighted age, and I am too old to bend, anyway.

Nathaniel called last night to give me the latest in the world of sports, since he refuses to believe there are newspapers, radios, or TV anywhere outside New York City. I knew both items already, but they were such good news that I didn't mind rehearing them. Howard Cosell's retirement from Monday Night Football means that I will be able to watch the games instead of playing solitaire at the tail end of the evening, and the USFL's decision to go to a fall schedule means that there'll be some respite from the blasted game. With the spring season gone, I can now concentrate on getting the regular season cut to the size it ought to be: September 1 through Thanksgiving Day. If this seems pushy, remember that football's only lasting contribution to American culture has been the Gipper.

Postscript

For a long time *The Village Voice* was changing its chararacter. Joel struggled against this change; but he still wanted to find a place in the paper. Eventually, the paper did not want to find a place for him. His withdrawal began gradually. His weekly column went to a bi-weekly column. When he handed in his final column he did not know that it was his last one. In the end, he did not have a chance to write a final piece, to say good-bye to his faithful readers, or just to say good-bye. He had remarried and moved to New Hampshire, which was a long way from Greenwich Village. He turned his attention to the vitality of his new spaces, and dedicated his later years to poetry, family, friends, and teaching.

Bibliography

Joel Oppenheimer
Publications in *The Village Voice*: 1969–1984
The following year-by-year listing accounts for Joel Oppenheimer's publications in *The Village Voice*. The majority of the entries are for his columns; poems have been identified as [poem]. The titles indicated are from the head of the columns not from the contents listing in each issue. At times there is a difference. As with the first entry, "Oppenheimer's Kvetch," some titles were supplied by the editorial staff of the *Voice*. Errors in numbering issues have been noted by the correct number appearing in square brackets following the published numbers. Beginning with "Fathers and Sons," which appeared in the issue of 31 October 1974, the titles appear in caps and lower case, whereas before that entry the titles appear in lower case only.

1969

[Reply to Sandra Hochman's review of Philip Roth's *Portnoy's Complaint, The Village Voice,* 14.20 (22 Feb 1969): 6, under an editorial title]: "Oppenheimer's Kvetch," 14.21 (6 March 1969): 12.
["Letter" in reply to Howard Smith's "Scenes" section (*The Village Voice*, 14.44 (14 Aug 1969)]: 22–23]; 14.45 (21 Aug 1969): 4.
" Edward Hoagland, *Notes from the Century Before*," 14.54 (23 Oct 1969): 7.

1970

"Charles Olson: 1910–1970—memoir of poet and teacher," 15.3 (15 Jan 1970): 9.

1971

"no, i can't stay away from the opening day of the baseball season," 16.15 (15 April 1971): 11.

"a modest reaction," 16.24 (17 June 1971): 6.

"the last game: hit the pitch of absolute beauty," 16.40 (7 Oct 1971): 13.

"a country that can't put up with its holidays," 16.43 (28 Oct 1971): 5.

"president nixon's thanksgiving day poem," [poem] 16.48 (2 Dec 1971): 52.

"hanukkah guilt: the best of one world twice," 16.50 (16 Dec 1971): 46.

"on the passing of the passing of the joint," 16.52 (30 Dec 1971): 5.

1972

"prejudice: the secret life of a fetal defender," 17.4 (27 Jan 1972): 19.

"life as it is lived: sergeant shoichi yokoi, 56," 17.5 (3 Feb 1972): 12.

"when in peking: what you see is what you get?," 17.9 (2 March 1972): 5.

"summer patriots: does ted williams know about this?," 17.11 (16 March 1972): 72.

"ingenuity is the lifeblood of the american system," 17.13 (30 March 1972): 20.

"the baseball strike: when worlds collide," 17.14 (6 April 1972): 17.

"the summer of 43: the best of time. . . ." 17.15 (13 April 1972): 28.

"if willie comes you bet new york ain't america," 17.19 (11 May 1972): 27.

"notes on language: life against death," 17.20 (18 May 1972): 22.

"mr gruen got sad when famous people acted human," 17.21 (25 May 1972): 25.

"heavy hitters, hard throwers, & amurricans," 17.23 (8 June 1972): 34.

"more notes on the ecology of language," 17.24 (15 June 1972): 22.

"agnes, antoine, etc.: come again another day," 17.26 (29 June 1972): 17.

"i like men who fool around within their framework," 17.29 (20 July 1972): 60.

"i can't believe i read the whole thing," 17.30 (27 July 1972): 21.

"to the citizens of westbeth," [poem] 17.30 (27 June 1972): 22.

"july 22: two deaths: chi-chi john dillinger, [poems] 17.31 (3 Aug 1972): 61.

"if god wanted us to be yankee fans. . . ," 17.34 (24 Aug 1972): 16.

"the other team: I go to a yankee game," 17.36 (7 Sept 1972): 37.

"the 72 olympics: switching back to real life," 17.37 (14 Sept 1972): 11.

"long distance," [poem] 17.37 (14 Sept 1972): 11.

"the life you save may be your own," 17.38 (21 Sept 1972): 27.

"the mother of us all," 17.40 (5 Oct 1972): 11, 77.

"what kind of toy do they make in hanoi?," 17.43 (26 Oct 1972): 35.

"dancing down the line: jackie robinson 1919–72," 17.44 (2 Nov 1972): 41.

"E.P. 1885–1972," [poem] 17.45 (9 Nov 1972): 33.

"by the dawn's early light: burrowing in again," 17.46 (16 Nov 1972): 42.

"holiday boo: skoal would be a terrific acronym," 17.47 (23 Nov 1972): 27.

"my high school's 25th reunion," 17.50 (14 Dec 1972): 5–6, 8.

"the class of 47," [poem] 17.50 (14 Dec 1972): 8.

"the 1972 traditional $mas book awards," 17.51 (21 Dec 1972): 28.

"things to come," [poem] 17.52 (28 Dec 1972): 18.

1973

"a little touch of harry s. in the night," 18.1 (4 Jan 1973): 8.

"and to the democrat for whom it stands. . . ," 18.2 (11 Jan 1973): 34.

"how to end a game without ever trying," 18.3 (18 Jan 1973): 19.

"LBJ goes away: the man we beat," 18.5 (1 Feb 1973): 15.

"not making head or tail of it," 18.5 (1 Feb 1973): 15.

"st. valentine's massacre: play melancholy baby," 18.7 (15 Feb 1973): 91.

"easing the energy crisis: we must go farther!," 18.8 (22 Feb 1973): 16.

"if there was sense," [poem] 18.10 (8 March 1973) 23.

"babble in arms: my mayoral dream ticket," 18.12 (22 March 1973): 5.

"further studies in time and space," 18.13 (29 March 1973): 19.

"an american shopping list," 18.14 (5 April 1973): 6.

"news special," [poem] 18.14. (5April 1973): 39.

"baseball season begins: how to observe the day?," 18.15 (12 April 1973): 23.

"checkers all over again: we will not be saved," 18.17 (26 April 1973): 87.

"the love song of j. lester oppenheimer," 18.18 (3 May 1973): 23.

"into the heartlands: no one will march," 18.20 (17 May 1973): 44.

"modest proposal for a past-watergate presidency," 18:21 (24 May 1973): 85.

"the little boy who cried national security," 18.22 (31 May 1973): 11.

"up early, changed underwear, went to a dirty movie," 18.24 (14 June 1973): 46.

"a return to normalcy," 18.25 (21 June 1973): 28.

"let's put the holy day back in holiday," 18.26 (28 June 1973): 21.

"about birthin' to help bear the pain," 18.29 (19 July 1973): 29, 37.

"what i did on my summer vacation," 18.30 (26 July 1973): 9.

"fair play: getting in the spirit," 18.31 (2 Aug 1973): 11.

"the little american: the era of john j. wilson," 18.32 (9 Aug 1973): 15.

"dog-day madness: our synapses one scrambled," 18.33 (16 Aug 1973): 19.

"theory & practice: a glossary for over-zealots," 18.34 (23 Aug 1973): 13.

"losses," 18.36 (6 Sept 1973): 7.

"weaving around in the social fabric," 18.37 (13 Sept 1973): 41.

"after we got through the humorous side," 18.39 (27 Sept 1973): 32.

"the rightest season: cincy in 3, oakland 4–1," 18.40 (4 Oct 1973): 5.

"of hangovers, orgasms, and the mets," 18.41 (11 Oct): 23.

"bush," 18.42 (18 Oct 1973): 39.

"losing the title: wait til next winter," 18.43 (25 Oct 1973): 16, 18.

"piece with honor: on the language of sex," 18.46 (15 Nov 1973): 42.

"a thanksgiving story," 18.47 (22 Nov 1973): 36.

"the family of man, american division," 18.48 (6 Dec 1973): 44.

"good pictures and good words," 18.50 (20 Dec 1973): 35.

1974

"silver linings for our times," 19.1 (3 Jan 1974): 66.

"hiding places," 19.3 (17 Jan 1974): 43.

"a loss of energy," 19.5 (31 Jan 1974): 39.

"the best is yet to come," 19.9 (28 Feb 1974): 74.

"can't anybody here play this game?," 19.10 (7 March 1974): 73.

"any wednesday," 19.12 (21 March 1974): 37.

"anomalies of everyday life," 19.13 (28 March 1974): 37.

"you oughta believe," 19.14 (4 April 1974): 19.

"it was just another home run," 19.15 (11 April 1914): 7.

"in his own rite," 9.16 (18 April 1974): 42.

"pendulum swing," 19.18 (2 May 1974): 51.

"fouling out," 19.20 (16 May 1974): 66.

"heroes to go with," 19.21 (23 May 1974): 51.

"corrected vision," 19.25 (20 June 1974): 29.

"my day," 19.26 (27 June 1974): 35.

"gloryosky," 19.28 (11–17 July 1974): 29.

"city mice, country mice," 19.29 (18 April 1974): 27.

"Stuart Perkoff," 19.29 (18 July 1974): 32.

"the all stars," 19.31 (1 Aug 1974): 37.

"after the ball is over," 19.32 (8 Aug 1974): 73.

"games," 19.32 [19.33] (15 Aug 1974): 30.

"what will we write about now?," 19.34 (22 Aug 1974): 45.

"on losing weight & other fallings off," 19.35 (29 Aug 1974): 55.

"law & order," [poem] 19.37 (12 Sept 1974): 87.

"language & sexism in today's world: a code of honor," 19.39 (26 Sept 1974): 97.

"meanwhile, down in the gap: sports, children and philosophy," 19.40 (3 Oct 1974): 95.

"the wrap-up," 19.41 (10 Oct 1974): 22.

"master of deceit & other sports news," 19.42 (17 Oct 1974): 29.

"the 74 series: searching for magic in today's world," 19.43 (24 Oct 1974): 48.

"Fathers and Sons," 19.44 (31 Oct 1974): 48.

"The Medicine Men," 19.46 (14 Nov 1974): 52.

"New Old Lifestyles," 19.47 (21 Nov 1974): 44.

"Rich Man, Poor Man," 19.49 (9 Dec 1974):44.

"An Apple for the Kids," 19.51 (23 Dec 1974): 53.

"Like We Say, The Holidays," 19.52 (30 Dec 1974): 34.

1975

"Wringing the New," 20.1 (6 Jan 1975): 40.

"Heating up the Stove," 20.2 (13 Jan 1975): 38.

"In the Dark Month," 20.3 (20 Jan 1975): 48.

"$mas Blues," 20.4 (27 Jan 1975): 32.

"The Free Market," 20.5 (3 Feb 1975): 42.

"Truth and Destiny, Both Manifest," 20.7 (17 Feb 1975): 25.

"Seasoning," 20.9 (3 March 1975): 25.

"Waltz Us Around Again, Jerry," 20.11 (17 March 1975): 25.

"The Springing of America," 20. 13 (31 March 1975): 34.

"The Question of Victory," 20.15 (14 April 1975): 44.

"Starting," 20.16 (21 April 1975): 32.

"Simple Pleasures," 20.18 (5 May 1975): 29.

"Guile 1, Rape 0: England No Yes?," 20.19 (12 May 1975): 73.

"Urban Marines," 20.21 (26 May 1975): 30.

"Making Practice Perfect," 20.23 (9 June 1975): 34.

"On His Way," 20.26 (30 June 1975): 24

"No More Pencils, No More Books," 20.29 (21 July 1975): 35.

"What I Did on Meine Vacation," 20.32 (11 Aug 1975): 27.

"Barely Managing," 20.33 (18 Aug 1975): 36.

"New Right Vs. Old Left," 20.36 (8 Sept 1975): 22.

"From Each According," 20.38 (22 Sept 1975): 46.

"Passing the National Time," 20.42 (20 Oct 1975): 122.

"This Series Was Top-10 Stuff," 20.44 (3 Nov 1975): 43, 45.

"Let's Say Farewell to Endless Summer," 20.45 (10 Nov 1975): 107.

"No Room for Magics: Screaming Poem'- Death Poem'," [two poems] 20.46 (17 Nov 1975): 46.

"How to Lose a School System," 20.47 (24 Nov 1975): 47.

"Franco Is Dead, Viva la Muerte," 20.49 (8 Dec 1975): 49.

"Support Your Local Poet," 20.51 (22 Dec 1975): 46.

"Stuff It," 20.52 (29 Dec 1975): 37.

1976

"Does It Change? Can It Hurt?," 21.2 (12 Jan 1976): 37.

"Angry at the Hall of Fame," 21.5 (2 Feb 1976): 47.

"The Tin Ear Listens," 21.7 (16 Feb 1976): 142.

"Ageism Comes Home," 21.11 (15 March 1976): 39.

"Writer Warms Up," 21.12 (22 March 1976): 36.

"Poet Digs Out," 21.14 (5 April 1976): 39.

"Swoboda Takes a Second Chance," 21.15 (12 April 1976): 112.
"Whither the University?," 21.18 (3 May 1976): 40.
"The Plot Thickens," 21.20 (17 May 1976): 49.
"I Didn't Expect Trumpets," 21.22 (31 May 1976): 129.
"Poet Gets Hair Cut, Retains Strength," 21.25 (21 June 1976): 49.
"Commish Goes Into Extra Innings," 21.26 (28 June 1976): 47.
"Country Gorge Rises!," 21.33 (16 Aug 1976): 89.
"Reliving Baseball When the Mets Were Green," 21.37 (13 Sept 1976): 43.
"Get Ready and Fall," 21.38 (20 Sept 1976): 41.
"A Is for Anker, B Is for Banker," 21.40 (4 Oct 1976): 59.
"," 21.42 (18 Oct 1976): 165.
"Yanks Can't Go Home Enough," 21.44 (1Nov 1976): 96.
"Funny, We Don't Look Jewish," 21.45 (8 Nov 1976): 45.
"What Will Ford Do Now," 21.47 (22 Nov 1976): 47.
"Inside the Winter Wonderland," 21.50 (13 Dec 1976): 57.

1977

"Ars Longa, Life Ever More So," 22.1 (3 Jan 1977): 73.
"to tip a cap," 22.3 (17 Jan 1977): 47
"Basketmaking 101," 22.7 (14 Feb 1977): 33.
"Capping It," 21.9 [22.9] (28 Feb 1977): 65.
"Stop the Presses," 22.12 (21 March 1977): 36.
"The Hot Cash Season," 22.16 (18 April 1977): 41.
"Spring Fever," 22.20 (16 March 1977): 38.
"This Little Phobia Went to Market," 22.23 (6 June 1977): 35.
"And Away He Run," 22.26 (27 June 1977): 36.
"Valst Tryst," 22.37 (12 Sept 1977): 63.
"Good-bye to Big John," 22.40 (3 Oct 1977): 8.
"Checks and Balances," 22.41 (10 Oct 1977): 8.
"," 22.42 (17 Oct 1977): 8.
"Salt-and-Pepper Lonely Hearts Club Band," 22.44 (31 Oct 1977): 8.

"Mix and Mask," 22.46 (14 Nov 1977): 8.
"A Time for Everything," 22.50 (12 Dec 1977): 8.

1978

"And So to Bread," 23.2 (9 Jan 1978): 8.
"The Tall and Short of It," 23.4 (23 Jan 1978): 8.
"Persephone Rising," 23.6 (6 Feb 1978): 8.
"Points South," 23.8 (20 Feb 1978): 8.
"Whither Billiards?," 23.9 (27 Feb 1978): 8.
"Comfort Me with Applause," 23.12 (20 March 1978): 8.
"Brazil and Hudson," 23.16 (17 April 1978): 102.
"The Games' Afoot." 23.19 (8 May 1978): 8.
"Why I Don't Rate," 23.19 (8 May 1978): 92.
"Piece in Our Time," 23.21 (22 May 1978): 8.
"Currying Favor," 23.21 (22 May 1978): 90.
"Counting the Measure," 23.23 (5 June 1978): 8.
"Avec Plaisir," 23.24 (12 June 1978): 84.
"Who's Counting," 23.27 (3 July 1978): 8.
"Oyster Bar None," 23.34 (21 Aug 1978): 123.
"Sweet Mastery of Life," 23.38 (18 Sept 1978): 10.
"You Can Go Back Again," 23.39 (25 Sept 1978): 133.
"All Booked Up," 23.40 (2 Oct 1978): 14.
"The Season Ends, I Think," 23.41 (9 Oct 1978): 40, 146.
"Maven Haven," 23.41 (9 Oct 1978): 148.
"Foreign Correspondence," 23.43 (6 Nov 1978): 8.
"The Bottom Lions," 23.47 (20 Nov 1978): 8.
"Restoring Appetite," 23.47 (20 Nov 1978): 116.
" Andrei Voznesensky, *Poems: Nostalgia for the Present*," 23.48
    (27 Nov 1978): 106.
"The Little Disturbance of Man," 23.49 (4 Dec 1978): 8.
"Running True to Form," 23.51 (18 Dec 1978): 8.
"The Last of the Old Bunch [review of Adrienne Rich, *The Dream
    of A Common Language:* Poems 1974–1977; Mark Strand,

The Monument; Judith Johnson Sherwin, *How the Dead Count*; Philip Schultz, *Likewise*; Hayden Carruth, *Brothers, I loved YouAll*]," 23.51 (18 Dec 1978): 117, 118, 120.

1979

"As American As Refried Beans," 24.1 (1 Jan 1979): 8.
"This is Your Country [review of *William Carlos Williams and the American Scene* at Whitney Museum of American Art]," 24.2 (8 Jan 1979): 57.
"Born Again," 24.3 (15 Jan 1979): 6.
"A Fan for Most Seasons," 24.5 (29 Jan 1979): 8.
"Teng and Death," 24.7 (12 Feb 1979): 8.
"The Ear Has Walls," 24.7 (12 Feb 1979): 101.
" Proensa: *An Anthology of Troubadour Poetry*, Selected and Edited by Paul Blackburn; and John Howland *Little Lives*," 24.7 (12 Feb 1979): 90.
"Mets Bow to Milwaukee," 24.9 (26 Feb 1979): 8.
"The Disco of Dialectic," 24.11 (12 March 1979): 8.
"Debts," 24.13 (26 March 1979): 8.
"Listening Toward Bethlehem," 24.16 (23 April 1979): 8.
"Take Two, Hit to Write," 24.18 (7 May 1979): 8.
"Cornered," 24.18 (7 May 1979): 113.
"To Sweep, Perchance to Dream," 24.21 (21 May 1979): 8.
"Head of the Class," 24.21 (21 May 1979): 120.
"No Runes, No Wits, No Airers," 24.23 (4 June 1979): 8.
"A Thousand Flowers," 24.25 (18 June 1979): 8.
"Campy," 24.27 (2 July 1979): 8.
"Old Dogs, New Tricks," 24.29 (16 July 1979): 8.
"Other Places," 24.31 (30 July 1979): 8.
"Plumb Wrong," 24.33 (13 Aug 1979): 8.
"Bushed," 24.35 (27 Aug 1979): 8.
"Bitter Living Through Sophistry," 24.37 (10 Sept 1979): 8.
"Shifting Gears," 24.39 (24 Sept 1979): 8.

"Small-Town Streets," 24.41 (8 Oct 1979): 8.

"Once More with Ceiling," 24.45 [24.43] (22 Oct 1979): 8.

"Hanging In," 24.45 (5 Nov 1979): 8.

"Careless Love," 24.47 (19 Nov 1979): 8.

"Catching Casey, [review of] Maury Allen, *You Could Look It Up: The Life of Casey Stengel*," 24.46 (12 Nov 1979): 40.

"The Endless Simmer," 24.49 (3 Dec 1979): 8.

"Creeley Now [review of Robert Creeley *Later*]," 24.50 (10 Dec 1979): 57–58.

"Rites of Passage," 24.51 (17 Dec 1979): 8.

"Wring Out the Old," 24.53 (31 Dec 1979): 8.

1980

"Lots of Gaul [review of Goscinny and Uderzo *Asterix: Adventures in English Series*]," 25.1 (7 Jan 1980): 31.

"Promises, Promises. . . ," 25.2 (14 Jan 1980): 8.

"In the Gold Old Summertime," 25.4 (28 Jan 1980): 8.

"Word Magic," 25.6 (11 Feb 1980): 8.

"Fate of Grace [review of Anthony Hecht, *The Venetian Vespers*]" 25.7 (18 Feb 1980): 44–45.

"Stolen Holidays," 25.8 (25 Feb 1980): 8.

"Muriel Rukeyser (1913–1980)," 25.9 (3 March 1980): 34.

"Water Babies," 25.12 (24 March 1980): 8.

"Frozen Debits," 25.16 (21 April 1980): 34.

"The Right Way [review of Dave Smith, Goshawk, *Antelope: Poems*]," 25.18 (5 May 1980): 36–37.

"Points," 25.20 (19 May 1980): 37.

"Walkin'," 25.24 (16 June 1980): 28.

"The With-Us Generation," 25.28 (9–15 July 1980): 30.

"Billie's Blues," [poem] 25.30 (23–29 July 1980): 40.

"Minding the Store," 25.32 (6–12 Aug 1980): 30.

"A Mid-Summer Night's Dream," 25.36 (3–9 Sept 1980): 26.

"After the Fall," 25.40 (1–7 Oct 1980): 38.

"A Likely Story," 25.44 (29 Oct-4 Nov 1980): 40.
" Norman Rosten, *Selected Poems,*" 25.47 (19–25 Nov 1980): 48.
"Keep Your Bags Packed," 25.48 (26 Nov-2 Dec 1980): 34.
"For John Lennon," [poem] 25.20 [25.51] (17–23 Dec 1980): 48.

1981

"Whether," 26.4 (21–27 Jan 1981): 34.
"Burger Heaven [review of Thomas Frosch *Plum Gut*]," 26.5 (28 Jan-3 Feb): 40.
"The Fullest Month," 26.8 (18–24 Feb 1981): 30.
"Preppies in My Garden," 26.12 (18–24 March 1981): 34.
"Persephone, Preserving," 26.16 (15–21 March 1981): 42.
"Thieves Like Us," 26.20 (13–19 May 1981): 36.
"Dreams of Glory," 26.24 (10–16 June 1981): 32.
"The Lourdes of Baseball," 26.28 (8–14 July 1981): 24.
"Three Nights," 26.32 (5–11 Aug 1981): 24.
"Running in Place," 26.36 (2–8 Sept 1981): 28.
"Mobility," 26.40 (30 Sept-6 Oct 1981): 30.
"The Descent," 26.44 (28 Oct-3 Nov 1981): 38.
"Playing for Time," 26.48 (25 Nov-1 Dec 1981): 36.
"Listlessly," 26.52 (23–29 Dec 1981): 52.

1982

"Moves," 27.8 (23 Feb 1982): 32.
"Leading the Union," 27.12 (23 March 1982): 36.
"Nature Boy," 27.16 (20 April): 32.
"Sun and Substance," 27.20 (18 May 1982): 34.
"Little Wars," 27.24 (15 June 1982): 34.
"Limply Yours," 27.28 (13 July 1982): 30.
"The State of the Rest," 27.32 (10 Aug 1982): 36.
"In Scale," 27.36 (7 Sept 1982): 32.
"The Operative Phrase," 27.44 (2 Nov 1982): 36.
"Homework," 27.48 (30 Nov 1982): 48.

"Xmas Presence," 27.52 (28 Dec 1982): 41.

1983

"Northern Rites," 28.4 (25 Jan 1983): 36.
"Phobophilia," 28.8 (22 Feb 1983): 38.
"Good News Tonight," 28.15 (12 April 1983): 40.
"The Beat Begins," 28.16 (19 April 1983): 32.
"Semper Illegitimati," 28.20 (17 May 1983): 36.
"Friends," 28.25 (21 June 1983): 38.
"No Change," 28.28 (12 July 1983): 38.
"Headlines," 28.33 (10–16 Aug 1983): 40.
"Summer Gone," 28.36 (6 Sept 1983): 32.
"Colding Up" 28.40 (4 Oct 1983): 44.
"Boop-Boop-A-Doop," 28.45 (8 Nov 1983): 40.
"Peace in Our Time," 28.48 (29 Nov 1983): 38.
"Family Trees," 28.52 (27 Dec 1983): 46.

1984

"Running in Show," 29.5 (31 Jan 1984): 28.
"Road Work," 29.5 (31 Jan 1984): 28, 98.
"Trivial Pursuits," 29.10 (6 March 1984): 34, 53.
"The Blackbird Cometh," 29.15 (10 April 1984): 26.
"Breakfast Reading," 29:16 (17 April 1984): 28.
"Dirty Thoughts," 29.21 (22 May 1984): 36.
"On the Road," 29.27 (3 July 1984): 42.
"The Long View," 29.29 (17 July 1984): 34.
"Selling the Gold," 29.34 (21 Aug 1984): 38.
"Dogged Days," 29.37 (11 Sept 1984): 36.

1989

"The Uses of Adversity," [poem] 34.5 (31 Jan 1989): 23–25.